RAIN: A Sailor's Story

Richard Elliott

Copyright © 2011 Richard Elliott

ISBN 978-1-61434-294-6

All rights reserved. No part of this publication may be reproduced, stored in a retrieval system, or transmitted in any form or by any means, electronic, mechanical, recording or otherwise, without the prior written permission of the author.

Although inspired in part by true incidents, the following story is fictional.

Printed in the United States of America.

First Edition

Dedication

To Beth - without your encouragement I would not have written this book

Chapter 1:
Little Things Trigger Long Forgotten Memories

Every day I walk my dog down back to the lake. Rain, cold, hot, every day.

Today was extremely hot. The humidity was like a steam room. That's when it hit me – the smell. The lake is more like a swamp, the lily pads, weeds, birds, turtles, dead fish all added to the smell.

It's like I'm back in the jungle on my machine guns on top of the pilot house on the swift boat. Waiting to pick up our Seal team and take them on a mission. It's amazing how something as unlikely as a smell can bring that all back as if it was beginning right now -- or never really ended.

I have a dock on the lake twenty feet long with an eight-foot "T" on the end. I brought a chair down with me and set it out on the end of the dock. I sit there every morning. Sometimes I'm lucky enough to see the sun come up: nature's rebirth. This morning the sun came up big and red. It ain't often you see a red sunrise. It reminded me of the morning on the delta.

The Seal team was late getting back. We were at the pick-up location waiting for them to come in. We wanted to get out of there before sunrise and they were late. The sun was rising big, red and bright.

If we didn't find cover, we would be sitting ducks. The captain (CW4 warrant officer ex chief boson's mate) decided to move off up the river and find a place where the jungle canopy overhangs the river so we could hide under it and wait for the Seals to call in for an extraction. I was on my 30s (30-caliber, air-cooled machine guns) and Bill Cooper, my loader, was standing by prepping ammo in case they came in hot.

Sitting here on the dock gives me time to think. While waiting for my dog to do his business, I sit and let my mind wander. For some reason, the last few days it wandered back to the jungle. Something's on my mind? The smell? The red sunrise? The sound of the water trickling by my dock?

Everyone and everything was real quiet. The only thing you could hear was the trickle of the river as it went by. Then we got the call: they're coming to the rally point and they're coming in hot. In a blink, the motors were running and we were on the move. I put my headphones on and immediately could hear them calling for support fire.

Rain, give us a look-see, give us a look-see.

They called me Rain mainly because they don't remember my name, and also because I rain lead on the enemy. A look-see is a machine gun burst of tracer bullets so they know where I'm aiming.

Coop was already loading a belt of tracers in the guns. He knew the drill. I let off a stream of tracers and hear "left, left, left, come left". I swung left without letting off the triggers, raking the jungle. "Stop! Come low, lower, Rain, lower." I lowered the barrels still raking the jungle along the edge of the river.

I knew they were in deep shit by the excitement in his voice, so I had Coop keep the tracers coming. Normally, I would take the tracers out of the belt and put them all in one belt and leave other belts without tracers.

I would shoot tracers until I was on target and then put in the non-tracers so that the enemy couldn't follow the tracers back to me and the boat. But today, I decided to leave the tracers in. The sun was at my back and my Seals were in deep shit, so the most effective support was to keep the tracers going so my team members could monitor my gun fire and direct it to the enemy continuously.

"You on, Rain; you on, Rain! Make it rain, Rain, make it rain!" I kept it up – Coop loading and me shooting. "One click lower, Rain, one click lower. OK. You back on, Rain, you back on. Make it rain, Rain, make it rain!"

My left barrel overheated and, in a second, Coop had twisted it off, grabbed a new one from its place in front of the pilot house, and clicked it in place. I was back shooting almost immediately. I was shooting almost straight out into the jungle and I knew the Seals were close. I hoped they were coming low so I wouldn't shoot any of them.

Then I saw them breaking through the bamboo heading for the boat. I also heard the 50s (the 50-caliber machine guns) in the back of the boat opening up.

Charlie was hot on their heels coming through the jungle right behind them. You could see the fright in their eyes when the 50s opened up. They thought my 30s were bad, but when the 50s opened up, it was like their whole world came to an end.

The Seals closer to the boat turned and helped give cover fire for the rest of their team. The Zipper Heads caught out in the open were cut to shreds.

Now our objective was to keep the dinks who took cover down until we landed the team with their wounded on board and got the hell out of Dodge.

The heat and humidity, the smell of the lake, and the sunrise have all added to my thought process to bring me back in time to the part of my life that made the most impact on it. After my 2nd day in-country, I really didn't believe I was ever coming home. From that day on, I wasn't afraid I was going to die – I knew it, and being afraid of dying and knowing you're going to die are two different things. Apprehensive, yes. Bone-chilling fear, no.

I really wanted to go to college, but even though I got a football scholarship, I couldn't afford it. End of story. A friend of mine told me about a program the Navy has that if you enlist in the regular Navy, when you get discharged, they will pay for your education. I went to the recruiter and asked him about it, and he confirmed it: Yes, they will pay for your education under the G.I. Bill.

I talked to my parents about joining the Navy. My Dad thought it was a good idea. My Mom wanted me to wait a year. After thinking about it for a week, I decided to join up. It was June, 1962 before anyone heard of Vietnam.

On a warm Thursday in June, I signed the paperwork to join the Navy. I was sent to Boston Monday morning for a physical. It was probably the most embarrassing day of my life. I played football and was used to being naked in front of other guys, but this was different. Bend over and spread your cheeks, pull back your foreskin. I was totally disgusted. The people giving the physicals weren't real doctors – they were corpsmen. One guy's penis wasn't as clean as they liked, so he got an ass-reaming or, as we call it, he got chewed out. They checked everything – eyes, ears, throat, even your feet. They checked for color blindness, flat feet, blood, heart, dexterity, everything you could think of and some things you never heard of. Finally, you see a real doctor; turn your head and cough. That's all he said – "turn your head and cough." So that's what we called him.

I passed my physical and, a week later, I went to Boston, got sworn in, and took a plane to Great Lakes, Illinois – boot camp.

The flight to Chicago sucked out loud. It was turbulent and the guy beside me puked three times, using up all three barf bags in our section. By the time we got there, I think everyone was feeling a bit queasy. When we got off the plane, the busses were waiting to take us to the base. When we got there, we got off the busses and lined up into two lines, turned left, and marched us off to our new barracks. We dropped off what little bit of our civilian gear that we had, and were marched off to the chow hall. Welcome to Camp Barry!

It was funny watching everyone march, who weren't trained to march. Some were strutting, some goose-stepping, some hippity-hopping, and the rest of us just walking. Talking was not allowed, and when we got to the chow hall, we were directed to stand in two lines, face forward and no talking. A couple of guys thought they were far enough back in line as they could get away with whispering. They were yelled at and both were told to drop down and do pushups. Later, all they had to say was "give me 20" which meant drop down and give me twenty pushups.

Surprisingly, the food was pretty good. I'm a meat-eater, and we had beef and all to go with it. It's true the Navy has the best food. After chow, we were marched back to the barracks and left to our own thoughts. The smoking lamp was lit – not really a lamp, but a saying meaning you could smoke. Unless you were told the smoking lamp was lit, you could not smoke. Ronny and I, the guy that threw up on the airplane, started hanging out together. Our last names started with the same letter, so we were close throughout indoctrination week.

Morning came early – around 5am. They woke us up by walking through the barracks with a billy club and a trash can cover and beating on it like a cymbal. "Rise and shine! "Drop your cocks and grab your socks! Everybody up! Line up at the end of your bunks! You have 30 minutes to wash up, get dressed and form up outside according to height. Tallest to the right – my right – your left."

We formed up outside the barracks and our drill instructor was waiting. He had us straighten our lines out and marched us to the chow hall to start our day.

Indoctrination week was more physicals, testing, getting our clothes, sending our civilian clothes home, learning how to march, etc.

Camp Barry lasted one week – not really enough time to get to know many people. So I hung with people I knew. Ronny, the fire hydrant that puked on the plane; Glen, the muscle head – tough on the outside, mush on the inside. Preacher, a black, religious guy that seemed to always have a bible with him. For some unexplained reason, he took a liking to us and hung around our group, becoming one of us.

One of the first things you learned was the term "Hurry up and wait." They hurried you from the barracks to chow, where you waited in line. From chow to where you got your uniforms. We waited in line forever. We couldn't wait to move on to Camp Moffat, our next step in boot camp.

Our last night in Camp Barry, we packed everything we owned into our sea bags in preparation to Camp Moffat. That night, Ronny and I were all packed up and sitting at the tables in the middle of the barracks talking about what's next and looking forward to the day we finish boot camp. Next day, we marched into Camp Moffat.

Next stop, Camp Moffat – the real start of boot camp. The group of us and part of the group before us were divided into two companies – Company 317 and 318. I was in Company 317.

We were to stay at Camp Moffat from 3-4 weeks. While there, we learned how to fold and store our clothes, how to make up our bunks, how to tie our ditty bags (little laundry bags) on the end of our bunks. We learned how to wash our clothes – the laundry room, drying room, etc. We stamped our names and service number into all our clothes, hats, pea coats, everything.

During our weeks at Camp Moffat, we got our ranks by our company commander. I ended up as 1st Platoon Leader. Billy Campbell was our Recruit Chief Petty Officer and Billy Ray was our 2nd Platoon Leader. We also have an Intelligence Officer, Athletic Officer, Religious Officer, and chow runners.

The chow runners ran to the chow hall and reported to the Petty Officer in charge that company 317 was ready for chow. The fastest chow runner from all the companies determined where in line you waited for chow. First one to report got to go first. With nine companies, 60 men to a company, you either ate first or 540th.

Luckily, our Religious Officer, a black man from North Carolina, could also run. We never ate less than 3rd company in line.

During the day, we learned marching, discipline, classes on military and weapons. We stood personal inspection every morning.

More than one recruit had to dry shave using the Company Commanders belt buckle as a mirror.

At night, we were back in our barracks where we wrote letters, did laundry, stood watch. We had a watch in the barracks 24-7, 4 hour shifts. We also did laundry, studied our military assignments, and generally hung out with each other.

Men are supposed to be tough – they are not supposed to cry. You can cut their fingers and toes off and they won't cry. But hurt them emotionally, and all men cry. Some can control the tears and only cry on the inside. I have seen some of the toughest men cry. I myself have bawled like a baby when something hurt me inside. At first, I get angry and lash out at what caused the pain. But eventually, when the anger is gone and the hurt can't be ignored, I find out how human I am and find a place to be alone and release my pain.

One night in the barracks, I was awakened by muffled sobbing. Glen, the muscle head from Camp Barry, was crying. I wanted to go over to him and find out what was wrong but, instead, I let him cry himself to sleep.

Glen was big and strong and physically fit. It seemed unlikely he would be crying, Next morning, I asked him about why he was crying. At first, he wouldn't talk about it, but finally he opened up. He was homesick.

Although he was big and strong, he was emotionally a little immature, and showed his emotions, wore his heart on his sleeve. Although I was the same age as Glen, I looked at him as a younger brother. I loved him as a brother, a bond you feel for a teammate, like the other players on your football team. That bond lives on 'til this day.

Our company was as diversified as you can get. We had white, black, Asian, Hispanic and mixed racial profiles. They were big, small, thin, fat, short and tall. You learned that size doesn't make the man –the size of his heart makes the man.

We all had to work together to make our company the best it could be. I was surprised at how alike we all were – city boys, country boys and the boys in between. Basically, we were all the same.

I met this black guy who didn't go through Camp Barry with us but was part of another group that got split up. He was a Golden Gloves boxer from Philly and we got into an argument because he was talking in the chow line and I sent him down to the chow line Master at Arms to do pushups.

That night, back in the barracks, he called me on it. We went into the drying room to fight it out.

I knew he could box, so I decided it would be best to wrestle. I took a couple of punches, but was able to grapple him to the ground and get him into a submission hold. After that, we shook hands and soon became best friends. Eventually, I even was best at his wedding. His name was Jefferson White, and we all called him Snowball. You know, a black man named White. The name just seemed to fit. Snowball not only could box, he could sing too. Many a night, he entertained us with songs he knew from Motown.

Every night after we washed our clothes, wrote our letters, straightened out our lockers, we would hang out at the tables in the middle of the barracks smoking cigarettes and talking. That's when Snowball would sing. Others would get up and sing with him, but Snowball was the star.

It was in the third week that some of the guys couldn't take the pressure. Me? I kinda liked boot camp. It sounds funny, but it was a little like football practice. You know being with the guys and working through it all was like being with your teammates and practicing football. The only difference is you didn't get to go home at night. In football, you practiced during the day. In boot camp, it went 24-7.

The first to break down was a kid from Indiana. He lived on a farm out in the country. Came from a real small town, and had never been away from home before. Not even on vacation. He just shut down. At first, he just got quiet, stared off into space. The he lost interest in everything and was just going through the motions. Finally, he wouldn't get out of his bunk. He went for psych evaluation and was sent home.

The next one to break down to everyone's surprise, was our Recruit Chief Petty Officer, our Recruit Company Commander, Bill Campbell. One evening, he just started screaming that he couldn't take it anymore. He ran through the barracks turning bunks and lockers over and bouncing off the walls. It took five of us to subdue him. Then he started crying. Next day, he went for psych evaluation and was gone.

I was elevated to Recruit Chief Petty Officer – Company Commander, and Billy Ray became 1st Platoon leader. Billy and I thought that the Athletic Recruit Petty Officer would be elevated to 2nd Platoon leader, but to our surprise, the Company Commander appointed a kid from Chicago named Joe Oshinski. Joe was a cool guy, always joking and clowning around. Referred to himself as "Joe the Pole" because of his Polish decent.

Through the course of the next few weeks, we found Joe to be a natural. His laid-back attitude offset Billy Ray's sternness and, when they were both doing their jobs, it made my job a lot easier.

We got into a routine: Training during the day, writing letter, doing laundry and hanging out in the evening.

My group now expanded to eight. Ron: a real good guy built like a fire hydrant and with natural bulk and strength to match. Glen: the muscle head, everyone's little brother although he was bigger, taller and stronger than all of us. Preacher: our chow runner and Religious Officer, the more level-headed of the bunch. Snowball: the Golden Gloves kid from Philly, his pleasant attitude and singing made him a favorite of everybody. Billy Ray: a southerner that had an attitude like he was in the Marines. Honest, fair, serious, helpful to everyone, but he seemed to be on point all the time – never relaxed and never let his guard down. Then there was Joe Oshinski, the newest member to our group: Joe the Pole, real laid back, easy going, but smart, knew how to judge people, a born leader. Another kid that joined our group, a friend of Joe the Pole, was Gary Buntley. Gary was a small, blond kid with pimples, an infectious smile, tried his best to stay squared away, and was one of our chow runners. Then, of course, there was me. Thrown into a position I didn't really want, but determined to make the best of it. The rest of the groups or clicks in the company looked up to use for direction. One group did not segregate itself from the other; we all got along real good. It was almost as if we were all one.

Our Company Commander was a Reserve Chief Petty Officer on temporary active duty. Master Chief Schrom. He didn't seem to have a personality, a real matter-of-fact type person. He told me what had to be done during the day, more or less let me do it, and that was that.

Every morning, we fell in for inspection. After inspection, our chow runners raced to the chow hall to secure our position in line, and the rest of us marched in order to the chow hall. While we waited in line, my 2nd Platoon Leader took over the company while I discussed what our Company Commander wanted us to do that day. Things like close-order drill, the 26-count manual of arms, marching. Add different classes on military training, etc. After three weeks in Camp Moffat, and before you went to Camp Porter you had to do a service week.

Service Week is a week in which all recruits work in some capacity to service the other recruits.

First and foremost are the mess cooks. There are three mess halls – one in each camp – Barry, Moffat and Porter. These mess halls need mess cooks to help cook, clean, do dishes, scour pots and pans, etc. Each company has to go through it. When your week is up, you leave, and the next company behind you moves in.

Next, we have recruits called service weeks. These are the Recruit Petty Officers that help the new recruits through indoctrination week and being a secretary-gofer for the Company Commanding Officers.

I was a service week at Camp Barry. On Friday, the end of the third week in Camp Moffat, we marched to our new barracks in Camp Porter.

We had all day Friday to get accustomed to our new barracks, put our clothes away and learn what our assignments were for service week.

Saturday was the beginning of our service week. Most went to their jobs in the chow hall, the rest of us marched to Camp Moffat to our service week jobs. Because my company had the highest scores in classes, drilling and personal inspection, I was placed in charge of all the other Recruit Petty Officers and marched them to Camp Barry at 4am to start our day.

Day one we ran the new recruits through their physicals. They took their clothes off at one end of this huge building, stood in line naked, and slowly but steadily walked through each stage of their physical. At the end of the line, they got their new clothes and found out that they had gone around in a big circle and ended up at the beginning. After they dressed in thief new clothes, they were directed to mail their civilian clothes home. You were only allowed to keep your wallet, cigarette lighters, and pen and paper for letter writing. Everything else was sent home.

Sunday, the recruits were given the day off. Go to church or just hang in the barracks putting their clothes away and shining shoes. The smoking lamp was lit.

Monday, we marched the recruits to chow, and then to a building where they were taught the proper way to fold and store their clothes in their lockers. The class was tedious – 300 recruits learning how to fold each individual piece of clothing. They were also given a stencil with their name and service number on it and told where each piece of clothing was to be stamped with their identification. After lunch, just to break up the monotony, we lined them up and taught them how to march. First day, march straight and about face. Each day, they learned something different – left face, March, right face, March, oblique, right, oblique left. That's a turn of about 45 degrees instead of the 90-degree left and right face. At the end of the day, we marched them to the chow hall for supper, and then back to the barracks where we turned them loose. Hopefully, they were doing their laundry (by hand) and properly folding their clothes and putting them in their lockers.

Tuesday, 4:30am: "Drop your cocks and grab your socks. Line up at the end of your bunks. You have 30 minutes to get cleaned up and line up in front of your barracks. You know the drill. Get going!"

Tuesday, we marched the recruits to the chow hall and then on to the medical building where they got their shots. Flu shots, infectious disease shots and penicillin shots. From there, we marched back to the chow hall for lunch and then to the indoctrination building for their dog tags. I don't know why, but everybody looks forward to getting their dog tags. I guess it means you're finally in.

After that, we drilled the recruits in marching, marched them to the chow hall for their evening meal, marched them back to their barracks and turned them loose.

As I looked at the other service weeks, and back at the recruits, I was surprised at the difference three weeks did. The recruits looked so young and apprehensive, while the service weeks looked older and more confident, even though they were all approximately the same age.

Wednesday, after breakfast, we were back at the medical building for classes on cleanliness. We learned CPR, battle dressing wounds, splints for broken bones and tourniquets to stop the bleeding. They showed us movies on all of this as they told us about the dos and don'ts of emergency medical treatment.

After the noontime meal, we marched them back to the barracks and told them to prepare for inspections on Thursday.

We regrouped them at 5pm and marched them to chow and then turned them loose for the day.

Thursday was inspection day. Fun for the service weeks, hell for the recruits. I learned early that, after you admonish someone for an infraction, you give them encouragement for something they got right. Positive reinforcement is a stronger training device than criticism.

We woke the recruits at 4:30, lined them up, and marched to the chow hall. After chow, we marched back to the barracks and lined them up for personal inspection. We inspected their white hats, t-shirts, haircuts, shaves and shoe shines. Everyone spends a lot of time shining the front of their shoes, but not the backs.

A lot of them got pushups for not polishing the backs of their shoes. "You wipe your ass, don't you? So polish the back of your shoes! Now get down and give me twenty!" Some didn't shave quite close enough, and some had dirty white hats.

After personal inspection, we inspected the barracks, latrines, bunk windows, door ledges, jambs and the floors. Basically, it was pretty good, but nothing's perfect so we found a couple of infractions. Next we inspected their lockers. If their clothes weren't properly folded or stored on the proper shelves, they were pulled out and strewn all over the floor and they were made to do it all over. But basically, they were pretty good.

Friday, the recruits were divided into companies and told where to line up on Saturday for the move to Camp Moffat. So after the midday chow call, they were back at the barracks packing their sea bags and preparing for the real start of boot camp.

Saturday is moving day. Timing is crucial. We're marching the recruits out and the buses are bringing the newbie's in.

As always, we woke them up at 4:30, marched them to chow and then back to their barracks to get their gear. Then we marched them to the parade grounds, separated them into their assigned companies and marched them to their new homes in Camp Moffat.

Sunday, we got to sleep in an extra half-hour, got up, lined up on the parade grounds and marched off to the chow hall. After chow, some of us went with Preacher to church. The rest of us went back to the barracks. At 10am, our Company Commander came into the barracks and told us to line up outside. He told us that we were to pick an athletic activity to join and that every Sunday we would compete for the Athletic Flag. Everything we did in Camp Porter was judged and the company with the highest score got to carry the flag representing that activity. As long as you stayed on top, you kept the flag. If another company got a higher score, next week they got the flag.

There were five different flags. The "I" Flag – Intelligence – highest scores in the classroom; the "A" Flag – best in athletics; the "D" Flag – best in drilling and marching; the "P" Flag – personal inspections and the "B" Flag – barracks inspection.

Sunday, we all chose an athletic activity. Volleyball, swim team, softball team, boxing team. The events were scheduled at different times of the day so we all got to watch each other compete.

Me, I joined the relay team along with Preacher, Snowball and Gary Buntley, the little pimply-faced kid. We didn't know if, but soon found out he could really run. I was the anchor man kid went first, Snowball second, Preacher third. They called me the train – I had a slow start, but kept on picking up speed and, at the end, I was really flying. We never lost a race.

It wasn't mandatory that you watch the other events, so sometimes we went back to the barracks to catch up on laundry and things.

As the weeks went along and our teams were doing pretty good, we would try to see one or two events before going back. I remember one time going to the boxing match. Ron, the fire hydrant, decided to box. He had won two bouts and lost one. This was to be his big test. He was fighting an amateur heavyweight boxer from New York – a guy named Tucker. The first round, Ron and Tucker just danced around testing each other out. In the second round, Tucker opened up a little and started jabbing Ron, bobbing and weaving and generally frustrating him.

In the third round, I could see Ron was really getting pissed off. He swung a round-house at Tucker, missed and fell on his ass. He was pissed. He got up, ran across the ring, got Tucker in a head-lock, pummeled him into the mat and hit him in the back of the head when he was down. Needless to say, he got disqualified and Tucker won the fight. Ron was told if he ever did that again, he would be thrown off the boxing team. After the fight, Tucker came over to Ronny's corner and said something to him. When we got back to the barracks, I asked him what he said. Tucker told him "You may not be a very good boxer, but I'd sure hate to meet you in a back alley." Our company was fortunate to win the A Flag every week except one, and we would carry it when we graduated boot camp.

Monday, our first real training day in Porter, started off like all the rest. 4:30 am they woke us up by blowing Reveille over the loud speakers. We all got up, got cleaned up and lined up in our usual positions on the parade grounds. The parade grounds were a big asphalt area in the middle of all the barracks, and each company had their own spot on it. When you were all lined up, the Company Commanders inspected you and, if everything was ok, they sent the chow runners off to secure you a place in the chow line.

RAIN: A Sailor's Story

While waiting in the chow line, the Company Commander took me aside and outlined the day for us. I had a small notebook and pen with me that I kept in my sock, and took notes and directions. After that, he left us and I was in charge of the company. After chow, we lined up at the parade grounds and marched off to our first class.

There were four companies going through boot camp at the same time. Four companies the week ahead of you, and four the week behind. So the times each company was at a class, the other three companies were at a different class.

So the classes rotated. When we were marching to the next class, the other company was marching to the class we just left and we attended the class some other company just left. Add in the time waiting in the chow lines three times a day, and the days were moving along in a boring sequence.

To keep the boredom to a minimum, we had to drill, march, stand inspections, and barracks inspections. Also, on Sundays, we had athletics. In the third week of Camp Barry, we had our swim test. Everyone was required to climb a ten-foot platform, jump off and swim to the other side of the pool. If you failed the swim test, you were sent home. With only 2 ½ weeks left of boot camp, nobody wanted to fail.

I marched my company to the gym, a combination of gym and pool, racquetball courts, basketball, volleyball, all that.

Each of us brought our Navy-issue bathing suit. Once inside the building, we stripped down, put our bathing suits on and went into the shower room and took a shower. When you finished your turn in the pool, you were allowed to get dressed.

The Petty Officers in charge of this class did everything to help you pass. They scolded you, ridiculed you, cajoled you and praised you. Whatever it took to get you through.

The black guys in our class had the most problems. Some refused to jump off the tower; some, when they did jump in, simply sat on the bottom of the pool and had to be pulled out. Some that failed the first time were given a second chance. While the rest of us were jumping in, they were taken to another pool and given lessons and allowed to jump in again.

I was happy to see Preacher and Snowball make it. Out of the whole company, we only lost two men.

We went back to the pool a couple of days later to learn how your uniform can save your life if you're out in the ocean with no flotation devices around. They taught us how to tie the ends of your shirt sleeves together, flip it over your head filling it with air, and using it as a flotation device. Same thing with your pants and white hat. First of all, they must be wet and then kept wet, occasionally re-flipping and filling back up with air.

The Navy white hat, although good on ship, wasn't worth a damn on land. I learned that in the jungle. The Marine's boonie hat was a lot better. The brim can be bent in such a way as to help keep the water off you when it rained, which it seemed to do every day. Also, the band around the crown of the hat can be used to store such things in like cigarettes, lighters, stub pencils, waterproof matches, etc.

I found the Australian bush hat to be the best. The brim was larger, giving a larger umbrella effect, and the way the brim was adjusted, high on the left side, tapered from front to back. You wear the hat slightly turned to the right for two reasons: First so that the rain water will run from front to back toward your left shoulder blade, not down the back of your neck. The second, most people are right handed and though, if you have 20/20 vision, your right eye is your dominant eye, your left eye will normally have the most peripheral vision. You'll see things out of the corner of your left eye quicker than you will out of the right. You can concentrate on and recognize things better out of the right eye. Most people who hear something, their first instinct is to turn to the right. Subconsciously, you know that you haven't seen anything in the peripheral vision, so it is probably coming from the right. So basically, that's why the Aussie's bush hat has the brim turned up on the left – to give the left eye a better vision. It sound trivial, but it just might save your life sometime.

The day after the pool and flotation training, we went to the rifle range. We were all excited about shooting. When we got to the range, each company had to wait at the parade rest until the company ahead of them went through the class on how to handle a rifle safely. Basically a safety course. There were three companies ahead of us; the class takes a half-hour to forty five minutes. So after standing on the parade grounds for two hours give or take, we were antsy to say the least. Finally, we were allowed into the classroom to take the safety class. Interesting at first, but soon turned boring. After the class, it was almost lunch time so we marched to the chow hall and ate lunch, then marched back to the range to shoot. Another disappointment!. We each took three shots; it didn't matter if you hit anything as long as it was done safely. The other disappointment was that the rifles were only 22s – the smallest caliber made. I guess they figured sailors really didn't need rifle training.

After our first four weeks in Porter, and with only three weeks left to go, we got our first weekend pass.

We were all pretty excited. Some of us went to Chicago, others went to Milwaukee. Ronnie and Glen wanted to go to Milwaukee, and Snowball and I went to Chicago. So on Friday at 4:00pm, we got our passes and, in our dress whites, boarded buses to the train station.

A couple hundred sailors left Camp Porter and they almost equally separated – some to Chicago, some to Milwaukee, although I think Milwaukee had the edge because the drinking age in Wisconsin was 18, while in Illinois, you had to be 21.

But at that time, there were a few bars in Chicago that served sailors no matter what their age.

When Snowball and I got to Chicago, we checked into the Planter Hotel. It was $19.80 each night Friday and Saturday, so we each paid for a night. Our room had two single beds, two small bureaus, a nightstand with a clock and telephone and our own bath. We paid a little extra for the room because we wanted a private bath instead of a community bath down the hall.

After checking in and dropping our ditty bags in the room - we brought our ditty bags with some underwear and toiletries - we went out on the town.

We heard of a few bars through the grape vine that served sailors, so we asked directions at the desk. The desk clerk told us about another bar that served sailors and had more girls there and we would probably have a better time. So off we went, all excited about our first "liberty" and going to our first bar. Downtown Chicago had a group of streets that formed a sort of oblong loop and was called the Loop. The major street was State Street and that is where Snowball and I were headed.

We were headed to a place called the Palomino and, sure enough, they let us in without asking for identification. The place was packed chock full of sailors. A few girls, older, not real good looking, and it took us 15 minutes to finally get a beer. The entertainment was a juke box, and it was loud. The whole place was loud and shoulder-to-shoulder with sailors talking about boot camp and going home in three weeks. I came there to have fun, forget about boot camp and maybe find a pretty girl, so after the second beer, Snowball and I left.

We were walking down State Street when we saw some sailors walking back toward us. We asked them where they were going. They said they were bringing their drunken friend back to the hotel and then going back to Mahoney's Bar. I asked if it was any good and they said "yeah, great." A friend told them about it and it was a little offbeat, but wasn't totally full of sailors, and there were some decent looking girls there. They told us where it was and Snowball and I were off.

When we got there, the place was jumping, the dance floor was full and people were having fun. We both had that look on our face, this is the place. We walked in and, before you know it, we were right in the middle of it. Dancing, drinking beer, and talking to pretty girls. We didn't score any girls that night, but one of the girls told us about a live concert at a club uptown. The Shirelles were going to be there and it would be great. The Shirelles were a Motown group that Snowball really liked. He wanted to go see the Shirelles and I wanted to go back to Mahoney's. At the end, Snowball wanted to see the Shirelles more than I wanted to go to Mahoney's.

So we went to the concert and I was glad we did. The Shirelles were awesome. They sang their top hits, songs like "Will You Still Love Me Tomorrow," "Mama Said," "Please, Mr. Postman," and when they sang "Soldier Boy" the place went wild – soldier or sailor, it all meant the same.

When they took a break, Snowball got up on stage and asked the drummer if he could sing. The drummer asked him what song he wanted and Snowball said the Mary Wells song "Two Lovers."

The drummer asked one of the guitarists, they both said yes, and next thing you know, there's Snowball singing, and he was great. He sang two other Mary Wells songs. By then the Shirelles were ready to get back on stage.

Snowball had one last song to sing. It was a Shirelles song, "This is dedicated to the One I Love," and when they heard him, they rushed out on the stage and joined in.

The crowd went wild. To see one of our own sailors singing that beautifully with the Shirelles was a great moment.

We were all yelling and cheering and, at the end, we grabbed Snowball and carried him off the stage.

At the end of the concert, Snowball and I made our way back to the Planters Hotel. We were exhilarated by the great time we had, but we were also tired. It was late and we had been partying hard and had to go back to base the next day.

We weren't looking forward to the 1-1/2 hour train ride, and the twenty minute shuttle back to the base. We had to be back by 6pm at the latest. I, not wanting to be late, thought we should catch the 1:55 train, Snowball agreed. We would probably be back to the barracks by 4:30, the latest. That would give us plenty of time to do our laundry, clean up our lockers and get ready for the last three weeks of boot camp.

Sunday morning, we got up around 7:30. After getting used to getting up at 5:00am, it's hard to sleep late. Snowball and I were just tossing and turning, not really sleeping. I said, "Hey, long as you're awake as I am, let's go get breakfast, I'm starved." All we had to eat the day before was a street vendor's hot dog on our way to the concert.

So we got up, got dresses and headed to this place called O'nosko's on Clark Street, a Polish restaurant that we heard had a great breakfast. Good food and plenty of it. You just had to have the breakfast sausage – it's what they're famous for. We went to O'nosko's and the food was great. As Snowball said, "Better than Mom's."

After breakfast, we just walked around the Loop window shopping and talking about going home after boot camp. We went back to the room, got our stuff, checked out and caught the train back.

Monday morning came and went before you knew it: Reveille on the PA speakers, drop your cocks and grab your socks, another day in Paradise.

RAIN: A Sailor's Story

Our Company Commander, Master Chief Petty Officer Schromm, met me at the chow hall and gave me my orders. Normally, he would give me my orders for the day. Today, he gave them to me for the whole week. After that, we hardly saw hide nor hair of him until the next Monday. I sort of took over his job, and Billy Ray, mine. With his no-nonsense attitude and string military attitude, we soon had more flags than any other company.

It soon became apparent to the other Company Commanders that ours wasn't around much. They all asked me at one time or another where he was. I always gave an answer like "I think he's at the logistics school setting up class," or "Down at the gym going over athletic schedules," and finally, "I really don't know."

In the last week at Porter, an incident came up that changed things for me that bothers me to this day. It was raining, and we were waiting on the parade ground to be paraded to the chow hall. Our runners got there a little late and we waited a little longer than usual. The men got a little grumpy and started talking. No matter what Billy Ray said, he couldn't quite them down. Without the Company Commander there, I had to do something to keep things from getting out of hand. A Recruit Petty Officer cannot make recruits do pushups. But without our Chief there, I took it upon myself to order them all – the whole company – to get down in the rain and give me twenty pushups. The other Company Commanders on seeing this came over and asked me who gave these men order to do pushups. I said "I did, sir." "Who authorized you to do it?" "No one, sir." They put me on report, relieved me of duty, and sent me down to the officer's quarters while they hunted up my Division Officer to report what happened.

I waited at attention for about an hour when I finally got called into a small office. The only one in there was my

Division Officer. He really lit into me, asking who the fuck did I think I was, and he lost a lot of respect for me, and I was no longer Recruit Chief Petty Officer – just regular recruit.

And then he asked me if I had anything to say for myself. I should have just shut up, but I did have something to say. I told him if he had been with the company, more like the other Company Commanders, maybe it wouldn't have happened. That really pissed him off. He jumped up and slapped me in the face. And out of instinct, I punched him back. Knocked him back over his chair and bloodied his nose. He jumped up and called in a couple other Company Commanders and had me arrested for assault on a Chief Petty Officer. Ten minutes later, two Marine MPs marched me off to the brig.

The first thing they did was strip me, power wash me, redress me in blue pajamas with a white stripe, and place me in cell one, rack three. My number was 13, the worst number you could have. Even though I was the only prisoner in cell one, they gave me rack three which was on top.

There were three racks in each cell – number one on the bottom, number two in the middle and number three on top. The only place I had to sit was on the second bunk. All the other prisoners were out in the general area playing cards, working out, watching TV or reading. I was locked in. I didn't have to wait long to find out what's next. The Sergeant of the Guard came to my cell. He unlocked my cell, yelled "At-en-hut!", and walked in. I stood at attention and answered his questions.

"So you like to strike officers, is that right?" Answer: "No sir. It was an accident. When he slapped me, I instinctively struck back." "Don't call me sir. I'm not an officer. I'm an enlisted man like you, sailor."

This was the first time I was called sailor and it surprised me. "What's your name, sailor?" "Richard Elliott, Seaman Recruit, 668-32-38." "Not any more, sailor. From now on, you're inmate number 13. Now what's your name?" "Inmate number 13, Sergeant." "While you're here, you will keep the general area clean and do whatever else needs doing; do we understand each other inmate number 13?" "Yes, Sergeant."

He then unlocked my cell and let me out into the general public. Most of the inmates were recruits like me; some were regular Navy who went AWOL for one reason or another. They were there awaiting either a trial or captain's mast and then sent to a real prison or busted in rank, fined or whatever.

My first job was to clean up the general area, empty ashtrays, rubbish buckets, wipe down the tables and sweep the floor. When I finished cleaning up, I asked one of the other inmates where the head was. He told me it isn't called a head in here – it's called a latrine. The Marines run this place and, in the Marines, it's a latrine. "OK, where's the latrine?" He said "You see that red line over there? The latrine is on the other side of that line and, before you can cross that line, you have to ask permission to cross."

So I walked to the red line and asked permission to cross. The Marine said "Why do you want to cross the line?" I said, "To use the latrine, sir." He said, "Don't call me sir. Permission is not granted."

I was standing there thinking "Are you shitting me? I don't have permission to take a leak?" "What are you standing there for? I told you, permission not granted." I started to get angry but held my temper and went back to the general area. I asked one of the guys what's up with that. He said "You have to ask permission properly. Say 'Sergeant, inmate number 13 requests permission to use the latrine, Sergeant." And stand at attention, eyes forward; do not look at the Sergeant. Ten minutes later I was at the line to ask permission again. "Sergeant, inmate 13 requests permission to use the latrine, Sergeant." All he said was, "Permission not granted."

I went back to the guys and asked what I did wrong. They said nothing, I did just fine; he's just messing with you, putting you in your place.

Ten minutes later I asked again – I really had to go. Again, no. I was pissed off. Now I really, really had to go.

Ten minutes later, I asked again. He said no again. I whipped it out right there and pissed all over the floor. Boy was the Sergeant mad. He grabbed me, threw me in my cell and locked the door. He then ordered the rest of the inmates into their cells and called in a few more guards.

About six minutes later, they unlocked my cell and three of them came in. I really didn't believe the stories you hear about getting beat with rubber hoses. I am now a believer. They beat me silly. After the beating, they dragged me out, made me wash and wax and buff the whole area including the hallways. When I was finished, they put me back in my cell and let everyone else out. About an hour and a half later, the Sergeant of the Guard came back to talk to me again.

He stood me at attention and asked, "What didn't you understand about what I explained to you earlier?" I said, "Sergeant, I had to use the latrine. I asked properly three times and, for no reason, he kept refusing my request, Sergeant." He said, "How do you know he had no reason? Maybe the water was temporarily shut off. Maybe the floor was wet. I'm sure he had his reason for refusing your request. You will not be allowed to go to the chow hall for two days. You will be on limited rations."

I didn't know what limited rations meant, but I soon found out. Bread and water – no shit – bread and water. The first thing you learn when you're on bread and water: No matter how hungry you are, eat only the crust. The doughy part will make you constipated.

RAIN: A Sailor's Story

My third day in the brig, I got a visit from my legal officer, Lieutenant Junior Grade, Mike Creighton. He told me I was charged with striking a Senior Petty Officer, and could be discharged with a bad conduct discharge which would follow me the rest of my life. He asked me if I liked the Navy. I told him, "Up 'til now I did," but I really didn't think I was treated fairly. He said I better get used to it. As you get older, you'll realize life ain't fair.

Then he asked me my side of the story. I told the whole thing. My Division Officer never being around, my guys would not stop talking, the slap in the face, and my instinctive reaction.

After he heard my story, he seemed to change his attitude against me a little. He went on to say that I had a real good record prior to this incident and my company was top shelf. He said hang tight and he would get back to me.

I found out later that he went to see Chief Schromm and confronted him with the fact that he hit me first, and that he had no right to do that. Chief Schromm said it was my word against his and he's the one with the bloody nose. Mike said you also were derelict in your duty to supervise your company and he had testimony from other Company Commanders that you were never around, and left the responsibility of running your company to Recruit Chief Petty Officer Elliott. I might add he's done a helluva job.

So before this gets out of hand and charges are lodged against you as well as recruit Elliott, I suggest we squash this thing right away.

Chief Schromm said he is willing to do that providing I wasn't allowed back into his company. It would be too embarrassing for him. Mike agreed. I was also told I had to apologize to Chief Schromm.

By then I had enough of jail and bread and water, I would have done almost anything to get out of the brig.

So on Saturday morning, graduation day, they pulled me out of the brig dressed in my Navy work clothes, brought me to the barracks to apologize to Chief Schromm, pack my sea bag and take the shuttle bus to the train station.

My company was on the parade ground ready to march in review down to the stage where they would listen to speeches, get their graduation papers and assignments in one huge ceremony.

After apologizing to Schromm, I walked into the barracks to pack my sea bag. The only one in there was the guy on watch, and he was getting ready to join the others on the parade ground. He was surprised to see me and only had a few seconds to talk. I asked him to tell Snowball I would meet his at the train station.

I packed my sea bag, was escorted to the shuttle bus, and headed to the train station. It was one of the most heart-wrenching rides of my life. We had to go right past the parade grounds.

There was my company, first in line. We had done it. We were the honor company. We had the most flags. Billy Ray was out in front leading them. I was happy for my company, but my heart hurt for me. I should have been leading them. I started to count the flags, but knew if I did I would start crying, so I faced forward and thought about going on leave.

Snowball was going home to marry his girlfriend, Madeline and had asked me to stop in Philly for a few days and to go to his wedding. I was to stay with him and his family. I said I would love to.

I really liked Snowball. One of his eyes didn't match the other, and he had a few scars from boxing. He was of average size, but he had a charismatic personality – everybody liked being around him. When he told everyone he was going to marry Madeline, someone said, "So then you'll be paddlin' Madeline?" And soon everyone was saying it. You ask Snowball, "What are you doing?" "I'm thinking about paddlin' Madeline." That broke up everybody – we just laughed and laughed.

Thoughts like this helped me pass the time. Three hours I had to wait for the train and Snowball. I was looking forward to meeting his family and seeing his side of the world.

With five minutes left, I figured I better get on the train. I thought that Snowball wasn't going to make it. I took one last look over my shoulder and there he was, running through the crowd with his sea bag over his shoulder. I started yelling, "Over here, over here!" He saw me and ran over to the doorway to get on the train. I grabbed his sea bag and helped him on. I put his sea bag beside mine and we collapsed into a seat. We made it. We graduated boot camp and were going home on leave. Yahoo!

All the way to Philly, 12 hours, Snowball talked about his plans with Paddlin'. We had started calling her 'Paddlin' in boot camp, and now even Snowball called her that. I told him we better go back to calling her Madeline, or we might slip and call her Paddlin' in front of her. He laughed and said "yeah, and then she'd kill me." At that we both laughed. He talked about getting an apartment, furniture, her new job, and all the important things to a newlywed. And of course the wedding. He was really excited, and it was contagious. By the time we got to Philly, I was as excited as he was.

We really didn't have much money as they don't pay recruits a lot. So we planned on taking the bus, a pain in the ass with our sea bags and all. But to our surprise, his mother and his uncle were there with an old Mercury station wagon to pick us up. They knew Snowball was bringing a friend home, but they didn't know he's e white. Boy, were they surprised. His mother said, "What's this, a white boy?" His uncle just shook his head. She said, "Jefferson, you know no white boy belongs in our neighborhood, especially with all those white clothes on." Then she turned to me and said, "I don't mean no disrespect, and I know you Jefferson's friend, but this ain't no place for you."

Snowball said, "Mom, Richard's my best friend and I want him at my wedding. Please, Mom, please." His Mom's name was Judy, Judy White. His uncle was John Washington, Judy's brother. I learned that his father would see us at home as he had to work. Jefferson, Sr., would meet us back at the house later along with his two sisters. Angela, the oldest, was married and expecting her first child, and Deidra, a couple years older than Snowball, had her own place with her boyfriend and he would also be there.

I was a little put off by Snowball's mother's attitude toward me, and more than just a little apprehensive. On the way to Snowballs house, nobody said much, just "how are you, how's it going, are you glad to be home?" Real small talk. I felt I had made a big mistake agreeing to come here.

When we got to the house, there was a whole bunch of people there. Friends, relatives, it was great to see that Snowball was so well liked. Me, I felt like a fish out of water.

Nobody was mean to me, but I didn't get that warm, fuzzy feeling either. I found a place in the corner out of the way and sat there. I guess Angela felt bad for me and, after a while, brought me a plate of food and a cold drink. After I relaxed a little bit, I just sat and watched everybody, and it was a really great family affair. You could actually feel the love they had for each other. One of Snowball's friends came over to talk to me. I was surprised, but enjoyed the company. We talked about boot camp and how Snowball and I had become friends. And a little while into the conversation, I let it slip that we called him

Snowball. At first, his friend just looked at me. I thought how I really fucked up, so I quickly added, "It ain't no racist thing – it just, you know, a black guy named white."I just kinda happened and it stuck.

His friend started laughing and, next thing you know, he told everybody. They all started teasing Snowball, even Madeline. She'd say "Oh Snowball" real sweet-like and everyone would laugh. Well that kind of broke the ice and everyone wanted to know how he got the name. Soon, I was telling everyone about boot camp, Snowball and me and our trip to Chicago, him singing with the Shirelles and, by the end of the night, I felt like one of the family.

The next morning, we all got up to a big breakfast. Judy and the girls all worked together in the kitchen. While I was waiting to eat, Jefferson, Sr. came over to me to talk. He said, "I want to apologize for my wife and the way she acted at the train station. It was just that she was surprised by you being white, that's all." I said, "Forget about it, I have, and I totally understand." Then he turned to me and said, "I like you, Richard. You seem like a real nice guy. Snowball's lucky to have a friend like you." Just then, breakfast was ready. We all ate and got ready to go to the church.

Then John, Snowball's uncle, came in and dropped a bomb. Snowball's best friend, Roosevelt, had been hurt last night and was in the hospital. It seems he was at a club and a problem erupted over a girl. Roosevelt wasn't even really involved, but went to the aid of a girl that was being hit by her boyfriend. Then the boyfriend and a couple of his friends turned on him and beat him pretty bad, and now he's in the hospital.

Roosevelt was supposed to be the best man at the wedding, and now he couldn't make it. What are we going to do? Everyone started talking at once. His mother said, "John, can you do it? Can you be best man?" John said, "I don't know. I'm a little older than Jefferson." Deidra said that her boyfriend can do it. Then Jefferson, Sr. spoke up. He looked at me and said, "Richard, you're Snowball's best friend. You do it." I was surprised at two things: One, he called his son Snowball and two, he named me to be his best man. Before I could answer him, Snowball stepped up and said, "Yes, I want Richard to be my best man." Jefferson, Sr. said, "Well, it's settled then, OK Richard?" I said it would be an honor.

So off to church we went. I was a nervous wreck. I didn't know what I was supposed to do. Everyone was telling me this and telling me that. I was confused to say the least. But I was determined not to let Snowball down.

At the church, Snowball and I waited in a small room beside the altar. We were looking out the door at the people in the church. I was told that, when the music started playing, you know, "Here Comes the Bride", Snowball and I were to walk to the altar.

The people in the church will be looking back at the bride walking down the aisle and wouldn't see us walk out. We would appear as if by magic. It worked like a charm. I felt good. Snowball and I in our dress whites, all the people watching the bride walking with her bridesmaids and flower girl, ring bearer, and her father on her arm. It was a beautiful scene. When they got to the altar, her father turned her over to Snowball, and they turned and stood before the minister, the maid of honor on Madeline's left, and me on Snowball's right. I kept fingering the rings in my pocket to make sure I was ready. The whole ceremony went smooth and, when the ministers said "you may kiss the bride," the whole place erupted with applause and cheers.

Madeline's sister was the maid of honor. She was cute as a button, and smiled at me as she took my arm to walk back down the aisle to the cars waiting out front. When we got to the reception hall, we were lead to the head table and seated. We waited for the rest of the people to come in and sit down. Before the speeches, cutting of the cake, and the mother-and-son and father-and-daughter, then everybody started dancing.

I was still sitting at the head table when Audra, the maid of honor, asked me to dance. I said, "Do you think that's a good idea, me being white and all?" She said, "You the best man, nobody's gonna say nuthin." So I got up and danced. I danced with a couple other bridesmaids and then back to her again. She said, "You sure don't dance like no white man, you can dance." That made me feel good and I added a few more moves I'd been working on. After a while, I had to go. Snowball and Madeleine left on their honeymoon, and I had to catch the train. I asked Audra where to catch a cab as I had to get to the train station. She said, "You don't need no cab. The best man needs a ride. I'll get Uncle John to take you." So Uncle John, Audra and I left for the train station. Audra was a doll. She said that she thought I was nice and she would write to me. Uncle John treated me as one of the family, like we knew each other for a long time. It was a fun ride. I got to the station on time and, to my surprise, Audra kissed me just before I got on the train. I looked over at Uncle John and he just raised an eyebrow and smiled. I remembered that kiss the whole train ride home.

My brother was supposed to pick me up at the train but, when I pulled into Fairfield, there was nobody there. Fairfield was the next town over from my hometown and we had a football rivalry with them. I figured if I hitch hiked, I could get a ride, especially with my uniform on, but it would be rough carrying my sea bag and papers and all. So I went to the ticket window, got a handful of change for the pay phone, and started calling. Nobody home at my house, and cousins, aunts, uncles – no luck. Finally, I called my next door neighbor. He was home waiting to go into the Army. A week later and I would have missed him. He was surprised to hear from me, and said he would be right over to pick me up. Jimmy came about 25 minutes later. We had been neighbors for about 15 years and were really good friends. We made small talk on the way home, how I liked boot camp, he going into the Army and, before you knew it, I was home. I thanked him for the ride and walked up my driveway to the house.

Back then, nobody in town ever locked their door. It's a good thing because there was nobody home and I didn't have a key. Unlike Snowball, there was no party, nothing. I was a little bummed out, but I guess they had their lives to get on with and, whereas Snowball got home in the evening, I got home at 2 o'clock in the afternoon.

The first to see me was my younger brother. He got home from school at 2:30. Boy was he surprised. He said nobody knew I was coming home. I told him I wrote Brendan that I was coming home, and he was supposed to pick me up at the train station. He said Brendan had to go back to college and had a pile of mail sitting on his desk and probably never got the letter.

I learned then never take anything for granted. I just sort of figured that he would tell everyone that I was coming home, and he would pick me up at the train station.

So I hung out with my younger brother, Peter, and waited for my Mom and Dad to get home from work and my sister from cheerleader practice.

My Mom was the first to get home. She hugged and kissed me and said she would make my favorite supper. My sister was the next to come in and she was happy to see me and talked for an hour about what she had been doing. And my Dad came in around 6pm. He smiled when he saw me, asked me to stand up so he could get a good look at me in my Navy uniform. Then he shook my hand and said I looked real grown up.

When I got home, I wanted to put my civvies on, but left my uniform on so my father could see me in it. Now I went to change for supper so I wouldn't spill anything on my whites.

Super was great – roast beef, mashed potatoes, corn, mushroom gravy, my favorite. From the way everyone ate, I think it was all our favorites. After supper, friends and family came by. I really wanted to go uptown and hang with my old buds, but because it was my first night home and all, I decided it would make everyone happy if I stayed in. I still had a week and a half to see my friends.

Next day, Peter and Elizabeth went to school, Dad to work and Mom said I could use her car if I drive her to work and pick her up by 4. After I dropped her off at work, I went looking for my friends. All my friends were either in college or working. I had a coffee at the coffee shop, hung around town for a couple of hours and, when school got out, went to the ball field to watch football practice and see my old coach. Nothing much changed except the kids seemed so much younger and the coaches treated me as more of an equal, like I was a grownup like them.

I felt like a fish out of water – weird. I picked up my Mom, went home, had supper, and after supper, went to see some of my friends who were still around. We hung out on the corner as usual and talked a little about boot camp, and mostly about girls. That's about how my week went. Kinda boring, but still good to see my friends.

Saturday night they had a dance at a ballroom by the lake. They'd been having it for a few years, so I went with my friends. When I first went, I was a sophomore in high school. I was so excited to be going to a dance with all the older kids. This night, I was kinda ho hum and really wasn't into it. I danced with a few girls, hung out with my friends, had an OK time and went home by midnight. I guess I'm starting to grow up. Three days later, I was on a train back to Chicago and "A" school.

I got to Chicago around 8pm, took the bus to the base, and pulled up to the main gate around 10. At the gate, I was instructed to go to barracks 40 and check in with the Master at Arms. When I got to barracks 40, there was no Master at Arms available – he was gone home for the night. So the man on watch showed me to an empty bunk and told me to see the Master at Arms in the morning.

He checked my name off a list he had and left. I got undressed, laid my clothes over my sea bag and went to sleep. In the morning, I was surprised to see Snowball in the bunk a little down from mine. He got in around 11. We checked in with the watch and he said to go to chow and check with the Master at Arms when we got back.

Snowball and I talked about our leave, his new apartment and furniture and all, and he thanked me for being his best man.

When we got back to the barracks, the Master at Arms was there. He was a 2nd Class Boatswains Mate name Vye. That's it – I don't know if he had a first name or last name – he was just called Vye. I learned now that I'm out of boot camp, Petty Officers are called by their name. At first, I kept calling him "Sir", but after a couple days, it was just plain Vye.

He told Snowball and I our schools are full-up for the month and, while we were waiting, we would be house mousing for him. A house mouse is a person who cleans the barracks. There were six buildings in the shape of an "H". They were three stories high, six barracks to a building, with the line between the two legs being showers and head on the right and offices on the left. We had about 40 house mouses to clean six buildings or 36 barracks plus our own.

RAIN: A Sailor's Story

Our building had the mess cooks and house mouses in it. The mess cooks worked three mess halls on main side. Offices mess, enlisted men's mess and chiefs' mess.

I was glad I was house mousing instead of mess cooking. The mess cooks got up at 4:30am and didn't finish work until 7 at night. They had a 2 hour break in the morning and one in the afternoon.

About a week after we started house mousing, we were informed that ten mess cooks were going to be starting school and he needed ten house mouses to replace them. Anyone who didn't want to get on the list had to pay him, the Master at Arms, twenty dollars to stay off the list.

If I had been the first one to go to his office, I probably would have paid the twenty bucks. But as I waited my turn, I started thinking this ain't right. It ain't fair for him to make money off of us over not going mess cooking. When I finally did get to see him, I told him I'm not going to pay him and if he put me on the list, I would request a Captains Mast and report him. He told me all requests had to go through him and he would deny it. So I next told him if he put my name on the list I would kick his ass. He leaned over, put my name on the list and said, "You are now on the list." I let him have it. After the second punch, his Seaman stepped in and grabbed me. Vye punched me in the eye. Before he could hit me again, Snowball jumped in. Where he came from, I don't know, but I was sure happy to see him. Snowball and I beat the hell out of those two and went back to our barracks. About twenty minutes later, the MPs were there to arrest Snowball and me. All I could think of was cell one, rack three, here we go again.

The MPs didn't take us to the brig. They took us to the administration building where they put us in a holding room where we waited for a couple hours to see the Captain in charge of main side.

While we were waiting, the 3rd Class Petty Officer, Vye, and his Seaman told the Captain their lies, and we were interviewed by a Navy Lieutenant. I told my side of the story and Snowball backed me up. When we were finished, the Lieutenant asked us if we were absolutely sure that is what happened. Yes, we are sure, and he can ask the other house mouses. He left. About three hours later, we were brought before the Captain. We marched in, stood at attention, saluted and sounded off. "Richard Elliott, Seaman Apprentice, 668-32-38" And Snowball saluted and sounded off. The Captain saluted back, left us standing at attention and told us what he had found out about the situation and if it was true.

I guess the Lieutenant has interviewed some of the other house mouses, and they all backed up my story, so basically the Captain got it right, and we told him, "Yes, that's right."

He then asked me why I didn't request permission to see my commanding officer. I told him what Vye had said about the chain of command and how he wouldn't approve my chit. He said, "So you think that gave you the right to strike a Senior Petty Officer?" I said what he was doing was against all laws civilian and military, and in doing so I lost all respect for his position and in my opinion he was no longer a Senior Petty Officer, but a criminal who was not only extorting me, but all the other sailors under his command. He obviously had done this before and felt as he could get away with it again and there wasn't anything I could do about it. Well, the only way I could think of to stop him was to fight him and bring to light his criminal activity. The Captain looked at me for a few minutes and said, "You have been thinking about what you were going to say for a while, haven't you?" I said, "Yes, Sir, Snowball and I have been talking about for the last few hours while waiting to see you." He looked over at Snowball and said, "You call him Snowball?" I blushed a little and said, "Yes, Sir. Someone called him that in boot camp and it kinda stuck." He looked at Snowball and said, "Does that bother you?" Snowball said, "No, Sir. I kinda like it." With that, the Captain said, "Take a seat out in the office while I decide what I'm going to do with you two."

We both said, "Yes, Sir," about faced and left his office. While sitting in the outer office, we saw a lot of people coming and going. Offices and enlisted men alike coming and going.

It seemed like forever, but at 7pm, we were finally brought back in before the Captain.

The first thing the Captain said was "Richard, it seems like that this is not the first time you struck a Senior Petty Officer. You like hitting Petty Officers?" "No, Sir. You see, Sir, things happen." "That's enough, Elliott. I don't want to hear it. What you did was wrong, even though your intentions were right. And Snowball...you don't mind if I call you Snowball?" Snowball said, "I would be proud, Sir." "Well, I think that you got involved because of your loyalty to your friend. I've decided that you two will go on KP duty until your classes open up. Dismissed."

Even though we hated to go mess cooking, we both felt we dodged a bullet. Things could have been a lot worse. As for Vye, he was dishonorably discharged and his Seaman was busted to Apprentice and sent back to the fleet.

Snowball and I walked back to the barracks not saying much. We talked a little about getting up early and reporting for mess duty and, although Snowball had been mess cooked in boot camp, I had never been there before.

When we got back to the barracks a bit after 7pm, we got a real surprise. Our barracks was full of people. House mouses, mess cooks, they all lined the stairs and hallways and the barracks 2nd floor where Snowball and I had our bunks and lockers. They were all cheering. These were the people that Vye had screwed over, and were happy that he got what he deserved.

They also thought that Snowball and I had a lot of balls to do what we did. After everyone congratulated us and things quieted down, we went to bed and prepared for mess cooking.

The next morning, we were up at 4am. Headed for the mess hall in out white pants, white t-shirts, boondockers which are the short boots that all sailors were issued in boot camp, and our white hats.

When we got to the mess hall, the Master at Arms was waiting for us. I expected a talking-to, but was surprised that all he did was assign us to a specific duty and told us to report to the Petty Officer in charge.

Bill Callahan was a Second Class Cook E5. He would be in charge of our section. We were assigned to the serving line. Our duties were to heat up the steam table, get the food from the cooks, put it in the steam table and serve it. When the meal was finished, we broke down the steam table, cleaned out the food pans, cleaned up our area and got ready for the next meal. Not too bad, but made for a long day.

Problems started right away. Students were a little demanding. "I want that piece. No, I said that piece." If you just gave them the piece of meat you had ready, they would move the tray and the meat would fall on the steam table or in the gravy or mashed potatoes or on the floor causing a mess that we had to clean up. After the third day of this bullshit, I got real quick at putting their meat on the tray. Then they started tipping it off on purpose. So I started picking it back up and throwing it so it hit them causing a stain on their whites, which had to be clean for class. Now they had to go back to the barracks and put on clean whites. Things started escalating. Most of the students were OK, but some were real assholes.

So the more they made a mess, the more we messed them up. Things got out of hand in the second week. They moved me and Snowball to the scullery. That's where the students dropped off their trays to be washed. Well, the assholes that had been causing the problems in the serving line did the same in the scullery.

Instead of handing in their trays, they started throwing them through the slot at us, sometimes past the deep sinks onto the floor which, of course, we had to pick up and clean. They didn't think we could do anything because there was a divider between us and only a slot to put their trays through. But we had soapy water and, when we saw them coming, we splashed water through the slot and got them soaked. Picture six mess cooks splashing water through six slots as the students went by.

The students were led by a Seaman named Michael Smith. He was a little older than the rest of the guys, had spent time in the fleet before coming to "A" school, and was an E3. The rest of us were E2.

One afternoon, he told me to get my men together, that after the evening meal he and his students were coming back to kick the shit out of us. He said, "Meet us out at the steam shed behind the mess hall or you're a coward." We found out he had about 90 students coming to beat us up.

We had about 40 mess cooks willing to fight. So after the evening meal, we went behind the steam shack where they had just finished steaming out the garbage cans. We had our gear on. We had pots, steel bowls and colanders on our heads. Some of the pots had handles sticking out. For weapons, we had ladles and serving spoons. What I did was put 25 men in front of the steam shed with Snowball and me and the other 15 men were behind the shed. When the students came down the hill, there looked to be more than 90, but my guys held tight. Just as the first group got to my guys, they got hit by ladles and spoons, but couldn't pull back because other students were pushing in from the back. At that point, me and my men came racing out from behind the sheds screaming, yelling and swinging our spoons. We must have looked a sight: pots with handles sticking out on our heads, swinging those huge serving spoons and ladles, and screaming our lungs out. Scared the shit out of the students. When they saw us, they turned and ran. Snowball and his guys started screaming and we chased them all the way back up the hill. But when we turned to walk back to the mess hall, we saw the MPs pull up. They rounded up everybody – students and mess cooks alike. When everything got straightened out and everyone had given their name, rank and service number, we were allowed to go back to our barracks. We didn't get back until around 9pm. We didn't know what was going to happen the next day, but we were sure it wasn't going to be nice.

We got up the next morning at the usual time – 4am – got cleaned up and reported for duty at the mess hall.

Everyone was abuzz about what happened and what was going to happen. At 10 o'clock, we found out. The mess cooks who were involved in the melee yesterday were to report down to long desk. Long desk is slang for administration building. I figured 10am was a good time so to get us back for the midday meal.

We all marched over together and were ushered into a large hall at the back in the end of the building.

There were half a dozen MPs and two officers waiting to see us. We were told that our actions of the day before were not to be tolerated and, if we had anything to say, to speak up now. Well, of course, I had something to say. I told him that the students attacked us and we were just defending ourselves. He told me that we knew the attack was coming and that we should have reported it to our superiors.

Next, he handed out our punishment. Everyone got 30 days restriction to base, and Snowball and I were told to wait right where we were while the rest of the mess cooks went back to work.

As this was going on, the students got the same ass-chewing and punishment, and Michael Smith was told to remain. Twenty minutes later, Snowball, me, and Mike were outside the Captains office awaiting our fate.

Mike was the first to go in. When he came out, he told us he was busted back to Seaman Apprentice and, if he didn't get into any more trouble, he would get his stripe back when he graduated "A" school. He was also restricted to base for 30 days.

Snowball and I were next. We went in, stood at attention and sounded off. The Captain returned our salute and told us to stand at parade rest. That usually means we're going to be there a while.

He started off by saying "Didn't I make myself clear? You were sent to KP duty to keep you out f trouble and for punishment because of the problems you had cleaning the barracks. Richard, you've proven you're a natural leader, and it aggravates me to see you wasting your talents. You're heading in the wrong direction. Instead of bucking the system, you should try working with it. And you, Snowball, can't you think for yourself? Do you have to do everything Richard tells you? If he told you to jump off the Brooklyn Bridge, would you? Well, would you??"

Snowball spoke up and said, "No, Sir. I wouldn't. I'm from South Philly. I wouldn't be caught dead in Brooklyn." He was dead serious when he said it. He wasn't trying to be a wise ass. The Captain knew it too, and the irony of the statement made the Captain do his best to suppress a smile. The Captain then turned to me and said, "Apparently, you have no respect for the chain of command. What's your problem?"

I finally said, "When I was in boot camp, my company commander was never around. He left everything on me. I had to read a list of classes I had to attend for the week. That was all the training I got from him. I followed what the other companies were doing and managed to win honor company, and when I needed him to reprimand the company, he was nowhere around, so I took it upon myself to correct their behavior and I'm the one that got in trouble for it. You expect me to respect a man who shirks his duty? And when I came to main side for "A" school, I am put to work for a 2nd Class Petty Officer who extorts money from the men in his command. From everything I seen so far in this man's Navy, I've yet to meet a Petty Officer who deserves my respect, Sir. That's not to say that I disrespect everyone. I have met some decent people, which gives me hope that things will get better. I have to say that you taking the time to investigate things and not just hand out punishment has gained a tremendous amount of respect from me. I know what I did was wrong, but also it solidified the mess cooks and made us respect each other more. The skirmish was not that bad. I do realize someone could have been hurt bad but, on the other hand, it set the boundaries between the mess cooks and students and gained some respect for the mess cooks."

The Captain looked as us for a long minute and finally said, "You two go back to work. I'll notify you when I figure out what to do with you."

Snowball and I went back to the mess hall. We were asked by everyone what happened, and we told them they haven't figured that out.

Things changed at the mess hall. The mess cooks were a tighter group and a little proud of themselves. The cooks and other Petty Officers even treated us a little better. The bickering between the students and mess cooks stopped and we even made some new friends.

Michael Smith and I started talking and soon became friends, visiting each other's barracks after work to talk, mostly about school and his experience in the fleet.

It took the Captain three days to figure what to do with Snowball and me. The punishment he handed down was a complete surprise and, two days later, we were on a bus heading for the airport.

Snowball and I had weekend duty at the mess hall, so we just hung out on our time off at the barracks worrying about what was in store for us.

Monday morning at 10 o'clock, we got the word that the Captain wanted to see us. Everybody started saying shit like "What you two got going with the Captain? You're in there all the time." They laughed. Not us. We knew that this was it. To say we were nervous was to put it mildly.

When we got there, we waited in the outside office for about ten minutes. Then we went in, stood at attention and sounded off.

The Captain returned our salute and told us to stand at parade rest. He said, "I tried to find an adequate way to teach you to respect your chain of command. I think I came upon something that will give us the answer, one way or another. Richard, you and Theodore are going to Vietnam for six months duty at a crypto lab outside of Saigon. Your flight leaves in two days. Furthermore, in order to be eligible for this assignment, you have to hold the rate of E3. So as of today, you two will have to sew your new stripes on. Are there any questions?"

I know I had a million questions and I didn't know where to start. What the fuck is a Vietnam and where the fuck is it? What is a crypto lab? Who is gonna pay for the flight? Do we get leave before we go? And so on and so on. But all I did is just stand there. Snowball didn't ask any questions either. So the Captain said, "Report to the Officer of the Day. You two are dismissed."

When we got out to the outer office, Snowball turned to me and said, "Hot damn! We got promoted to E3." I said to him, "Yeah, but what and where is Vietnam?" Snowball said, "I guess we'll find out when we check in with the Officer of the Day."

We walked down the hall to the office where the Officer of the Day was already standing there waiting for us. We saluted and started to sound off when he just waved it aside and told us to sit down. He said, "I know you've got a lot of questions, so let's get started. You two are being sent to South Vietnam. South Vietnam is part of Indochina, just south of China. At this point, Vietnam is separated into two halves – North Vietnam and South Vietnam."

"North Vietnam is communist and South Vietnam is a democracy. We have close to 20,000 military advisors helping the South Vietnamese government. We also have a large part of the sixth fleet in the South China Sea and the Tonkin Gulf just outside of South Vietnam. Do you understand what I've just explained to you? "We both said, "Yes, Sir." "Before you ask any questions, I am going to explain your duties to you. In order for you to have passed the test for "A" school, your particular school requires you to have passed a security check and get a top secret clearance. That clearance is what was needed in sending you to your next duty station. A crypto clearance lab outside of Saigon. A crypto lab has the ability to decipher encrypted messages. At this point in time, few ships have crypto deciphering equipment on board so these messages will be deciphered at the crypto lab and hand delivered to the ships at anchor out in the Tonkin Gulf. You will be trained at your new duty station as to what your jobs entail. In the next two days,

RAIN: A Sailor's Story

you will sew your stripes on and get ready to leave Thursday am. You two are dismissed. You will meet back here tomorrow at 1000 hours for your orders. At that time, you can ask questions that you haven't figured out for yourselves. I suggest you use the library. Dismissed."

Great Lakes training center in Illinois is a large training center. It covers about 30 square miles in all. If you stood it the center, you could walk two miles in any direction and still be on base. It has everything it needs to sustain itself. Boot camp has three camps with their own barracks, chow hall, administration building, classrooms and parade grounds. Main side has five mess halls, two administration buildings, four churches, 36 barracks, 12 different "A" schools, a library, a hospital, a movie theatre, three parade grounds, nurses quarters, officers quarters, chiefs quarters, first and second class quarters, chiefs' club, acey ducey first and second class petty officers club, two geedonks, which are like a combination deli-coffee shop, the brig and the Marine barracks and chow hall. So the place is quite large.

Snowball and I decided he would take our clothes to the laundry and also our dress clothes to the tailor and have our stripes sewn on. He was really excited to be getting his third stripe. Me, on the other hand, would go to the library and find out what I could about Vietnam.

When I got to the library, I was surprised to find that the librarian was a civilian and a man. I asked where I might find information on Vietnam and a world atlas so I could find it on a map.
At first, he just looked at me for a few minutes and asked why I was interested in that particular area. I told him I was being transferred and it was my next duty station.

A strange look came over his face and he said, "If you've got the time, I can tell you most of what you want to know."

I'm being shipped out in two days, all I have to do it pack my sea bag, so I guess I got the time.

He said. "Sit over here. This will take a while, and I may have to get up if someone comes in and needs something. When we first started showing an interest in Vietnam back in the late 50's, I started studying up on it. In the late 1600s, France with its Foreign Legions invaded Vietnam and made it a colony of theirs. There has been an ongoing struggle between the Vietnamese people and the French since that time. In 1941 when the Japanese joined the 2nd World War by bombing Pearl Harbor and dragging us into it, the French, even though they were invaded by the Germans, still had their Foreign Legion in Vietnam. The French wanted to pull their Legions out of Southeast Asia and join the allies in Europe. So the United States went to Vietnam and basically told them that, if they would allow us to use their air bases for our military planes in the fight against Japan, the French would pull out and we would turn the country back over to the Vietnamese people when the war was over.

When the war was over, the French basically told us we had no right to make that deal and, against our advice, moved back into Vietnam. After World War 2, Russia retained all European countries it liberated from the Germans, including East Germany, making them communists.

Also, right after the war, the Chinese embraced communism and tried spreading the communist philosophy to their neighboring countries including Korea and Vietnam.

The United States joined the Korean War to stem the flow of communism, but the socialist philosophy in its purest form was very attractive to the masses, and the democratic philosophy was also attractive to the people. SO part of the people wanted communism and part wanted a democracy. Communism is basically socialism.

RAIN: A Sailor's Story

People are not born equal. Some are bigger, stronger, better looking, smarter, have better reactions, eyesight, instincts, etc., while others are not as gifted. Socialism basically figures that people should be treated equally. If you're smarter and can work at a better job, then someone who is not so smart, because we are all equal in this society, we should all share equally in the wealth. We all work to our potential and share equally in the wealth.

In a democracy, we should all work to our fullest potential, but the money we earn is taxed to the more you earn, the more you're taxed. Those taxes are used to take care of the society as a whole. So if you are gifted enough to earn more money, you keep more of it as everyone pays the same percentage in taxes to the government to run the country and assist the poor.

In the early 50's, we fought a war in Korea and it ended by splitting the country in half. At the same time, the French were in an unannounced war with the Vietnamese. It finally ended in 1958, dividing Vietnam in half. In 1959, the United States sent military advisors into South Vietnam to help train their military to defend themselves against the flow of Communism. And now we have more than 20,000 advisors in South Vietnam. We only admit to 5,000. That, basically, is what you're walking into.

I was a little bit stunned by the information. I knew a little bit about the history of Korea, but had learned nothing about Vietnam. If the United States promised to leave the country in the hands of the Vietnamese people, why are we going back now?

Well, it is what it is, and I guess Snowball and I are headed to war. But being in a crypto lab can't be as bad as being on the front line. After talking to the librarian, I went over to the world atlas and looked up Indochina and Vietnam, found it and left to go back to the barracks and pack my gear.

Snowball and I walked down the hill to the chow hall. On the way, we talked about what I had learned from the librarian. Snowball knew nothing about our involvement in Vietnam. It was September, 1962. Not too many Americans realized how involved we were in the struggle against communism in Southeast Asia.

After lunch, we went to the tailor shop to pick up our uniforms with our new stripes. Snowball was all excited. He talked me into putting my dress whites on so we go to the chow hall and show off our new rate. Me, I was still apprehensive about our new assignment. I was preparing a mental list of questions I wanted to ask at our 10am meeting with the Officer of the Day.

When we walked into his office, he handed each of us a folder. In it were our orders and plane tickets. That answered some of my questions, 1. No leave. 2. The government pays for our flight. Next, he told us that there would be a 1-hour indoctrination class at 1300 hours in the Intelligence Office at the main administration building. "Now, are there any questions?" I had no questions for him, but some about crypto lab and our new duty assignments. I guess I'll find out about that at the indoctrination class.

Snowball and I walked to the chow hall. We were a little early, so we hung around for a while wondering what was going to happen. Snowball loved his new stripes and wasted no time in showing them off. After chow, we walked to the administration building and sat on a bench outside the class room. We looked around, but we were the only two there. The instructor came in and I was surprised to see he was a full Lieutenant. Most, if not all, instructors up 'til now had been Petty Officers.

We stood and saluted; he returned our salutes and waved us into the class room. It would be a private class for Snowball and me. He started off by introducing himself, a Lieutenant Curry, and acknowledged that we were Seamen Elliott and White.

He went on to explain about the crypto code and the equipment needed to send and receive code and decode messages that were secret or top secret. Snowball and I were being sent to Saigon to deliver the decoded messages to the ships anchored in the Tonkin Gulf just offshore. He lectured us for about two hours at what we were to expect, how we were to act and how to request permission to go on board a ship. Little things, but things we needed to know.

When he dismissed us, we walked back to our barracks to finish up any last-minute things to get ready to ship out the next day. We both felt that we were being sent to do an important job, and were kind of proud and looking forward to it.

The next day, we were on the bus headed to the airport, sea bags in hand along with our orders. We flew from Chicago to San Francisco. It took about 3-1/2 hours. We had about a 1-1/2 hour wait for our plane to Hawaii. Then we had to deplane and walk across the tarmac to the airport where we waited for our plane to Okinawa, Japan. By now, boredom had set in. We slept as much as we could and now we were just plain bored. On the flight to Japan, we were accompanied by a couple of Marines headed for the same place. They sat across the aisle from us and we talked about what we had heard about Vietnam. They we going to Da Nang to add to the support of the air strip. Talking to them made the flight go by faster. When we reached Okinawa, we needed to take a bus from the civilian airport to the military airstrip. When we got to the military base, we checked in and they gave us a place to sleep as we had to spend the night because the next flight to Da Nang was at 1000 hours the next day. We settled into our rooms, cleaned up and walked over to the chow hall. After chow, Snowball and I said goodbye to our two new friends as they had their own rooms, and went back to our room. We wrote letters home and finally got a good night's sleep after 22 hours of flying.

The next morning Reveille sounded at 6am. Snowball and I were well rested, hopped out of bed, cleaned up and headed to the chow hall for breakfast.

After breakfast, we picked up our gear and headed for the administrative building. There we were ushered into a waiting area with a bunch of Marines who were also waiting for a flight to Da Nang.

Snowball and I were the only sailors there. We felt out of place, but soon after talking to them they made us feel right at home. In fact, we were like celebrities as we were E3 in rate and most of them were E2 Privates.

The flight was 10 hours of misery. The air was turbulent and the seats were benches against the sides of the plane. Down the middle of the plane was cargo and supplies going with us.

We landed just as it was getting pretty dark. When we got off the plane, the first thing I noticed was the humidity. The air was saturated and smelled wet. It made the heat even more oppressive. Within five minutes, I was soaked with sweat.

Looking around, trying to get my bearings, I saw some buildings like warehouses to the left of the plane. To the rear and left, I saw what looked like the administration building and figured that was probably where we were going to go.

Not knowing what else to do, we lined up with the Marines. They were told to right face and were preparing to march in the direction of that administration building, so we fell in behind them. As we were about to start marching, a jeep pulled up and we heard, "Hey, sailors." We turned to see a 2nd Class Boatswain Mate driving toward us and waving us over. "Are you Elliott and White?" We said, "Yes." He told us he was there to pick us up and bring us to our new duty station.

It took us about 1-1/2 hours to get to where we were to spend the next six months of our lives. It was dark by then and we didn't get a real good look at our new duty station. We had Marines guarding the gate and about 1/3 of a mile ride to the building we were to check into.

The Petty Officer on duty took our orders and showed us to our room. The room they showed us to was decent. Two bunks, bureaus instead of lockers, and lamps on nightstands. They left us to ourselves, telling us that someone would formally check us in the morning. I had to take a leak and wanted a shower, so I went looking for the leak and shower room which, it turned out, were just down the hall. After taking care of business and getting cleaned up, we were ready for a good night's sleep. It had been a long 48 hours since we left Chicago.

At two o'clock in the morning, we were awakened by the sound of fireworks or something. Snowball and I ran out into the reception area to find out what was going on. There was a new sailor on watch and he told us that "Charlie" (the Viet Cong) was shelling the air base with mortars.

It usually happens a couple of times a week. Thinking of when we flew in, I remembered seeing craters in the runway and wondering why they didn't fix them. I asked if they ever bombed us and the guard told us, "Not yet, thank God." After that we went back to bed. I tossed and turned for about an hour, but finally got back to sleep. It seemed that I just got back to sleep and Reveille sounded.

Snowball and I jumped to our feet, both of us looking bewildered. Next thing, we started laughing. Whatever came next, we would face it together.

We got cleaned up and put on our work clothes figuring that was what we were supposed to report in for work, and went up the road to the chow hall. There was a small line, so we just fell in at the end and followed everyone else. After getting our tray full of scrambled eggs, sausage, hash, home fries and coffee, we sat at a table with two 3rd Class Firemen. They don't fight fires. They fire up the engines. They told us they drove the boats that delivered the messages to the fleet. We also had engine men that drove and repaired the engines. After chow, we went back to the crypto lab to officially check in.

We were a little early as the time to check in was 7:30 and it was only 7 o'clock so that gave us a half hour to check things out.

Our building was good size. It had living quarters for 30 people. Along the back of the building were the enlisted men's quarters. Not like a barracks, but separate two-man rooms. At the end were the officers' quarters, three single rooms and one small apartment. The officers had their own latrine and the enlisted men had theirs at the opposite end of the hall. The hall to the front of the building had two offices on each side. One side had the crypto lab itself and on the other was the Captains office which, in this case, was a commander one step below Captain. The other office was the personnel office. They had all our records, pay master, duty roster and that stuff.

With Snowball and I coming on board, it brought the total of personnel to 29. Three officers and 26 enlisted men. We had 6 motor launches with 4 engine men and 2 fire men running them. With the addition of Snowball and me, that brought up the number of messengers to 7. We had 4 radio men that ran the crypto lab, 2 personnel men, a quartermaster, 2 officers, orderlies, and barracks chief, and 4 other Seamen that stood watch and cleaned the barracks. When we weren't out delivering messages, we were required to stand duty one day a week in a rotation. So it was a different day every week and one weekend a month.

Our guide through all this was an engine man named Earl Peavey. He was a 3rd Class Petty Officer and came from West by God Virginia. That's the way he called it. Fine with me. He told us things were kind of informal here, but be on our toes when we went on the ships. Also, we had to change into our dress white, no neckerchiefs. That would be our uniform of the day for delivering messages.

By the time our tour was over and we had changed into our whites, it was time to fall in. We fell in with the group of sailors who had lined up in the big room in the front part of the building. As the Captain or, in this case, the Commander walked in, the Officer of the Day yelled, "Attention on deck!" We all snapped to attention as the Commander stepped up and said, "At ease." He started by saying he would like to welcome two new sailors on board – Seaman White and Seaman Elliott. Then he told us that the Marines received mortar fire at the airport and there were no injuries, and everyone clapped at that, and told us to stay alert as things have escalated lately and Charlie is a little more daring in their attacks. Then he dismissed us and told us to carry on. Snowball and I reported to the Officer of the Day, an Ensign Peers who took us into the crypto lab, introduced us to the lab techs who were trained radio men, and started telling us what our duties would be.

On the table was a map of the Tonkin Gulf and on the map were placed ships with a name tag on it. When a ship sailed off, the name was taken off and a new tag was put on the ship that replaced it. At present, there were nine ships anchored outside out cove waiting for us to deliver their messages. The engine men were required to memorize the map, and it was a good idea if we memorized it also. Every morning, we would pick up our messages, take them down to the pier and board a motor launch. An engine man or fireman would drive us to whatever ship was on the envelope. Sounded easy. We watched as other sailors picked up their envelopes and headed out the door.

Ensign Peers directed us over to a 2nd Class Radio Man named Douglas Knight. Everyone called him Dougy. He was to be our next in command and our message officer. We introduced ourselves, shook hands all around, and were handed a message with a ships name and number on it. Then we were taken over to the map and shown where the ship was. Then they told us to go down to the pier and deliver the message. As luck would have it, my driver was 3rd Class Engine Man Peavey, and Snowball got 2nd Class Engine Man Penny. They hung together like Snowball and I, and I had a good feeling about our new assignment.

My next problem was to find the pier. We really didn't see much on our way up the road to the chow hall, but I figured it was probably around back.

So Snowball and I walked out the front door and headed down a pathway toward the back of the building. When we got around to the back, we saw a really awesome cove. It was shaped like a horseshoe with salt marsh flats on each side and a deeper channel that ran right up the middle. The pier was right in front of us and had berths for eight motor launches even though we had only six. I was told that sometimes the ships sent in their own launches and they tied up in the empty slots. In case there was no more room, we had an extra place at the end of the pier for another launch.

The pier was a floating pier and raised and lowered with the tide.

This particular morning, it was low tide and we could see the mud flats. But at high tide, the cove was full of water. I thought the place was beautiful. I loved the smell of the ocean, the look and feel of everything. I knew I was going to like it here.

I saw Peavey and Snowball got introduced to Penny, and off we went. On the way to the first ship - I had two messages to two different ships – Peavey explained to me the proper procedure on bow to board the ship. They had a platform on the water that we would pull up to. I would then step off the launch and onto the platform, climb the ladder – actually a staircase, but in the Navy, all stairs are called ladders.

At the top, I would step on board, salute the Officer of the Day, and request permission to come on board. He would then return my salute and grant my request. Then he would ask me my reason for coming on board. I would tell him I have a message for his Captain and that I have to deliver it personally. He would then have the Petty Officer of the watch take me to see the Captain. When I stepped in front of the Captain, I would salute and tell him my name, rank and service number, and tell him I have a letter for him.

He would return my salute and take the letter. I would remain at attention -- or at ease if he gave me the command -- and wait for his reply. After reading the letter, most times he would dismiss me, but once in a while, he would give me a message to bring back to the lab.

At first I was a little nervous but, after a couple days, it was easy and I felt important. I really started to like it here.

After I delivered the mail – that's what we started calling it – Peavey and I went back to the base. I went up to the lab and Peavey checked out the boats refueling, oiling and general maintenance. We agreed to meet later for chow and he said we should go out for a beer if I didn't have duty that night. I couldn't wait.

Snowball got back a little before me and waited for me to go to chow. The mess hall was over for lunch, but they kept some food out for us lab rats – that's what they called us cause we worked at the crypto lab – and we didn't know exactly when we would be back from delivering the mail.

The whole base was there for the crypto lab. The Marines that guarded the base, the chow hall, the Marine barracks, the laundry and the PX - all there for our top-secret coding laboratory. It made me feel kind of special. After we ate, Snowball and I went back to the lab. We cleaned our room, checked in with the Master at Arms, got put on duty or watch list and learned more about our duties, watches and layout of the base.

Peavey, or Peave as he was called, and Penny, who everyone called Chris, got back in around 4:30, went to their rooms and got ready for chow. An hour later, we were all in the chow hall eating and talking about going up to the Little America bar which was the only place to go around there and have a few beers. After chow, we headed for the main gate, showed out ID cards and walked out towards the road. A little outside the gate was this Vietnamese kid with a three-wheel bicycle. It had a large bench seat in the back and he peddled from up front, kind of like a rickshaw.

The kid called to us and asked, "You want ride liksaw?" It was about ½ mile walk to the Little America, so Peave and I walked and Snowball and Chris rode in the liksaw. It cost 10 cents apiece each way as he would also ride you hack to base when the time came. I ended up riding in the liksaw a lot as the only thing to do at night was go to the Little America or hang around your room. Hanging around the room was boring, so Little America it was.

When we got to the Little America, the juke box was going and the place was already a little crowded. It was about 8:15, still light out, but it was getting dark. There were more Marines than sailors, but everyone got along OK.

The bar was directly across from the front door, against the back wall. Up to the left were some tables and chairs, a small dance floor and a juke box against the front wall a few feet from the door. To the right were a bunch more tables and chairs and up at the right end were three pool tables. Snowball, Peavey, Chris and I headed toward the tool tables and sat at an empty table. Peavey and I headed to the bar to pick up the beers.

Behind the bar was a pretty Vietnamese woman. She looked to be about 30 years old, but it was hard to tell. She could have been 10 years younger or 10 years older. Along the bar and out on the dance floor were more Vietnamese girls. They were mostly small, young – say 18 to 25 – and were cute. Some not so cute, some real cute, but all were sexy. They dressed sexy, acted sexy and talked dirty. Me, I like a little romance with my sex, but from the way these girls talked, it was strictly business. To me, that was kind of a turn-off. I was raised different than that and, don't get me wrong, I'm not gay or nothing, but it was a little too impersonal to me.

For a girl to just walk up and say, "You want to boom-boom? Me make you happy for you one dollar, two dollar for room." There was no discussion, no getting to know you, just a straight business deal. All four of us said no. Peavey and I returned to the table with the beers. Chris was a good pool player and had his challenge up for the next game. Me, I just wanted to have a few beers and get the feel of the place. Snowball was at the juke box putting some money in and picking out some songs. When he got back to the table, he said there isn't much on there, but I found some decent stuff. He said, "You know there is even some French stuff on there – must be left over from when the French were here." Peavey said, "Yeah, the bartended speaks French, English and Vietnamese. Speaks all three fairly fluently." Chris said, "Yeah, and she can swear pretty good in all three too."

We just sat around playing music, drinking beer and shooting pool. I played a couple games – won one, lost two. Chris beat me. He was like the guy to beat. Snowball sang along with the music and Peavey drank beer and talked and flirted with the whores. There was one that caught my eye, but I wasn't ready for that just yet. I figured I'd wait, get more used to the place and see how things shake out. Around 10 o'clock, I decided to go back to base. It was our first day there and I had done a lot, was kind of tired, wanted to be ready for tomorrow and digest everything that had happened.

Snowball said he would go with me and Chris and Peave said they wanted to stay a little longer and they would see us tomorrow. When Snowball and I stepped out the door, the liksaw was there so we gave the kid twenty cents and rode back to the base in style. We showed our IDs at the gate and walked the 1/3 of a mile to our building.

We checked in with the Watch and went to our room and went right to sleep. It was a long, difficult day for both of us. I felt not only tired, but good. I had a good feeling about this place. Little did I know that, in a few days, all that was going to change?

The next day, Snowball and I went to chow, met up with Peave and Chris. Peave went with one of the girls and said it was the best three dollars he ever spent. Chris said, "I hope you wore a hat (meaning a rubber) or your dick's gonna fall off." We all laughed. Peave blushed and laughed and we walked back to the morning meeting at the lab.

After checking in at the meeting, Peave and Chris went to the boats, and Snowball and I went into the lab to pick up the messages.

Time to deliver the mail. Boy did I like the job. The cove, the boat, driving around the ocean from ship to ship and back to the cove. It was great – the smell of the ocean, always a breeze, and everyone going out of their way to help me in any way to make things easier for me. My job was real important and I loved it.

That night we went back to the Little America. We did about the same things, but this time I started a conversation with the little cutie I saw the night before. She actually talked to me and wasn't all business like. She talked some small talk but, after a few minutes, asked the usual question: "You want boom-boom?" I said no, figuring she'd probably walk away and was pleasantly surprised when she stayed, seemed more relaxed and talked a while longer.

At about 10pm, some Marines in battle gear came in and told us to go back to the base. Everyone is on alert. Charlie's been acting up lately and the shits hit the fan up at Da Nang.

So we all got out and walked back to the base. Peave and Chris went to their rooms and Snowball and I went to ours.

Next morning, the base was abuzz about the attack on Da Nang. A bunch of Viet Cong guerilla fighters attacked the base and were driven off by the Marines. There were all kinds of rumors about casualties, dead count and prisoners. Everyone heard something from someone but, by the time it got to us, everyone got a different rumor. But the chatter kept going, mostly all misinformation.

I figured we would get the real info at the morning meeting with the Commander. When the Commander came in, Ensign Peers yelled, "Attention on deck!" We all came to attention. Things seemed a little tense. The commander had a tight look on his face and didn't give us the order to parade rest for a few minutes. He just looked at us while he got his thoughts together. When he finally put us at ease, he said "I suppose you all heard the rumors about Charlie attacking the airbase at Da Nang?

Well, they did. The Marines repelled the attack, killing 18, wounding 9 more and taking 6 prisoners. The Marines received 1 dead and 3 wounded. Three planes were heavily damaged and the administration building took some damage.

We are all currently on high alert and will remain that way until told otherwise. After this meeting you will be issued flak jackets and will report to the armory and pick up a weapon. The Marines at the armory will instruct you on how to use your weapon. You will then return here and carry out your duties. If you have any questions, Ensign Peers will answer them. 2nd Class Petty Officer Penny and 2nd Class Petty Officer Knight will be in charge, along with the Marines, of handing out your weapons. Ensign Peers will now take over the meeting." The only question I had was 'Is Charlie heading this way?' Nobody had that answer and the next thing you know was Penny and Dougy handing out flak jackets and lining us up to go to the armory for a weapon.

When we got there, the Marines were waiting for us. The Marines carried M14s, but the Navy carried 30 caliber carbine and Thompson submachine guns. Peavey, Dougy and Penny chose a 45 caliber handgun. I would have chosen one, but there weren't any more when it came my time to choose. With the job I had, it was easier to carry a sidearm than a rifle. Snowball chose a 45-caliber Thompson submachine gun. With three fully-loaded 30-round clips, it weighed in the neighborhood of 25 pounds. He said he saw one on a TV show and since then always wanted one. I chose a 30-caliber carbine. Loaded with a 10-round clip, it weighed less than 9 pounds. With the sling, I could easily carry it over my shoulder, so I guess it was second-best to a sidearm.

The Marines spent the next 4 hours instructing us on the use of the individual weapons. We all got to load and fire them. Snowball had a grin from ear to ear when he fired that Thompson. He even let me fire it. I had to admit it was impressive. I almost second-guessed myself on my choice of weapon, but then I figured it may be fun to shoot, but carrying it

RAIN: A Sailor's Story

every day would be a pain in the ass. I'd much rather be carrying 9 lbs. instead of 25.

When we got back to the lab, our mail was ready so we packed up and went down to the boats and delivered the mail. Because of the late start, we didn't finish delivery until just before evening chow. With the activities of the day, we missed noon chow, so all of us were pretty hungry.

Because of the high alert status, we were restricted to base, so we hung around the pier that evening and familiarized ourselves with our weapons and each others. I liked my carbine, and Peavy and Chris's 45s. And we all were impressed with Snowball's Thompson submachine gun.

After firing the guns trying to hit a rock here or a piece of driftwood over there, we picked up and went back to the lab. It was starting to get dark and we needed to get ready for the next day.

The next day, we had a new ship on the map – a large, heavy cruiser called the Bainbridge. It was an older model, not yet equipped with a crypto lab of their own, so I had two messages to deliver to them. I also had one to deliver to a destroyer that was anchored closer to shore so Peavey figured we would go there first and hit the cruiser second.

When we got to the cruiser, I couldn't believe the size of the thing. It was 2-1/2 times bigger than a destroyer. We mostly deliver messages to destroyers as most of the larger ships have their own deciphering equipment.

The Bainbridge hadn't gotten their yet, but were in line to get it as soon as they got back to the states.

The ship being anchored so far out took us a whole to get there. With a stop off at the first ship and travel time to cruise out there, it took us about 2 to 2-1/2 hours to reach the Bainbridge.

The ladder to get on board was about 30 steps, so I was a little winded when I got on deck. I saluted the Officer of the Deck and requested permission to come on board. The first thing he said was, "Where the hell have you been? The Captain calls every 5 minutes looking for his order. You left base over two hours ago." I told him that I had to deliver a message to a destroyer on the way out and, because they were anchored out so far, it took us a little longer than usual to get there. He told me in no uncertain terms that a cruiser was much more important than a destroyer, and I was duty obligated to deliver their messages first. I just said, "Yes Sir. Understood, Sir." Next, he said, "Petty Officer O'Neil will escort you to see the Captain."
    When I got into the Captains office, saluted and sounded off, he saluted back and took the messages. I stood there waiting for his to read the messages in case he wanted to send a reply back to the lab. He said, "You can go now, sailor." I said, "Excuse me Captain, but it's customary for me to wait until you have read your message just in case you want to have me return a message to the lab." He looked at me for a second and said, "I told you can leave now. Is that clear, sailor?" I said "Yes, Sir," saluted, he returned my salute, I about faced and got out of there as quickly as I could without running. When I got back to the launch, I told Peavey what an asshole the Captain was. "Yeah," he said, "You're going to run into one of them once in a while."
    Peavey's an E4, Penny's an E5, and Snowball and I ware E3. We all talk and hang out together just like we're all the same, but I know that if a decision has to be made, the senior man among us makes the decision. Other military personnel are treated the same way. Non-commissioned officers like Sergeants in the Marines and Petty Officers in the Navy are superior to Privates, Corporals and Navy Seamen. But they don't usually throw their weight around. But once in a while,

you run across a prick. That being said, it happens more back in the states at training facilities, more than when you're out in the fleet. And it happens a lot less when you're in combat situations. Everyone knows what each other is capable of, and you rely on your training and follow your orders from the senior people in your unit.

Peavey got us back to the lab late that afternoon. We missed lunch by a couple hours and, even though we were hungry, we waited until evening chow to eat.

Snowball and I hung around the base down by the water talking about our day and carrying our flak jackets and rifles. Even though we were off duty, with the base being on high alert, we had to keep our weapons with us at all times.

The next morning, we were told that the alert status had been lowered from high to just plain alert. By then we had all stopped wearing our vests and just carried them with us. They made the wooden seats on the motor launch a lot more comfortable. After the meeting, we delivered the mail and, when we got back, we were told that, if we didn't have the duty, we could leave the base on liberty that night. So the four of us went back to the Little America, sang songs, played pool, drank beer, flirted with the girls and generally had a good time. Chris and I took the liksaw back to the base, as Snowball and Peavey had left a little earlier.

One day stretched into the next. The newness of our assignments started to wear off. I still enjoyed my job, and the cove and boat and stuff, but it was starting to become more ho-hum and less exciting.

Then one morning it happened – what we all had in the back of our minds, but no one talked about.

As Snowball and I were leaving, we heard a lot of pops like fireworks and, from our experience with getting our weapons, we knew right away it was machine gun fire. But who was

Richard Elliott

shooting and who were they shooting at? When I saw the dirt around us popping up, I knew they were shooting at us. I yelled, "Snowball, let's get back to the lab. They're shooting at us!" So he and I started running. I dropped my flak jacket and messages because I could run faster without them. Snowball also dropped his, I still had my carbine and Snowball's machine gun was still strapped across his back. A lot of good that did us – we didn't have time to use them.

I was a little ahead of Snowball and, from the sound of his footsteps and the noise his machine bun made bouncing on his back; I knew he was right behind me. I turned to check on Snowball and he wasn't there. I looked back and saw him lying on the ground, bullets kicking up dirt all around. I started to run back to get Snowball when I got yanked backwards off my feet and pulled into the lab. The door slamming shut behind me.

I jumped to my feet yelling, "Let me go. I gotta get Snowball. They're shooting at him!" They told me I can't go back out the door, that Snowball was probably already dead. I refused to believe it. I ran to the window, but the metal shutters that cover the windows in situations like this had already been closed. So all I could look out were the little gun ports beside the window. When I looked out, I could see Snowball still moving. I yelled, "He's still moving." Dougy was looking out the other port and said, "He's still moving because they're still shooting at him." Then I became angry those bastards are killing my best friend. I stuck my carbine out the gun port and started shooting back in the direction the bullets were coming from.

I guess the others got the same idea because pretty soon we had rifles sticking out of every gun port blasting away. A few minutes later, we were told to hold our fire. The Marines sent a squad in to get that machine gun and we didn't want to hit them. About ten minutes later, we heard a lot of gunfire and a few muffled blasts, which we later learned were hand grenades. Within minutes, the Marines came out to the road in full battle gear. They had one prisoner and were dragging three dead Zipper Heads. I started toward the door and Snowball, but was told to wait for the Marines to get here and give us the all-clear.

I left my rifle against the wall by the gun port. I was out of ammo anyway. But when the Marines came and gave us the all-clear and I was able to get to Snowball, what I saw really pissed me off. They shot the hell out of him. Part of his head and one eye was missing. He had bullet holes everywhere. I turned to look for help. I didn't know what kind of help, but some kind of help. Then I spotted the zipper head. The little son-of-a-bitch that had killed Snowball. I wanted to kill him but I didn't have a weapon.

I ran to Ensign Peers, grabbed his 45 out of his holster and headed for the gook. Before I could move one step, Chris and Peavey grabbed me. "No, Rich, don't. They need to interrogate him." Next thing I know, I'm face first in the dirt with Peavey and Chris holding me down. To say I was bullshit was to put it mildly. That was the maddest I've ever been in my whole life, and it was going to take some time to get over it. When I calmed down, they let me up. I walked back into the lab, went to the head and washed up. After I pulled myself together, I went to my room, put on a clean jumper and went back to the meeting room. The Marines and their prisoner had gone, Snowball had been taken away and the rest of the guys were standing around waiting to be told what to do next.

Ensign Peers stepped up and told us to pick up our messages and deliver them. I was amazed after what just happened he expected us to go about our duties as if nothing happened. Then he looked at me and asked me if I was going to be alright. I didn't know what else to say, so I said yes, and went looking for my messages. Someone had picked up mine and Snowballs messages and flak jackets. I put my flak jacket on, picked up the messages – Snowballs and mine – and looked around for my rifle.

I spotted Snowballs Thompson against the wall. My rifle was empty, and his was full and had a lot more firepower than mine, so I took his. If anyone decided to shoot at me again, this time I won't run. I'll take cover and shoot back.

Peavey, Penny and I walked to the pier together. I guess we were all going out together to calm our nerves. As we were getting to the dock, one of the other delivery boats was pulling in. I forgot some of the others had pulled out before the shooting started. Chris went over to talk to them and told them about Snowball being killed. They came up to me and said, "Sorry, man. I know he was your friend." That's when it hit me. My heart turned cold. I'd never see my friend again. My eyes filled up. I didn't want to cry. That's when my anger kicked in. I was going to find and kill every VC I could. And I was going to start that night.

Peavey was angry about the fact the Marines who are supposed to guard our facility and protect us from this shit let their guard down. Even though we were on high alert, they didn't step up their duties. He blamed them for Snowball's death.

It was then I made my plans for what I was going to do – to hunt the VC and protect the base.

When I got back from delivering the mail, I went back to my room. I dressed in my dungaree pants, black sweater and black watch cap. I put my boondockers on, grabbed my machine gun and headed into the woods in front of our laboratory.

The base is approximately 1 mile wide by 3/4 of a mile long, with our lab at the bottom of the peninsula and the Marine

RAIN: A Sailor's Story

guard shack at the top. Along the road in front of our base is a chain link fence.

Down the middle of the base is a dirt road that runs from the guard shack to the crypto lab. Up at the front of the base is the Marine barracks, the PX store and the chow hall. Then there's about 1/4 mile of woods before you get to the lab. So there's woods behind the barracks on the right side of the base and woods on the left side behind the PX and the chow hall, and it comes to within 50 feet of the front of the lab. So 70 percent of our base is heavily wooded. It's not real jungle, but mostly dense foliage and trees and thickets.

This was to be the area I was going to patrol. I would deliver the mail in the morning, sleep in the afternoon and early evening, and patrol the woods at night. I would not be caught by surprise again.

When I got into the woods, it was about 2pm in the afternoon, or 1400 hours military time. I was hot as hell, no sea breeze in there. I almost regretted wearing the sweater. But I knew I had to get used to it. It would be my night uniform from now on.

My self-appointed mission this afternoon was to familiarize myself with the wooded area around my base. I wanted to find trails and the spot where the enemy had set up the machine gun. I checked the front, right corner of the base where the Marines brought the girls instead of paying two dollars for a room. That was going to stop. I believe one of the girls showed the VC this Lover's Lane and how to enter the base. For the Marines to allow this breach of security and to turn a blind eye even though we were in high alert was inexcusable.

I scoured the woods on the right side and discovered the animal trails and clearings. I designed the way I would patrol the area, and then moved to the west side. The left side of the woods was a lot thicker and harder to move through.

Some of the trails I found through the thickets were so small I had to get down on my hands and knees to get through them. By the time I went to chow, I had a good plan of how I was going to patrol that night. After chow, I went back to my room to get some sleep before I went out. I figured I would get there just as it was getting dark around 9:30pm, and I would hunt VC until around 4am when it started to get light. I laid out my clothes, set my alarm for 9, or 2100 hours military time, and went to sleep.

I awoke right on time, dressed in my black sweater and watch cap and headed up the road. I figured I would check in at the Marine guard shack and give them a heads-up of what I was doing.

When I got to the guard shack, one of the Marines said, "Where are you going with that machine gun?" I told him I didn't plan on leaving the base, that I would be patrolling the woods behind them. I told them to let people know I would be out there because I have an itchy trigger finger and I shoot anything that moves.

I then turned around and disappeared into the woods. I followed the path I had planned in my head, crossing the road from one side to the other twice in each patrol. A patrol took about 2-1/2 hours. I figured three patrols a night. I had to actually force myself to move slowly and stay attentive to my surroundings. More than once, I found myself walking too quickly and daydreaming.

Then about 2:15am, I saw movement. My adrenaline kicked in and I was on full alert. I knew I saw something. I wasn't daydreaming. But where was it? I used a trick I learned in Scouts when I was a kid.

Your peripheral vision is keener at night when looking straight at something. So I looked to the right of where I saw movement. The right eye being my dominant eye, meaning the peripheral vision in my left eye should give me my best night vision. Bingo. I saw it again. Whatever he was doing, he was down low and moving slow. I figured he was crawling through the woods toward the lab. I got down on my hands and knees and inched forward with my machine gun cradled in my arms. I lost sight of him for a few minutes. When I saw him again, he was coming up over a small hump in the ground and moving a little faster. I got to one knee into a shooting position. As soon as he got to the top of the rise, I opened up. The noise from the gun broke the silence with a staccato of noise that made me jump, not only from the recoil, but from the deafening blast coming out of the machine gun. I had forgotten how loud it was and how it kept shooting as long as you hold back on the trigger.

I heard a squealing, screaming sound and knew I got him. I got to my feet, held my machine gun on him and walked over to get a closer look.

When I got there, I said to myself, "Oh shit. I just shot someone's pig." What the hell was a pig doing out here?

I decided to drag it to the road because I knew the Marines heard me shooting and would want to know what I was shooting at. Maybe now they would know I was serious about patrolling the area.

When I got out to the road, two Marine sentries were walking down the road toward me. They were walking slow, guns at the ready and staying in the shadows.

When they saw me pulling out the pig, they said, "Hey, are you Elliott?" I said, "Yes, I am." "Were you the one shooting?" I said, 'Yes, that was me." "What were you shooting at?" I said, "I saw something moving in the woods. I thought it was a VC crawling toward the lab. So I opened up on him. It turned out to be a pig." They came down and looked at the pig. They said,

"You know the farmer across the main road has pigs. It's probably one of his."

I said, "Well, now it's dead. It shouldn't have been trespassing on a top-secret restricted Naval installation." They said, "What are you going to do with him?" I said, "I don't know. Give it to the cook and see what he can do with it." I turned and walked back to the lab. They yelled out, "Yeah, great white hunter. Goes out on patrol and kills a pig!" I did feel kind of silly, but now I think they will realize how serious I am, and the word will get out that I'm out there and willing to shoot at anything that's not supposed to be there.

It wasn't quite time for me to end my patrol, but I figured with all the shooting and noise going on if anyone was sneaking in, they would change their mind and back out.

So I went back to my room to get a couple hours sleep before Reveille. Next morning, I went to chow. Everyone was talking about me killing a pig. The guys were busting my balls, calling me a great white hunter and shit like that. I was surprised when Peavey came up to me. I was expecting him to bust my balls, but instead he patted me on the back and said, "Good job, Rich. At least someone's watching our back out there."

At the meeting that morning, Ensign Peers said, "Our self-appointed protector killed a pig last night. Let's have a round of applause for Richard Elliott." Everyone was cheering and hooting. I'm sure some were making fun of me, but also some really appreciated it. Whatever, I would still be back out there tonight.

When I got back from delivering the mail, I went to chow then back to my room. I brought back a sandwich because I knew I would miss evening chow. I got to sleep around three, woke at 9 and walked to the Marine guard house to let them know I would be out again tonight. When I got to the guard

RAIN: A Sailor's Story

house, one of the Marines handed me a small jar of ointment. It was camo paint to darken my face. He said my white face was as bright as the moon and I should cover it. I said "thanks" and walked into the woods. Once inside the woods, I sat and darkened my face.

That night went by uneventfully. 4:20 a.m., I was back in my room hoping to take a quick nap before Reveille. After chow and the meeting, Peavey and I walked to the boat. I had a few more messages, and it took more time to deliver them. Normally, I would get back around 1:30-2:00. Lately, I've been getting back 2:30-3:00 and that's with Peavey putting some giddy-up on them motors. I've been living off breakfast and sandwiches and lots of coffee. I woke again tonight at 9:00, got dressed and walked to the Marine guard post and checked in. They now expected me and asked how things were going. I really didn't want to make small talk as, like Peavey, I kinda blamed them for Snowball.

After I checked in, I slipped into the woods and started my rounds.

I heard him before I saw him. A little off to my right. I was on the left side of the road in the heaviest part of the woods. I was crawling out of a thicket on one of the game trails. I froze, looked to my right. I stared into the woods looking in the direction of the sound, trying to look around trees. Then I heard it again a little further to my right. I crawled out of the thicket into a small clearing real careful, scanning the trees to my right. Then I saw him. He was standing near a tree. He was not real big, but he must have heard me when I saw him. He froze, then jumped up and tried to climb the tree. I swung the machine gun around and shot him out of the tree – thump. He didn't let out a sound. Not like the pig. Just fell, or actually was knocked out of the tree. I walked over to him.

I felt like a real asshole. This time I killed a monkey. A fucking monkey. I'll never hear the end of this. I dragged him to the road and the Marines were on the way to see what happened. When they got to me and saw the monkey, they started laughing. "Well, it looks more like a zipper head than the pig. Well, Rich, it looks like you're getting closer. Maybe in a few years, you might just get it right." So they think I'm some kind of a joke, sneaking through the woods with face camo and dressed in black. Well, I don't care. That won't stop me. My safety and the safety of others depends on me.

That's what I thought anyway. The Marines have not proven to me that they can secure this base. Until they do, I will continue to patrol it.

Next morning at the meeting, not much was said about last night, but when I went to get my messages, one of the radio men was walking back and forth scratching his side and going "coo-coo" like a monkey. Everyone started to laugh. Me too. I thought it was funny too.

On the way to the boat, Peavey said, "Rich, what's happening to you? I know how close you were to Snowball, but don't you think you're taking things a little too far? Today was the first time I saw you crack a smile since that day. Some of the guys are starting to think that there might be something wrong with you."

I looked at Peave and said, "The only thing wrong with me is I don't want to be killed. So I patrol at night to protect myself. Why are you complaining? I'm protecting you too." He said, "Are you, really? So far all you did was kill a pig and a monkey. Are you really out there protecting us or just looking for something to kill?"

I looked at Peave for a long two minutes and said, "To tell you the truth, I don't really know." He said, "Don't you think it's about time you found out?"

I thought about that all morning but, by the time I got back, I still had no answers.

The alarm went off at 9 on the button. I was getting into a routine. Go to the head, put on face paint, get dressed, and check gear – flashlight, parachute cord, watch cap, black gloves, ka-bar knife and machine gun.

At 9:30 sharp, I checked in with the Marines and slipped into the woods. I was getting to know the woods real well. I patrolled the right side first, slipped across the road down below the chow hall and patrolled the left side back up to behind the PX where I again crossed the road and worked my way up to the right where the Marines had their Lover's Lane. But tonight, before I could get to the corner, I saw two people in a clearing about 30 yards away. I got a pretty good look at one of them, and I could tell it was a gook. I immediately raised the Tommy gun and started shooting. A second alter, I heard a yell, "Stop shooting, I'm a Marine!"

I thought, "Oh shit! What is he doing here, and who the fuck is the gook?" I walked over to him, my gun at the ready. When I got there, he was standing beside one of the prostitutes from the Little America.

He started yelling at me, "What the hell do you think you're doing?" Before he could say anything else, I said, "You're under arrest for trespassing in a restricted area on a top-secret Naval base. And she is under arrest for being a spy. He yelled, "A spy? She's a whore!" I said, "Shut the fuck up. Both of you are in deep shit" I looked over at the girl, and she had blood coming out of her shoulder. One of the bullets had ripped a chunk off her left arm and she was bleeding pretty good.

I told them to head toward the road and marched them toward the guard shack. When we got there, one of the guards was heading our way. He saw I had my gun on the Marine and had wounded the girl. He said, "What is this all about?" I told him that I arrested these two for trespassing on a restricted top-secret Naval installation without permission, and her for being a spy.

The guard saw her bleeding and said, "Holy shit, you've gone and done it now Rich. You're in deep shit." He called back to the guard shack, "Call the Captain. We've got a situation here." We walked up to the guard shack and I stood my ground. I told them I wanted these two placed under arrest. I knew if I backed down now, I would be in deep shit. But if I held my ground and pushed the fact that they were trespassing on the base without authorization, they were the ones in deep shit.

Also, if I pressed on about her being a spy and that Lover's Lane was the only way for the VC to get on the base with a machine gun, I figured I was on firm ground. A few minutes later, a Marine Captain came to the guard shack. He said, "What's going on here?" Before one of the guards could answer, I said, "I want this Marine placed under arrest, and I also want this civilian placed under arrest." He said, "For what? What are the charges?" "He's charged with trespassing on a top-secret Naval installation without authority. She's charged with being a spy on the same installation." "Who gave you the authority to arrest these people?"

As this was going on, my Commander came up the road to the guard shack. I didn't know who called him, but I was glad he came.

He walked over and said, "What's going on here?" The Captain said, "Your sailor took it upon himself to patrol this installation. He shot one of my Marines and wounded a civilian." The Commander looked over and saw a Corps man bandaging the girls' arm. Then he looked at me and said, "Is this true Seaman Elliott?" I said, "Yes sir, it's true."

The Captain said, "What gives you the authority to arrest anybody? As far as I know, nobody authorized you to patrol this base, never mind arrest anybody."

I answered back even though we were on high alert; the Marines in charge of security on this base were lax duties resulting in the death of a sailor.

Now the Captain was pissed. He said, "So without authority, you took it upon yourself to shoot at a Marine?" I said, "No! Because the Marines assigned to provide the top-secret Naval installation I am presently serving at failed to provide adequate security, I took it upon myself to protect myself and other Navy personnel on the Naval installation." I kept stressing the fact that this was a Naval installation.

I also told him that the Marine was shot, not because he was a Marine, but because he was trespassing on a top-secret base in the company of a spy who gave information to the enemy on how to enter the base with a machine gun and kill a sailor. When the Marine identified himself, I stopped shooting and placed him and the spy under arrest.

The Commander looked over at the Captain and said, "Is this true?" The Captain said, "No. This Marine is assigned to this base. He has a right to be here."

The Commander said, "In the company of a spy? I don't think so." The Marine piped up and said, "She's no spy. She's a prostitute at the Little America" I said, "No way. She's a spy posing as a prostitute."

The Commander said, "Whether she is a spy or not has yet to be determined, but she is definitely not authorized to be on this base, and your Marine is not authorized to sneak her on this base without going through the main gate. Elliott, you can report back to the lab now." As he turned to talk to the Captain, I said, "Beg your pardon Commander, but we are in a war zone and you are unarmed. I would rather wait over here and escort you back to the lab." I said that just to rub salt into the fat that the Marines can't provide proper security and I can.

I saw a slight smile come across his face and he said, "As you please."

He then told the Captain to place those two under arrest and he would expect a full report on his desk in the morning.

On the way back to the lab, he said, "You've really done it now. You just opened up a whole can or worms. I understand what you've done and why you did it, but you're really stretching it with that spy things. But that's the only thing we have to hang our hat on." So I said, "You're not mad at me? You're going to help me?" He said, "Yes, I'm going to help you. Not because I approve of what you've been doing, but because I figured, if you stirred up enough shit, the Marines would be forced to increase security on this base. I'm as pissed off as you about Snowball's death. Now we have to circle the wagons and make sure this doesn't come around and bite us on the ass. Go to your room, get good night's sleep. In the morning, deliver your messages and report to me when you get back."

I didn't know what to think. The Commander knew all the time what I was doing, but didn't stop me, which realistically means he approves it, which also mean he's on the lookout for my actions as well as I am. To know he is on my side, and that he is two grades senior to the Marine Captain, that means a lot. I started breathing a little easier when I went to sleep.

Next morning, I went to chow and met Chris and Peavey. Both had heard about last night. News travels fast.

They asked me what happened. I told them and they seemed a little surprised. "You actually shot at a Marine and shot a prostitute?" I said, "Yes. I didn't get a good look at the Marine, but I could tell that the prostitute was Vietnamese. I couldn't tell man or woman. I just thought they were both Vietnamese, so I opened up."

Chris looked at me and said, "You are one crazy bastard." After the morning meeting, the Commander told me to report back to him when I got back from delivering the mail.

I expected Peavey to ask a lot of questions, but he hardly talked on the way out. But after we delivered all the messages, he asked what did I think would happen next. I told him I didn't know, but I would find out when I got back.

After chow, I went in to see the Commander. He told me to take a seat. I figured I would be a while.

He started by telling me he had a meeting with the Marine Captain and they came to a mutual agreement.

We would drop the charges against the Marine and the prostitute, and he would not press any charges against me. He also agreed to increase security by putting a guard post at each corner of the base and increasing the fence 500 feet down each side of the base and having his Marines do sentry duty along the fence.

He will also request for an additional 20 Marines to help protect our perimeter.

We also agreed that you would be transferred back to "A" school. I said, "What are you talking about? I can't go back. I have to stay here!" He said, "I thought you'd want to go back." I said, "I can't. What will I say to Madeline, Snowball's wife?" He said, "I think you will find a way to tell her. I really don't think she blames you. Anyway, we both think things would be better off if you went back to "A" school. The decision's made, and we secured you a flight to Yokosuka, Japan tomorrow at 800 hours. We have a jeep ready to take you to the airport at 600 hours. Take the rest of the day to get your things together. Pick your orders up from personnel at 1600 hours, and good luck, Rich. Try and put this all behind you. In the short time

I've know you, you've shown great promise and leadership ability. You'll be a good sailor."

I just looked at him, saluted, about faced and left. Going back to "A" school... I can't believe it. What will I tell the Captain back at main side? Wonder what he's going to think. I'm supposed to be gone for 6 months, and now I'm coming back in under one.

I went back to my room, packed my sea bag and got ready to ship out. At 4 o'clock, I picked up my orders, went to chow and went back to my room. I lay on my bed, staring at the ceiling thinking about everything that went on. How come I'm always getting into trouble? What's my problem? If I had just given Vye twenty dollars, none of this would have happened. I looked over at Snowball's bunk to ask him a question, then realized he wasn't there, and never would be.

That was the loneliest night of my life. I'm on a base with 30 other sailors and I'm so lonely it physically hurt. And I knew deep down inside, it would last a long time. I missed my best friend terribly. I miss the sound of him sleeping in the next bunk. The little put-put-put he made that was so annoying, now I miss it. I ended up crying myself to sleep that night.

Had weird dreams all night. Next morning was up at 5. Grabbed early chow and caught the jeep to the airport. I'd be back to main side and "A" school in 48 hours. What am I going to tell my Captain? What am I going to tell Madeline? Things aren't going to be easy. I saw someone in a movie once say, "Woe is me." That's exactly how I feel.

The plane ride back to Yokosuka was a lot faster than the one coming over. I guess it was because I was so wrapped up in my thoughts. Plus, the plane was practically empty. No cargo unless you call three passengers cargo. No one talked much. We all had that faraway look in the eyes. When I got to Yokosuka, there was a bus going to Okinawa and a commercial plane leaving for Hawaii right away. Great, I didn't have to spend the night in Yokosuka.

The flight to Hawaii was uneventful. It was real smooth and I just drifted a long not thinking, not feeling. Just drifting along in limbo.

I had been flying for close to twenty hours and hadn't slept a wink. I really wasn't tired. I didn't really feel anything. After a 2-hour layover, I caught a plane to San Francisco. It would take about 12 ½ hours flying time. On the way I started drifting in and out of sleep. At one point I was in the woods, and instead of hunting the Dinks, the Marines were hunting me. But every one of them that I saw had Gook eyes. Vietcong in marine uniforms. They had me surrounded and were forcing me to move into this clearing, where the Gooks had a machine gun set up. The Gooks firing the machine gun were the whores from the Little America. I thought, *I know they are spies*. I was trying to run but couldn't move. Bullets were kicking up dirt all around me. Then I realized somewhere down inside I knew I was asleep and this was a nightmare. I was trying to wake up. Crawling up from a deep sleep that I couldn't wake up from.

When I finally woke up, there was an old lady beside me shaking me. I looked over at her with a quizzical look on my face. She said, "You were having a bad dream. It must have been pretty bad over there." I shrugged my shoulders and said, "I guess you could say that," and turned back to look out the window. Then I turned back to her and said, "Thanks for waking me up." She said, "Thanks for protecting our country." That was the first time a civilian ever said that to me and the last time for at least twenty years.

We landed in Frisco at 8:30 p.m. and there was a plane leaving for Chicago at 11:15. So two and half hours later I was boarding a plane for Great Lakes, Illinois. What a difference a day and a half made.

It felt like my time in Vietnam was just a dream. A trick dream, like a horror movie. You know like you go on a vacation to a beautiful island and end up being chased by monsters. But it was real alright; real as a heart attack for Snowball. And now I have to go back and face the music. So what the fuck can they do to me now? Send me back to Vietnam? Been there, done that. What's next, the brig? Been there, done that. I guess I'll just have to wait and see. No use worrying about it.

Twelve hours later around noon on Sunday, I was on a bus to Great Lakes, Illinois Training Center. Going to "A" School for the second time.

I checked in at the guard shack and was told to report to Barracks 39.

Barracks 39 is for temporary quarters until you can check in on a week day. I walked across the parade field to the barracks and was assigned a bunk for the night and told to check in at the Administration Building the next day. That night wasn't so bad; it almost felt like I was coming home. Next morning I checked in at Admin and they took my paperwork, assigned me to a permanent barracks, and told me to report to school at the fire control classroom in the Electronics "A" school building.

I went to my new barracks, got a bunk and locker, dropped off my stuff, and reported to class.

The first day was mostly just getting books, meeting instructors, and getting to know your way around the building. So even though I was 2 hours late the first day, I really didn't miss anything.

The dress code for school was dungarees, white hats, and black shoes. The laundry on base actually pressed our dungarees, shirts, and pants. So the students looked pretty sharp. I'm glad I was an FT as the ETs or electronics technicians had to wear their dress whites.

After lunch we were all sitting around a classroom talking to each other and getting briefed on which classes to go to first and order of the day. When a petty officer came in, said something to the instructor and left. The instructor called me up to the front of the class and told me to report to the officer of the day at the Admin building.

I thought to myself, *here we go again*. I walked the length of the parade field, checked into the Admin building and went to see the officer of the day. After saluting, he told me that the captain wanted to see me and to wait outside his office until he called me in.

I didn't wait long; the captain came out to see me and called me into his office himself. When I stepped inside, I saluted and said, "Seaman Elliot: reporting as ordered, sir." He saluted back and said, "Take a seat, Rich." A little confused, I sat down. Sitting down means I'm going to be there for awhile, but this is the first time he called me Rich. I sat and waited as he picked up a file in front of him.

He started by saying, "I found out about Snowball and I feel bad about it. He was a good sailor. It says here that you feel personally responsible for what happened. But I'm here to tell you it wasn't your fault. If anything, it was mine. I'm the one who sent you over there. I thought it would do you some good. I never thought either one of you would get killed. I knew that I was sending you into a war zone. But I figured that being in a crypto lab surrounded by Marines; you would be in little danger. I was wrong. There were a lot of contributing factors that led up to the attack on the crypto lab and the death of Snowball."

"The Crypto lab is an important link in our fleet. The enemy realized that and attacked it. Because of its location, the

Marines felt that it was safe, and they were lax in their duties to protect it. You and Snowball were serving your country in an important military role. Snowball will receive a letter of commendation and a Purple Heart. You will receive a letter of commendation in your service record. Because of your patrolling the area around your post and the wounding of a marine, it brought to light the inadequate manner in which the lab was protected and in doing so increased the security significantly."

"Richard, you seem to have a knack for stepping over the line and doing things that somehow brings to light certain things that need fixing. Rich, this has to stop. You can't take things into your own hands. From now on, you have to use the chain of command. If you see something that doesn't seem right, go to a senior petty officer in your command. If the problem isn't resolved, you have my permission to report to me directly. Do you understand what I've just told you?"

I said, "Yes, Sir. I do."

He continued. "Now there is also a report that you may be suffering from battle fatigue. So just to be on the safe side, I made arrangement s for you to see a counselor. You will see her two days a week until she thinks you are okay."

I told him that I didn't really need to see anyone – that I was fine. He said that he preferred the counselor told him that. "You will see her tomorrow at 1600 hours at the hospital. That's all."

I stood up, saluted, and left.

Battle fatigue? That means they think I'm crazy. Maybe I am. Crazy things happen around me. Was I crazy when I went to Nam, or did I get crazy over there? I think maybe I was always s a little nuts; I think most of us are. Me a little more than others. Good thing? Bad thing? Who knows; I'll see what the counselor has to say. He did say she. Hope she's cute. See how I think? Maybe I am a little crazy.

I went back to class, caught up with my class on the third floor classroom 3B, and got filled in on what I missed – which wasn't much. Finished up, got my books, and went back to my barracks.

My new barracks was building II, closer to the school and Admin building, then 39 but farther from the chow hall. To get to the chow hall, we had to walk down the hill across the parade grounds and off to the right a little way. I was on the second floor, right side of my barracks. Because I was the last one there, my bunk was way back at the end, closest to the outside wall. I really didn't mind; I was away from the noise around the tables in the middle of the barracks and close to a window.

I really didn't feel like socializing anyway. So my location was perfect for me.

The next morning, after chow, and before classes started, we were lined up on the parade field and made to do P.T. (physical training). We did it every morning and I got to like the exercise. It relieved a lot of stress and felt good.

After exercising we went to class. I listened to the instructors, took notes, learned about capacitors, resistors, tubes, and circuits. Later we would learn circuit boards and transistors, which would eventually take over tube circuits.

That afternoon at 4 o'clock, 1600 hours, I went to the medical building and met with my counselor. Her name was Margaret Pearlman, and she was a naval lieutenant. She was in her early 30s with black hair, tall, with a trim figure, and all business.

I knocked on her door, and when she opened it, I saluted and said, "Seaman Elliott Reporting as ordered, Sir." She saluted back and asked me to come in.

"Have a seat over there and make yourself comfortable. I'll just get my notes and we'll get started."

She started off by saying, "It says here that you just got back from Vietnam when you were involved in the shooting of a marine. Would you like to tell me what happened?"

I knew I would have to talk to her about what went on over there, but I really didn't want to. So I figured I would answer her questions without getting into any real detail. So I told her that I didn't shoot a marine, I wounded a Vietnamese prostitute I thought was a spy – and still do.

"Tell me about it."

"Well, I was on patrol around the perimeter of the base when I saw the two of them sneaking around in the bush. It was dark and I didn't see them real well. As I got a little closer, I could see she was Vietnamese, but I couldn't tell if she was male or female. It didn't matter; she was in a restricted area of a top secret naval installation that was on high alert because we had been attacked three days before. So I opened up on them."

"What happened after that?" I told her after that, I was sent back to "A" School.

"What happened immediately after that?"

"They were placed under arrest"

"Then what happened"

"I was sent back here."

"Before that."

"I had a meeting with the commander in charge of the base."

"And what did he say?"

"That I was being sent back here."

"Richard, before I can help you, you're going to have to talk to me and explain what happened over there."

I said, "Excuse me, lieutenant, but you have the full report in that folder in front of you. So you know what happened over there."

"Well, I would like to hear your version. If you let me reread the report, I will tell you where it differs from what I believe to be the truth."

She said, "You know, Rich, this isn't getting us anywhere, so why don't we adjourn for today, and you come back next week at the same time and we'll try again. Dismissed."

I got up, saluted, about faced, and left. Half way back to my barracks, I started thinking, what does she want from me? Why doesn't she just leave me alone?

Instead of going back to the barracks, I walked over to the chow hall, had supper, and then went to the barracks.

By the time I got there, it was getting late. Everyone was around the tables talking. I noticed this one guy was playing a shell game using cards and a penny.

For a dollar, he would put a penny under a card. Then quickly move them around. If you picked which card the penny was under, you won the dollar. He hardly ever lost. He was really good. He let some of them win just enough to keep them interested. Besides, there was really nothing else to do. Me, I went back to my bunk to study.

The next day was more of the same. Physical Fitness classes, chow, back to the barracks, study, and so on.

There was a watch list and it was made out a week in advance. So it was up to you to check it. The person on watch was responsible to wake you up twenty minutes before your watch so you could get ready. You had probably one watch a month and one weekend duty a month. Any other time you could pick up your liberty card at the school office and go on liberty. Any night of the week or weekend as long as you didn't have the duty.

I didn't really feel like going on liberty, so I basically stayed in the barracks and studied. The weekend came and went; I basically stayed on base, went to the coffee shop, which we call a Gee dunk and saw a movie at the theater on the base.

Monday was like any other day, and things kind of fell into a rut. P.T. every morning, chow classes, studying in the barracks. Tuesday at 1600 hours I had another appointment with the counselor. This time the meeting started out a little differently.

She had me tell her about when I first got there and what I thought. I told her about everything. The cove, boats, the dock, the lab, and how much I liked it.

By that time it was late, and she said she thought we made some progress today. She dismissed me, and I had to run to reach the chow hall before it closed.

I felt pretty good walking back from chow – almost happy. When I got to the barracks, I decided to have a smoke. I didn't smoke much – maybe 4 or 5 a day, but after supper and in a good mood, I just felt like one. So I sat at the tables in the center of the barracks and lit up.

You couldn't smoke at your bunk, even though the smoking lamp was lit. You had to smoke at the tables where they had little coffee cans with water in the bottom to put your cigarettes out in. The big mouth was there playing his shell game, annoying as ever. I just tried to ignore him. I talked to some of the guys in class; small talk – nothing serious.

Then Big Mouth, who turned out to be Louie Pacheco, asked me to play. I said no thanks. He said, "Why? Afraid to lose a dollar? I'm too fast for you?"

I said, "No. I'm just not interested."

He said, "Yeah, just as I thought. You're afraid 'cause I'm better than you."

I knew he cheated, and I saw how he palmed the penny in the crease of his baby finger, so by now I was starting to get upset at this big mouth asshole. He really thinks he's something; he's got his group of young guys hanging around, and he cheats them and they don't know any better.

So I reached in my pocket, pulled out a dollar, and put it on the table. I watched as he went through his motions, moving the cards around, and when he stopped, he asked where the penny was. As quick as I could, like catching a fly off the table, I swept my right hand over, grabbed his right hand, and turned it over, forcing him to drop the penny.

Everyone saw then that he was a cheat. He had a cigarette in his left hand, and put it out in my face.

Talk about seeing red. Well it does happen because I saw red. All the shit that I had been going through. All the heartache and guilt feelings exploded at the same time. I don't remember the fight, but from what I was told, it was all one sided.

Before they could pull me off him, I beat him pretty bad. He had a broken nose and dislocated collar bone.

As I looked down at him lying on the floor bleeding, I thought, *I'm in the shit again. The captain just told me not to take things into my own hands. What is wrong with me? Maybe I do need counseling.*

The man on watch had two of the other guys walk with him over to the hospital side to the emergency room. Me? I went and sat on my bunk and waited for the MPs.

An hour later, one of the sailors that went with Louie to the hospital said that he talked with Louie, and they all agreed that he would say he fell down the stairs. He didn't want anyone to find out he was cheating.

So he wants to know if you'd go along with that and he said he's sorry he put a cigarette out on your face. I was so relieved I could dance a jig. But all I did was say no problem, as long as he apologized.

Next day at school it was more of the same PT classroom, chow, and back to the barracks. When I got back to the barracks, I saw Louie was back at his bunk talking to a couple of the guys he usually hangs with. At first I thought they might be conspiring with each other to get back at me. But on second thought, I didn't think that was likely. Too many other sailors in our barracks were annoyed by Louie and his cheating card tricks.

I went over to my bunk, put my stuff away, and went to the tables to have a smoke before I went back to my bunk to study.

While I was at the table, which is more like a picnic table with a bench seat on each side, Louie and his two buddies came walking toward me. I was m ore curious than worried, but just to be on the safe side, I put one leg on each side of the bench seat and sat sideways so I could get up faster and wouldn't be trapped inside the bench seat, unable to get out.

When they got to me, I looked up at Louie and waited to see what he had to say. He said, "I understand you want an apology. Well, I'm sorry I put my cigarette out on your face."

Looking at him, he didn't look too tough with a bandage on his nose and his arm in a sling. I told him the apology isn't for me; it's for all the sailors that you've been cheating for the last two weeks.

There were probably 12 guys sitting at the tables and they all looked up when I said that. It was so quiet; you could hear a pin drop. He said, "Hey man, we were just having fun. What's a dollar? It ain't nothing – it was just for fun."

I said, "Try and find another way to have fun without cheating your shipmates. It isn't the dollar that matters, it's the cheating, and if you don't understand that, then I don't to have anything to do with you. Now apologize to your shipmates."

He looked at me for a long second, digesting what I had just told him, turned and in a loud voice said, "I apologize to you guys, I was just having a little fun." Then he turned and walked back to his bunk. His two friends stayed at the tables and talked to the other guys.

When I finished my cigarette, I walked down to Louie and said, "It took a big man to do what you just did. Maybe there's hope for you after all." I put out my hand, and he stood up, took it with his left hand because his right was in a sling. We shook hands, smiled, and went back to my bunk.

The next day and the days after were more of the same. Weekends I normally stayed on base, went to a movie with one or two of the guys and studied or wrote letters. Time has a way of going by. Before you know it, I was back at the hospital for my meeting with the head shrinker.

Margaret started off by asking me to tell her about the day that Snowball and I were ambushed as w left the crypto lab. I told her I didn't really want to talk about that. She told me that it might help if I just told her point blank what happened.

She said, "Try and look at it as if you were an outsider watching from a distance and not really involved." I didn't know where to begin. At chow that morning? At the morning meeting, or as we were leaving the crypto lab with the mail? I decided to start with the mail.

Snowball and I got our messages just like we did every morning. Our drivers Peavey and Penny were already down at the boats warming them up. Other guys had left before us and everything seemed normal. We left the lab, walked to the end of the building, and as we turned the corner, we heard pop-pop-pop-pop, like a string of firecrackers going off. At first we didn't know what it was. Then I saw the dirt kicking up around us and said, "Snowball, Run! They're shooting at us!" Snowball and I had gotten into the habit of carrying our flak jackets instead of wearing them because of the heat and they were basically uncomfortable. So when we started running back to the lab, we dropped our letters and our flak jackets so we could run faster. I was a little ahead of Snowball because I started running first. I know he was right behind me as I could hear him. But as I got to the door, I turned to see where he was. I saw him laying on the ground bleeding. I started to run back to get him when someone behind me yanked me back into the lab. They locked the door so I couldn't get back out. I ran to the window to see where Snowball was, but the windows were covered with steel shutters, so I couldn't see out.

On each side of the window were gun ports. I looked out the gun port and could see that they were still shooting at Snowball. It was horrible; he was shot to pieces. I picked up my rifle, stuck it out the port, and started shooting in the direction the machine gun fire as coming from. The other guys got the idea and they started shooting back to.

"And that's that," I said. "I don't want to talk about it anymore."

"So you think this is your fault that the enemy fired a machine gun at you?" Margaret asked.

I looked at her as if she was stupid. I said, "You don't really get it, do you? If I hadn't gotten us into trouble back here, we wouldn't have been sent over there and Snowball wouldn't have been killed. So yes, it's my fault. I keep thinking I should have paid Vye the twenty bucks. I keep doing things to try and make things better. But in making things better, other things get worse."

She said, "Tell me about it what exactly do you mean?"

"When I first got over here, my school was full up. So I was house mousing, cleaning the barracks. We had a second class bosunsmate named Vye in charge.

When people got finished mess cooking and started school, Vye had to send house mouses to the chow hall as mess cooks. He extorted money from the men in his command by telling you if you gave him twenty, you wouldn't have go mess cooking. I told him I would report him. He said I would need permission to go over his head, and he wouldn't approve it. So to bring to light his illegal activities, I started a fight with him. His seaman jumped in to help him and Snowball helped me.

After the investigation into this affair, Snowball and I were sent mess cooking and Vye was dishonorably discharged and his seaman was busted to apprentice and sent back to the fleet.

"Snowball chose to help you, you didn't ask him to," said Margaret. "But if you were mess cooking, what happened to get you sent to Vietnam?"

Again I just couldn't let things go. The students treated us mess cooks like shit. Instead of taking the food we put on their trays, they would want a different piece of meat or more potatoes or gravy on their meat and not their potatoes or vice versa. And if they didn't get their way, they would tip their tray and dump the food back on the steam table, making a mess that we had to clean up. Things escalated and we ended up in a big brawl after the evening meal. The MPs had to break it up. But after that, the mess cooks and school guys started getting along. But because I was the ring leader and Snowball my right arm, we were sent to Vietnam. So you see what I mean? The end result seems to work out, but I always get screwed. I don't know how I get sucked into doing things like that. Just the other day, one of the guys in my barracks had a card trick where he had the other guys bet. Well, I could see he was cheating. I tried not to get sucked into it, but it was bound to happen. I showed how he was cheating and ended up in a fist fight. As a result, he was hurt pretty bad, but no longer cheated his shipmates. He did apologize for cheating, and I think it made things a lot better in the barracks. See what I mean? I do things – not that I plan on doing them – it just seems like the right thing to do. Like shooting at that marine and wounding the prostitute, the end result greatly increased security at the base. But I didn't do it for the Marines to increase security, I took it upon myself to patrol the base and increase my own security. Everything I do has repercussions. It seems to end up okay, but things could have ended up a lot worse. And for Snowball, they did end up a lot worse, and that is my fault.

Margaret sat there for a few minutes trying to digest everything I just told her. Finally she said, "Richard, I think you're a good person but you have to lighten up little. You're a natural leader, and you take it upon yourself to look out for others. I'm not saying that's a bad thing, but the captain is right. If you see a problem, don't try and take care of it yourself. You don't have the authority. You'll just end up getting yourself into trouble. Report the problems to your chain of command and let them take it from there. Now go to chow, and see me next week." I was real late for chow, so I was half walking and half running to get to the chow hall before it closed. The mess cook that counted the line saw me coming and held the door open for me. I ran inside, and even though they had pulled the steam table down, they had set aside a tray of food for me!

The master at arms was standing there as I picked up my try and said, "How's it going with the head shrinker?" I said, "How do you know about that?" He said, "Everybody knows. They say you got screwed up in Vietnam and now you're little crazy."

I said, "Well, I'm not crazy and what I do is my business." He said, "I was here when you had that fight between the mess cooks and the students."

I said, "That was a long time ago."

"No it wasn't. It was just last month. And last week you broke a guy's nose and dislocated his shoulder. So if you ask me, you are a little crazy. What happened to you in Nam? Why are you back here so soon?"

I told him, "None of your business. Maybe you should watch your mouth."

He said, "I didn't mean anything by it; just conversation is ll. It's what everyone's talking about. "

I said, "No problem. Think what you like."

After I ate I walked back to my barracks. I was thinking, *Is that all these people have to talk about?* Maybe it's good that I'm seeing this counselor. I'll try and lay low for awhile. Hopefully no more trouble and no more gossip for these morons. I was thinking if everyone on base knows about the fight with Louie, does the captain know?

Well, he hasn't called me to his office yet, so I guess I'll just wait and see.

The next day was the same as the rest. PT in the morning, classes all day, and study at night. One day rolled into the next and the next, and soon the weekend was her before you knew it. And to my surprise, Louie asked if I wanted to go out for a beer with him and a couple of the guys. I said, "I don't know."

"Come on," he said, "all you do is sit on your bunk and look out the window. It will be fun. We'll take the bus to Kenosha. There's a nice little bar there – good juke box, some girls. Come on?"

Kenosha is a small town in Wisconsin, just over the state line a short distance from the training center, a five-minute ride by car. I thought, *what the Hell*, so I said, "Okay, but I don't want to stay out too long."

We picked up our liberty cards and walked out the gate, hailed a cab and for $2 apiece, Louie, me and his friend Paul were dropped off at his little bar in Kenosha, Wisconsin. I was a little skeptical on how Louie was going to act, but he and Paul turned out to be a lot of fun. They went out of their way to make sure I had a good time. The juke box had some good tunes on it, and the beer was flowing real good. I was having fun.

Then somewhere around 11:15, a girl got up to play the juke box. The song she played, "Two Lovers" by Mary Wells, brought back some memories. I just sat and listened. In the back of my mind, I could hear Snowball singing. I started tearing up and knew I had to get out of there.

I went to the men's room, splashed water on my face, and pulled myself together. I told Louie and Paul I had to get back and that I had had enough to drink. They tried to get me to stay a little longer, but I had to go. I caught a cab back to the base, went to my barracks, and went to sleep, dreaming about the song "Two Lovers."

The weekend flew by, and Monday morning, PT was here before you knew it. Classes chow, studying, and my Tuesday afternoon meeting with my head shrinker was here.

When I knocked on her door, she was sitting in her chair waiting for me. Usually she gets up and opens the door. Today she just said to come in. I walked in, saluted, and she returned my salute and I sat down.

She had my file in front of her and was studying my notes. She said, "Rich, we have been pretty much over everything, but I feel that there is something m ore bothering you. Is there something you want to tell me? Whatever you tell me in this room is strictly confidential. So you can feel free to tell me anything."

I sat for a few minutes, fidgeting in my chair, not knowing how to start.

Finally I just spit it out, "How am I supposed to tell Madeline that I got her husband killed? I haven't written her since I got back. I barely write home. I'm basically hiding up here at school not writing to anyone. I don't know what to say."

She was flipping her pencil from one had to the other, just staring at my file. Finally she looked up and said, "Rich, you have to write that letter. If you don't, you will never get over this. I know it isn't going to be easy, but don't you think that you have an obligation to tell them in your own words what happened to Snowball and not in the general way they were informed by the military? So for your own piece of mind, and their right to know, you should write that letter. Think about it and let me know what you decide. See you again next week, same time."

Out of habit I went to the chow hall. I wasn't really hungry. She just laid a big trip on me. I knew she was right, but I didn't know how to go about writing that letter.

All week during class my mind would slip back to that letter. I couldn't leave it alone. I knew that this weekend I would have to write it. I put it off long enough. And weekends, most of the guys are gone on liberty and the barracks are empty and quiet, and hopefully I could get it done. Friday came before you could say it. When you're not looking forward to something, it's here before you know it. Not like Christmas when you're little – it doesn't ever seem to get here. Saturday is going to be the day.

Random thoughts have been running through my head. Now I have to put them on paper. After six false starts and over five hours of letter writing, I painfully came up with a letter. Walking to the rubbish bucket to throw away the unacceptable drafts of the final letter helped me to think. I think better when I pace. So the walking helped.

The letter:

My Dearest Madeline,

It has taken me a long time for me to write this letter. I don't know what to say. I am deeply sorry for your loss, as it is my loss also. I know that the pain and heartache I feel cannot compare to yours. To add to that, I somehow feel responsible.

The Government has probably written you telling how Snowball died a hero, sending you his purple heart and a letter of commendation. And that he died for his country.

In reality, Snowball lived for his country. His confidence and uplifting and happy attitude made everyone around him feel better. It was contagious. I was fortunate to have him as my friend. Together, we went through boot camp and had each other to lean on through all the trials and tribulations. It sure made things easier to have a trusted friend to help you along.

Snowball invited me into his life, his family and his home. He bared his soul to me as only a trusted friend can do. And, in the end, I couldn't save him. Sometimes, I wish it was me that got killed. Snowball had his whole life planned out. His new wife, plans for a family, apartment, and education – he seemed to have a handle on everything. Me, I was just drifting along, taking one day at a time.

It was because of me that Snowball and I got sent over to Vietnam. The Captain thought that it would teach us the chain of command and the proper way of doing things. I feel so guilty that I can't forgive myself over what happened. I will always cherish our friendship and keep his memory alive.

Thinking of you in this time of sorrow.
Richard

The letter seemed a little short, but I didn't know what else to say. I didn't want to drag it out. I had to say it so as not to hurt her by the details. I didn't want her to know how he was shot to hell, and that all he talked about was her and their future.

Just before chow, I walked to the post office and mailed the letter. After chow, I went to my bunk, sat, looked out the window and thought maybe things would get better. I felt a little lighter.

RAIN: A Sailor's Story

Sunday morning I decided to go for a run. I did two laps around the parade field before going back to the barracks for a shower.

After the shower, I went to my locker to get dressed and check my notes to get ready for class on Monday.

As I was sitting on my bunk going over my notes, three of the guys came over to me. I was wondering what in Hell do they want? As they got up to me, Henry VanMartin started talking. He had a piece of paper in his hand. He said, "We know what happened in Vietnam, and we're sorry."

Then I recognized the paper. It was one of my rejected letters. That SOB went through the trash and read my personal letters. I leaped off my bunk and grabbed Henry by the neck I was bullshit. I wanted to break his neck. The two sailors with him pulled me off. We wrestled around for a few minutes until I got myself under control.

When they turned me loose, I said, "What gives you the right to read my personal mail? You're lucky I don't smash your face in." Henry said, "Everybody wonders what's up with you. You stay to yourself, look out the window, have no friends, and don't go anywhere but to school and to chow. Oh and you go to see a head shrinker every Tuesday. Just as we are Louie's shipmates, we're yours too, and you're ours."

I said, "Maybe you should mind your own business and get out of my face before I kick the shit out of you."

I was hurt and angry. They invaded my privacy. No matter that their intentions were good, what they did was wrong. I was so upset I hardly slept that night. Classes dragged by. I wanted to talk to my counselor. To Hell with Tuesday, I'm going to see her today.

I barged into her office without knocking. I said, "I need to talk to you right away!"

She said, "You can't just barge in here like this. You have an appointment for tomorrow. I said, "I have to talk to you right now." She said, "I am an officer in the Navy, and I will be treated as such." I said, "So that's it. When you want me to talk to you, you're my counselor, but when I need you, you're an officer in the Navy. Let's just forget it. You won't' see me again. Put me on report." I turned and walked away.

I didn't go back to the barracks for awhile. I walked around the base thinking, wondering what next. I ran off at the mouth to an officer. Well, I've got to think of something to tell the captain. I imagine I'll be seeing him soon.

I waited until just before lights out to return to the barracks. I didn't want to talk to anyone. If Henry or one of the others said anything to me, I was afraid I might hurt them.

As I was sitting on my bunk, the barracks was unusually quiet. The guys were in little groups whispering to each other. Then to my surprise, Louie walked over to me. I thought, *what's he want?* His arm was still in a sling so I was at ease when he came up beside me. He said, "We all know what happened in Nam. Henry told us."

I could feel the anger building up. I also thought that Louie's got balls coming to me like that. Then he put his hand o my shoulder and said, "I'm sorry, man, and I'm damn proud to be your shipmate. I'm here if you need to talk to someone."

He turned and walked away; I just slumped down and put my head in my hands. I thought to myself, *that Louie is turning out to be a good guy.*

When I was sitting there, some of the other guys came over. They just touched my shoulder and said, *Sorry, man.* Some just touched me and walked away. . Pretty soon everyone in the barracks had walked up to me and either grabbed my shoulder or touched my shoulder or rubbed my back. Some said, sorry and some didn't say anything. The last one to come by was a big guy named Jack Burger. This guy was huge – 6' 6'' tall – maybe 250 pounds. His nickname was whopper. When he came up, he walked around my bunk, stood in front of me and stuck out his hand. A little confused, I reached out and shook hands. When I did, he pulled me off my bunk, and gave me a big hug. He said, "You're a helluva sailor and we're all proud of you. Rich, you're not alone; you're our classmate and our ship mate and I for one am proud to call you friend. I'm sorry about your friend. If you need to talk, you can talk to me or you can talk to all of us." He turned and walked away and at that point, I was glad he did, as I was tearing up and needed to go to the latrine and pull myself together.

The next day at school, I was thinking about my appointment with the head shrinker. Should I go, or should I just forget about it? Finally I figured I should go. What have I got to lose? And besides, I think I owe her an apology. So at 1600 hours after classes that day, I went to my appointment.

I knocked on her door and she said, "Enter." I walked in, stood at attention, saluted, and sounded off, "Richard Elliott: reporting as ordered." I was waiting for an ass chewing, but all she said was, "please sit down. We have a lot to talk about."

As I was sitting down, I said, "First I would like to apologize for my conduct yesterday. I was upset and took my frustration out on you, and for that I'm sorry."

She said that she can understand that and that she apologizes too. She knows that trust between her and her patients is very important, and for her to pull the officer's card was totally inappropriate.

"Now that we have that out of the way, let's get started," she smiled. I relaxed and I think both of us felt better.

"Now, what was it that got you so upset? Something about a letter?

I told her about writing the letter to Madeline and how I threw the first few drafts away until I finally got it right and how one of the guys fished it out of the trash and read it. Then I told her about everything that happened, and how all the guys came to me and patted me on the back.

She said, "You know, Rich, his death is not your fault. He chose to do what he did. You can't take responsibility for everything. For example, let's say you and Snowball wanted to go on liberty together. You wanted to go to Milwaukee and he wanted to go to Chicago. Let's say that you won out and you went to Milwaukee. If Snowball got run over by a car and got killed, would that be your fault?"

I said, "That's not the same thing. We didn't choose to go to Vietnam. We were sent there because of my actions."

She said, "yes, but Snowball chose to do the same things as you. That was his choice, and because he chose to do it, he was sent with you. So you see, it was his choice. Same as it would have been his choice if you went to Milwaukee instead of Chicago and he got hit by a car. Can you see that?"

"Yes, I can see that, but it's not that simple. A lot of circumstances led up to us going over there."

"I realize that, but each one of those circumstances he had a choice. And he made his own decisions. I want you to think about that and see me in two weeks. Oh, and you seem to be thinking a little better. You didn't hurt Henry." I looked over at her and she was smiling. "Now get out of here before you're late for chow."

Somehow she started to make sense. I've got a lot to think about in the next 2 weeks. Interesting.

That night at the barracks, I walked up to the tables, lit up a cigarette, and told everyone to listen up. "I want to thank you guys for last night. But what Henry did was wrong; he should not have read my personal letters. Now you all have an idea about what happened to me in Nam. Let's just leave it at that. Please don't ask me any questions because I don't want to and I won't talk about it. And again, thanks for the support."

They all said, *yeah, okay*, and stuff like that. Me, I finished my cigarette and went back to my bunk to study and think. Basically with the support of my shipmates and the help from my counselor, I felt better than I had in many a day. That night, I slept like a baby.

The next day at school, things went along pretty good. My grades were right up there and I had a pretty good handle on how things were working. One day led into the next and before you knew it, it was the weekend. Everyone had plans for liberty but me and a couple other guys.

There was a small bar just over the line in Kenosha, Wisconsin. It was about a 40 minute walk, maybe 5 to 6 miles. I decided Saturday night to go and check the place out. It was a few miles closer than the bar Louie took me to, and supposedly not as much fun. All I wanted was a quiet beer and some good tunes on the juke box. As I was getting ready to go, one of the other guys in the barracks asked if he could go with me. I said, "Sure, we'll walk over together." His name as John Dresly. John was a total geek. He was tall, gangly, clumsy, and no matter what he did with his hair, he had a cowlick sticking up the top of his head. He wore horned rimmed glasses that he thought make him look good, but in reality made him look silly. He did his best to try and fit in. No matter how much he tried, you knew that it was not natural and he tried too hard.

But he was a real goodhearted guy and would do anything for anyone. He was just kind of embarrassing to be around, so nobody really hung out with him. He was very intelligent; real book smart, but on practical matters, he was lost. So John and I headed out to Lulu's.

It took us about 35 minutes to get there walking. I didn't realize the training center was that close to Wisconsin. When we walked into Lulu's, I immediately felt comfortable. The people were a little older, mostly petty officers and a bunch of waves. I figured they were going through nurses training on the hospital side.

The place was not real big but good sized. Decorated in naval paraphernalia and had been that way for a very long time. Lulu was the grandmother of the lady that runs the place now. She was in her late 30s, a little plump, and called herself Lulu. She was there every night and was more like a hostess. She welcomed everybody and was real friendly and likable. She made everyone feel at home. I had that warm and fuzzy feeling as soon as I walked in. A real friendly Navy bar.

John and I pulled up a couple seats at the bar, looked around and ordered a beer. On the dance floor, a couple waves were dancing. The music from the juke box was pretty good. At the end of the room was a couple pool tables, and I was debating whether to put up a challenge. At the end of the bar was a wave sitting alone. When I noticed her, she was looking at me and immediately turned her head. After my first beer, and halfway through my second, I decided to say Hi.

I walked up and asked if I could sit down. She said OK. I said, "You came here alone?" She said, "Yeah, my girlfriend will be here any minute." I asked if I could buy her a drink. She said, "No, I don't drink much. Thanks anyway." I said, "My name is Rich," and I put my hand out. She took my hand and said, "My name is Sheila."

I said, "Nice name."

"Not really," she said "It's funny how I got my name. You see, my father is Irish but came here from Australia with his parents when he was young. My mother is of Indian descent. In my mother's heritage, most children are named after things in nature. So instead of being named Running Deer or White Dove, my dad named me Sheila." A Sheila in Australia is a female kangaroo. So in reality, I'm named after a kangaroo."

With that, we both started laughing. At that moment her girlfriend came in. I was introduced to Cynthia, and I motioned for John to come over, hoping he would be cool and not blow it. I really didn't have to worry; she was as big a geek as John. They got along fabulously. We talked and laughed and soon it was time to go. I asked if they wanted to take a cab or walk. Unanimously, everyone wanted to walk. When we got to the base, the girls had to walk to Hospital side and their barracks, and we had to go to the left to ours. We stopped in the middle of the parade field to say goodbye. I leaned over to kiss her cheek, and to my surprise, she kissed me on the lips. A big wet one. It felt good. It was late October and a little chilly, but her kiss was warm and soft. She was a good kisser. After, I turned to see where John was, and he was kissing Cynthia. I smiled. John looked happy. The girls went their way and we went ours, not before promising to meet at the Geedonk the next day at noon.

John was beside himself. The best time he ever had. He had a girlfriend. The thanked me over and over. I said, "John, it was all you." He said, "No, if it wasn't for you, I would never have had the courage to talk to her."

The next day John came over to my bunk and said, "Let's go to chow." At chow he never stopped talking about last night and couldn't wait for noon and our date with the girls. John's enthusiasm was catchy, and I found myself almost as excited as him at seeing the girls again. We walked to hospital side and found the Geedonk. Sure enough the girls were there waiting. They looked real good in their uniforms. Cynthia was a blonde version of Olive Oil, Popeye's girlfriend. She and John were happy to see each other and looked good together. Sheila had a great body, and the Indian blood gave her an exotic look that was sexy and attractive. They both seemed genuinely glad to see us. They were in their dress whites, and we were in our dungarees. We didn't really decide what we were going to do, but we took it for granted we were going to stay on base. They thought we would go on liberty. At the end, we stayed on base and went to a movie.

At the end of the day, we made a date with them to go to Lulu's the next weekend. John and I went back to the barracks to get ready for school on Monday.

School on Monday was a little different. We got into algebra and I was having difficulties with it. All the A's and Y's = Z had me confused. So for the next couple nights, John helped me get it down. Finally I got the concept. After that it was easy.

The week went by quickly and before you knew it, we were back at lulus with the girls. Watching John and Cyndi dance was cute and funny. Neither one had a clue, but you could see they were having fun. The night ended too soon, and we promised to go back to Lulu's the next day. It was our new hangout and we felt comfortable there.

The days and weekends went by and I grew more comfortable. I was doing real good in school thanks to John and me learning algebra.

Sheila told me that she was graduating school at the end of the month. It was the second week in November, and we had changed uniforms from summer whites to winter blues. We were walking to Lulus and I was thinking how good she looked in her blue uniform. John and Cyndi were a little ahead of us. I felt a little tug on my heart; I knew I would miss her, but I knew this day would come.

That night we drank a little more than usual. Sheila and I decided to take a walk. We told John and Cyndi we would meet them back at the base and that we wanted to go for a walk.

RAIN: A Sailor's Story

We were looking for a secluded place to be alone so we could be together. We spotted an abandoned car in a field a little way off the street. So we went over and got into the back seat. I told her I would miss her, and she said she would miss me. We started making out, and I really liked the way she kissed. She was a great kisser. Her lips were warm and moist. She kissed me back, hard. I felt her hand on my thigh. I placed my hand on her breast, half hesitating, waiting for her to move it. She moved into my hand and moaned low and deep. Her hand moved into my pants and was unbuttoning my fly. I was pulling up her shirt. We made love right there in the back seat. At first we were in a hurry, like *let's hurry up before someone changes their mind*. But once we got into it, we slowed down and took our time. We made love twice; the first one was hurried and didn't last long. The second was beautiful. We explored each other, took our time, and it was exceptional for both of us. I made up my mind on the way back to the base that on our last weekend we would go to Milwaukee and get a nice hotel room.

We met at the Geedonk a couple times the next week, held hands like high school kids, and promised to write even though we knew we probably wouldn't.

The next weekend we were back at Lulu's and our little love nest in the back of that old car. She made love like she was on a mission. We definitely needed more room. On the way back to the base, I told her of my idea of getting a hotel room in Milwaukee. She was all for it. We would go right after classes on Friday and take the 4:15 train back early Monday morning so we could spend three whole nights together and get back to base before school starts. I couldn't wait.

When I told John about my plans, he was wondering if Cyndi would like to do the same thing. I asked if he had slept with her yet. He said no. I told him about the old car and maybe they should try that first, and that Sheila and I would really rather be alone anyway.

School dragged that week; we met at the Gee dunk every day and talked about our plans for the weekend. We avoided talking about her leaving.

Friday finally got here, we met at the gate, caught the train for Milwaukee and we were off. We hadn't reserved a room – we figured we could find one easy enough when we got off the train.

Not far from the train was the Prairie Hotel. We walked over and asked if they had a room and how much. They asked how long we were planning on staying. I said, "Three nights." It was $21.95 a night and that included tax. I said fine, paid, and got the key. We got Room 521 with a private bath and two beds. We both laughed and said that's just in case we break one! Neither one of us was really hungry. So we stripped off our clothes and hopped into bed. It was only 6 o'clock, but we didn't plan on sleeping. Next morning we went to breakfast, picked up some beer and a cheap Styrofoam cooler. They had ice at the hotel, so we were all set. We only left the hotel room to eat and buy beer. The rest of the time we made love, watched a little TV, and listened to the radio.

We talked about our future in the Navy. And finally I told her about Snowball. It was a long story, and she was a good listener. When I finally finished talking, she just held me to her breast and rocked me back and forth. I felt something wet on my head. I looked up, and Sheila was crying, and that made me cry. We cried for about 10 minutes. Then we made love. It was the most intense and passionate experience I ever had. We were totally into each other, hanging on tight and rocking back and forth. It was almost as if we were one person, like we melded together. I don't remember falling asleep, but Sunday morning came quick, and we were famished. At breakfast we ordered everything. The weekend was flying by, and Monday morning was there before we knew it. On the train back to the base, she told me she was graduating on Friday and hoped I could skip school and see her graduate. She said that on Saturday she was catching a plane home for 30-day leave, which means she'll be home for Christmas, and that she was going to a hospital ship out of Long Beach, California. She was happy about her new duty assignment. She always wanted to travel and hoped she wouldn't get stuck at a base hospital.

On Wednesday, I asked my instructor if I could skip out two hours early so I could see my cousin graduate from Nurses School over on hospital side. He said, 'Cousin?" and with a smile and a wink, he said, "Just check into your last class, and then leave."

So on Friday I ran from the school to my barracks, dressed into my dress blues, and ran to Hospital Side. It was chilly, and the ceremony was held inside. I was a little late, so I stood in back of the auditorium and tried to catch her eye as she sat on the stage. Finally she saw me and smiled. I waved and smiled back. The nurses came up one at a time, got their diplomas and orders, and walked off the stage and sat down in front in the seats reserved for them. After they all got their orders, the speeches started. A half hour later, everyone clapped and shouted, the girls threw their caps into the air, and we were free to leave. I waited outside the door for Sheila, and we walked to the Gee dunk. We went to the one over at my side of the base because hers was full up.

As we were having coffee, she told me she ordered a hotel room in Elgin, Illinois, a small town about twenty miles from the base. Not too many sailors went there, and she said she wanted us to be alone. I had to run back to school to get my liberty card, and she had to double check everything so she could just grab her sea bag and go to the airport the next day at 2.

We met at the main gate, took a bus to Elgin, and checked into our hotel room. Elgin seemed to be a nice Midwest town. Head a nice restaurant close to the hotel and a liquor store not too far away. We decided to buy a nice bottle of champagne to celebrate our last night together. I knew I would miss her a lot. I didn't know if I was in love with her; I didn't know what love was. I'm probably still a little confused about it. But I cared for Sheila, and it wasn't just the sex. She was just a real good person and a good friend.

After dinner we went and got the champagne and went back to our room. The night turned out perfect; it was all we thought it would be and more. I never wanted it to end. Bu all good things must come to an end. Next morning we caught a cab back to the base. I gave her my address and told her to write when she got to her new duty station and then I would have her new address so I could write back. We left each other at the main gate, knowing it would be better that way. Kissed goodbye and walked away. I had a lump in my throat and missed her already.

The rest of the weekend I hung around the barracks, tried to study, and basically just stared out the window. Sunday night John came in and told me about him and Cyndi. They were getting along just fine and were going to try and get stationed together when they got out of school. I didn't want to bust his bubble by telling him they didn't have any guns on a hospital ship. And any chances of his getting stationed with her were null and void.

The days at school turned into weeks; weeks into months, and before I knew it, it was almost Christmas. Everyone had a decision to make. When you finish "A" school, you usually get 30 days leave. They gave us a choice, 15 days for Christmas

RAIN: A Sailor's Story

and 15 days after graduation or 30 after graduation. I took the 15 for Christmas and the 15 after graduation.

A bunch of us were going to Boston, so we checked the airlines and got a group rate round trip for $78. So Friday night after school, we took the bus to the airport and were homeward bound.

This time my older brother was home from college, and he picked me up at the airport. We finally got home at 1 a.m. Mom and Dad were waiting up to see me. Hugs and kisses, a lot of small talk, and off to bed. I was exhausted.

Next day Saturday we had a big old fashioned home-style breakfast. Dad cooked. He is the best breakfast cook around. I toasted the toast, my brother buttered it, Mom made coffee, and my sister set the table. Boy it felt good to be home.

They asked how the Navy was going; I told them good. I had three more months of school. I told them about Sheila and how she got her name. They all laughed. I didn't mention the crypto lab or Snowball, and they didn't ask.

People were in and out all day. Relatives came to see me and also some of my friends. We made plans to go to the dance hall that night and I was looking forward to it.

That night Danny, a good friend from high school, picked me up. He had one of the older guys pick him up a six pack, and we drank it on the way to the dance. When we got there, the place was rocking; it was Saturday night, Christmas vacation, and everyone was out having fun.

When we went in we moved over to the corner where our group hung out. Said hi to everyone. How's the Navy small talk. One of the girls from high school came over and asked me to dance. We talked a little and then her girlfriends came over and everyone was talking.

I decided to walk around the place and see what was happening. Halfway around, I saw her. Prettiest blonde girl I

111

had ever seen. I caught her eye, and instead of turning away, she looked right at me. I was a little embarrassed that she caught me looking at her. I was tempted to turn away but instead I walked right up to her and asked her to dance. The band was playing a fast song, and at first she just looked at me. Then she took my hand and we went out on the dance floor. I'm a pretty good dancer, and she was excellent. We danced a lot, talked a little, and at the end of the night, the band started playing slow songs. We slow danced together, and she felt great in my arms. Our bodies seemed to fit perfectly together and we glided over the dance floor. I was in Heaven.

When the dance was over, I asked if I could give her a ride home. I knew Danny wouldn't mind. She said she came with a bunch of girls and had to go home with them. So said, "At least give me your phone number so I can call you." We went over to her purse; she took out a pen and paper and wrote down her phone number.

Linda Spillane....I put the number in my pocket, grabbed her hand, kissed her on the cheek, and said, "See you tomorrow."

I slept good that night; it was great to be home. I was used to getting up early in the Navy so my interior alarm got me up at 5:30 a.m., and as much as I tried, I couldn't get back to sleep. So not wanting to wake up the family, I decided to go for a run. I dressed quickly, pulled out an old pair of sneakers, and my favorite hoodie and out the door I went.

The neighborhood hadn't changed much. I didn't know what I expected. I had only been gone six months; it seemed like a whole different lifetime. I changed, so I expected everything else to change.

I was gone for about 2 hours and by the time I got home, everyone was up. Again, we had a big breakfast, and Mom reminded us that Sunday dinner would be at 3 – don't be late. I was thinking what time should I call Linda? I didn't want to seem too anxious. At around 10, I couldn't stand it anymore, and I called. She answered on the third ring. I told her it was me and I had a good time last night. She said she had a good time too. Then I asked if she would like to see a movie later, and she said sure. She gave me her address, and I agreed to pick her up at 6:30. She was from the next town over, and I knew where her street was. Mom said I could use the car; now I had to figure out what movie to see.

I wanted to see an action movie, and there was a good one playing at the Orpheum. So I planned on going there. When I picked her up, I asked if she wanted to see that movie. She said not really; there was a movie she wanted to see at the Union theater two towns over. I really didn't mind as long as we were together. The movie turned out to be more of a cartoon for children. I figured she may have made a mistake. But she was totally into it.

Although we were together last night and tonight, we didn't really talk much. So I didn't know a lot about her. As we watched the movie, she put her hand on my thigh, and after a while I put my hand on her breast. I expected her to push it away. Instead she just smiled up at me and snuggled in a little closer. After that, I could care less about the movie; I just enjoyed feeling her up and having her do the same to me. I couldn't wait for the movie to be over so we could go parking.

We finally left the theater and went up to the state forest. I found a perfect spot, parked, and we started making out. She played all the little games starting and stopping, going a little further each time. Saying I'll think she's a pig and all the time have her hand between my legs.

After about an hour of playing around, we finally got to it. I was about to burst. The first time went quick, and I could tell she was a little disappointed. But I was ready almost immediately. The second time it was great. We took our time and totally enjoyed ourselves.

When we were finished, we just sat in the car and talked. We talked for hours. Neither of us had to work the next day, so when I finally got her home at 2:30 a.m., it was no problem. We promised to go skating the next day after lunch. I hadn't been skating for about a year and was looking forward to it.

I picked her up at 12:-- sharp. To my surprise, Linda had a picnic lunch all packed. We drove back to my house, parked the car, and walked a short distance to the frog pond. The pond was perfect size for skating. I believe that back in the old days it was actually a farm pond. But now it was a nice round pond in the middle of a field that us kids in the neighborhood grew up skating on in the winter and catching frogs in the summer. Our mothers felt safe because it was shallow and there was little fear of drowning.

It was Christmas Eve and I still had shopping to do, and I added Linda to my list. It was a little bit colder than I thought, so we only skated for about a half hour. So with cold feet and rosy cheeks, we walked back to my house to eat our picnic lunch. I was planning to ask Linda to go shopping with me, but never got around to it. As we were eating a sandwich, I brought her into my room to see my Navy uniform. She asked me to try it on. I asked her to turn her back, and she said, "Remember last night. I've already seen you naked." She loved my uniform and kissed me. Next thing we were on the bed making love.

Both parents were working, my older brother, sister, and younger brother were at my grandmother's where I was going alter. So we had the whole house to ourselves. She was uninhibited, absolutely gorgeous, and I knew I was falling love. We both had family obligations that night; I still had shopping to do and I had to pick my mother up after work. So although I wanted to spend the rest of the day with her, I had to take Linda home and pick up my mom by 5 o'clock. I promised to call her later and hopefully we could get together that night for a couple of hours. She wanted me to meet her parents, and I wanted her to meet mine. Needless to say, I was going to have a busy Christmas Eve, and I still had shopping to do.

There is a small mall just up the street from where my mom works. So after I dropped Linda off, I went shopping at the mall. I made it to my mom's work right on time, picked her up, and we went home. I told her all about Linda and how much I liked her and maybe she could come to Grams and meet everyone later. My mom said she would love to meet her, and yes, I can use her car. I didn't have to ask; she knew I was going to. Mom made supper, and I wrapped gifts.

I called Linda and we agreed I would come to her house at 7:30 and then she would come to my grandmother's for our family party. I was excited and nervous at the same time. What if her parents didn't like me?

My sister helped me pick out some clothes and ironed my shirt and pants. As we were doing this, I told her all about Linda. She was dying to meet her.

I got to Linda's about 7:30 and knocked on the door. It was opened by her father. I was a little amazed by the way he looked. He was dressed in a suit with a frilly white shirt, silk tie, and wingtip shoes. I thought that maybe he had changed his mind and decided to go out. He shook my hand, ushered me inside, and said, "You must be Richard." I said, "Yes, that's me." Then he introduced himself. "I'm Jonathan Spillane, and this is my lovely wife Marilyn." I looked over at her and she was just as dressed as he was, in a gown and shawl with her hair done up and fancy high heel shoes on.

Then Linda came over and said, "I see you met my parents." I said, "Yes I did and they seem very nice." They ushered me into the living room and I sat down in a chair. Then they started pointing out to me different pieces of furniture, telling me things like *antique this* and *antique that*. And Mrs. Spillane was showing me her collection of Hummels and telling me that *this is a rare one, very expensive*. All the time I'm thinking to myself what a couple of phonies. He is a foreman on an assembly line at the local tool factory, and she doesn't work. They live in a small Cape, not in the best section of town, and they're coming on like they're high society. She's telling me about her flower gardens, and she's secretary of her garden club, like I'm supposed to be impressed. They live in a small house in a small town. Her garden club has maybe 10 of her neighbors in it. They were so pretentious that I was embarrassed by the whole ordeal and couldn't wait to get out of there. So after Jonathan got finished showing me his chess set with the real ivory and onyx pieces, I said that my family was waiting for us and we had to leave. Not before promising to play a game of chess with Jonathan before going back to school.

On the way to my grandmother's house, I got to thinking about little things that Linda did. She was always looking in her makeup mirror and checking her face. Adding a little makeup or lipstick, fixing her hair, always a little something. She was extremely superficial, but I just thought it was a girl thing that she took to extreme.

She seemed to expect things. I just thought that because we really didn't know each other real well that she was trying harder to be more ladylike and expected me to be more gentlemanly. When we went skating, she asked me to tie her skates. Fine, I didn't mind. I enjoyed doing it. She always waited for me to open up her door or hold her chair; I know it's the gentlemanly thing to do, but I think it was taken a little to the extreme. After meeting her folks, I understood it a little more.

When we got to my family's Christmas party, most of my family was already there. As I introduced her to everyone, she acted like she was a princess being nice to her subjects. I started to think that it was a mistake bringing her here. My sister is a couple years younger than me and couldn't wait to meet Linda. At first she thought Linda was very pretty and favorably impressed. After awhile, she wasn't so impressed. Linda treated my sister as her own personal maid. Expecting me to do things for her was one thing, but expecting my sister and other family members to is another story. She thought she was a queen and deserved to be waited on. Maybe not a queen, more like the guest of honor. Needless to say, she didn't fit in with the family real well. At first I thought it was because she was shy. But no, she really was that self-centered.

My first impression of her started to wane. I knew I had to go back in a little over a week. It would be interesting how I felt about her then. Right now her good looks and great sex had me head over heels in love. But now some doubts started surfacing. I thought to myself, *forget it; she'll be okay once she gets to know everyone. She'll be alright.*

The next ten days went by quickly. I spent as much time as I could with Linda. She really was stuck up. The way she acted and treated people was a real turn off. She really thought that because she was so pretty, she was better than everyone else. Men fell all over themselves being nice to her, and I considered myself lucky to be with her.

She told me that last summer after graduation she went to work in a nursery for her uncle. She designed landscaping for new houses. But the nursery closed on November 1st, and she was laid off for the winter. She put her application in with TWA Airlines to be a stewardess and got accepted. She was going to Texas to school after the first of the year. So it seems we'll be leaving home together.

I didn't know the difference between love and lust. What I did know was I didn't want to be without her. I really didn't want to go back. I didn't want her to go to Texas. I just wanted things to stay the same, but that could never happen; time goes on.

We were together every day and she told me she loved me. I told her the same thing. We talked about how I would come home after "A" School, and she may be able to come home for spring break. I said there was a good chance I could be stationed close to home because I was in the top 5 of my class and go preference when I asked for my next duty assignment. She said she would try to get based in Boston at Logan. I was sad about going back but happy about our plans for the future. She gave me a graduation picture of herself, and I gave her one of me. It was one of the happiest two weeks of my life.

But all good things must come to an end. She left three days before me, and her folks drove her to the airport. We said our goodbyes the night before, in the back seat of my mother's car. I didn't want her to go, but I had to leave soon, so reluctantly we said goodbye. I gave her my address at Great lakes and she promised to write and give me her new address in Texas.

Sunday morning I was on a plane for Great Lakes Training Center. Back to "A" School. I promised myself I would study hard and stay tops in my class so I would get the duty station of my choice.

When I got to my barracks, it was later when I had planned. Bad weather kept us in Boston getting de-iced before takeoff, and a snowstorm kept us in the air circling O'Hare longer than usual. So ultimately I was four hours late getting to the training center.

I had wanted to talk to John about school and see if we could study together. I was determined to be in the top 5 of my class. I got in around 9:15, even the bus was slow. All I had time for before lights out was a quick shower.

Monday morning was the start of my new agenda. I took a lot more notes than usual and paid strict attention. Asked more questions, some good and some not so good, and picked up extra reading handout at the main office.

Back at the barracks that night I hooked up with John. He handed me a stack of letters that came for me and he had volunteered to keep till I got back off leave.

We talked about studying together and hitting the library at least twice a week. We went over our notes and homework assignments for about an hour. Then I went back to my bunk to read my mail.

The first letter I read was from Sheila. She liked the hospital ship she was on and was leaving for Vietnam in a couple weeks. She was looking forward to helping the wounded over there. She also told me she missed me, John, and Cindy; the nights at Lulus and our alone time. *Say hi to John for me and write soon.* She had written her address although it was on the corner of the envelope. The next letter was from my little brother Peter. He had sent it just before I got home. He said he missed me and couldn't wait to see me at Christmas. It made me feel a little sad that I didn't spend more time with him and my family and less time with Linda. I got a letter from Peavy. I was real surprised he was transferred back to the states and was waiting for his new ship to get back from the Mediterranean. He was going on a destroyer out of Norfolk, Virginia. He gave me his address and asked me to write. He didn't mention anything about Penny or snowball. I now had some letter writing to catch up on and my studies. I also wanted to ask John about Cyndi.

I decided to write one letter a night, starting with my brother Peter. Growing up, although I was seven years older than him, we were close. So I decided to write him first because

I felt a little guilty about not spending more time with him at Christmas.

The next morning at chow I talked to John about Cyndi. He said they were still seeing each other and everything was great and would I like to go to Lulu's with them Saturday night. I said it would depend on how school as going and if I got caught up on my letter writing.

School was going good. The days went by and were piling up one on top of the other. I managed to stay in the top five of m y class, shifting between number 3 and 5. John as always was tops. I did go to Lulu's a couple of times, and usually left early after a couple beers. It wasn't the same without Sheila. I wrote her a couple times and she wrote back. I missed her. I had been at school for three weeks when I finally got a letter from Linda.

It wasn't at all what I expected. It was blunt and right to the point.

Rich,

I didn't know how to write this letter; that is why it has been so long. After getting here in Texas and thinking about us, I realized that it just wouldn't work. We're both too young and have a career ahead of us to get through. You in the Navy and me as a stewardess. So I'm sure you can see that it's too soon for either of us to settle down with someone.

I've met a lot of nice people down here and I'm really enjoying it. I'm doing well in school and am looking forward to when I start flying. So right now I want to concentrate on my career and give it all my attention. Good luck with the Navy.

Linda

My first Dear John. I was devastated. I kind of knew it was coming when she hadn't written in so long, but still it hurt. What really amazed me was I also had a feeling of relief. That feeling of relief is what I was thinking about. I had to figure it out.

What I decided to do was put emotion aside and look at this logically. So I made up a list; her good points on the left and things I didn't like on the right:

<u>Good</u><u>Bad</u>
Extremely pretty annoying
Great sexual appetite self-centered
Superficial
Snob
Unappreciative
Spoiled
Uncaring

After reading my list, I knew why I was somewhat relieved. Although I lusted after this girl, I didn't like her. I think lust is a very strong emotion. Hard to control! But now the situation has resolved itself. I just got dumped. Of course I was hurt; who wouldn't be? But at the same time, I was relieved.

At those times when I felt sorry for myself, I would look at my list. It made me appreciate Sheila that much more.

Time has a way of healing things like broken bones and broken hearts, and time was flying by. I still wanted to be in the top 5 of my class and studied hard, which helped with my feelings and moved time along.

In February we had the big move. That's when you go from the classroom to the lab. We actually get to work on electrical components. Testing resistors, capacitors, and building circuits.

Of course I teamed up with John. They wanted the more top rated guys teamed with the lower achievers, but I convinced the instructor to let John and I team up, and then we could help the others. He thought it was a pretty good idea and everything worked out perfectly.

I really liked working with John, and I know he liked working with me. Being such a geek, he really never had a real best friend. Now that I helped fix him up with Cyndi and went places with him, I was his best friend. Truth be told, I liked John a lot, and he was becoming my best friend. I got to know Cyndi a little better too and I liked her. She and John were good together.

Sheila and I were still writing; she was getting accustomed to shipboard living and would be arriving in the Tonkin Gulf and Vietnam real soon. I don't know how the mail was delivered to or taken off a ship while it was underway; I guess they dropped it off and picked it up at each port they stopped at.

Soon Sheila's letters would be getting more frantic. All the wounded soldiers, sailors, Marines, and even Vietnamese civilians were taking a toll on her. I promised myself to write her often to try and buck up her spirits with letters about me, John, Cyndi, and school. Telling her to hang in there, this is what she was taught to do. And she was helping out our military and should be proud.

I had a taste of war and didn't like it. I felt sorry for Sheila and would try and help her any way I could. It may be romantic in the movies; the Navy nurse meets the wounded aviator, nurses him back to life, falls in love, and lives happily ever after. But in reality that don't happen. War is Hell on Earth and hard on the soul.

"A" School was coming to an end. We would graduate April 3 on a Thursday. Normally you graduate on Friday, but because it was Good Friday and Sunday was Easter, we graduated a week early.

Two weeks earlier we filled out our dream sheets. That's where you wanted to go for your next duty station. I put in for Newport Naval Shipyard in Newport, Rhode Island and Boston Naval Shipyard in Boston, Massachusetts.

We would find out on Monday. Also we would all advance to the next pay grade. So on completion of "A" School, I would become an E4 3rd Class Petty Officer. I was in the Navy a little over 9 months and already an E4. That was unheard of. Usually it took minimum a 1 ½ years. In school, we also studied the Uniform Code of Military Justice. So I figured with my education, I was prepared for my promotion.

By the time we graduated on Thursday, I found out I would be stationed in Newport, Rhode Island on the repair ship, the Grand Canyon. AD27, I also sewed my petty officer stripes on my uniforms and instead of waiting for Friday to fly out, I reserved a flight for Thursday night at 7:15. Goodbye "A" school.

This time my father came to the airport to pick me up. I asked where Brendon was and he said he wasn't home from school yet. It was good to see my father, and he was as excited as I was about my promotion, and when I told him I would be stationed in Newport, he was real happy. Newport was only an hour from home, and I would be home on weekends if I didn't have the duty.

While I was home, I wanted to go to Newport, check it out so I would be more prepared when the time came to check in.

It was after 1 a.m. when I got home. My mom waited up to see me – Brendon too. But my younger brother and sister couldn't wait and were in bed sleeping. I would see them in the morning.

I couldn't wait for Easter Sunday dinner and then going to Grandma's house that night for the big family get-together. Aunts, uncles, cousins; it was fun because there were lots of them. And with all the friends that stopped in, it was a big party.

Saturday after breakfast and talking to everyone, I decided to go uptown to see if any of my friends were around. As luck would have it, I ran into Danny. Dan and I had been friends a long time, and I was happy to see him. We talked for awhile, caught up on what was going on, and decided to go to the dance that night.

I was a little apprehensive about it because it would bring back memories of Linda. And even though I was over being hurt, I still had a soft spot in my heart. I know I shouldn't have, but it was there and there was nothing I could do about it. But I liked to dance, all my friends would be there, and I really decided to go and have fun.

Danny picked me up at 8:20. He already had the beer, so we drove around for an hour and drank the six-pack before going to the ballroom. Once inside, we went over to our corner. All the kids were there. Everyone was home for Easter. We all said hi, shook hands, and gave hugs. It was good to see everyone. All my old girl and guy friends; I was glad I didn't let a bad experience keep me away.

With a few beers under my belt and the music blasting, I couldn't' wait to dance. I grabbed one of the girls I knew to be a good dancer, and off we went. We all danced with each other, the whole gang – what fun. The night went by too fast. Danny got me home about 1 a.m. I was tired but also felt good.

Easter Sunday we all went to St. Mary's Church for Easter mass. The beginning of a good day. I wasn't disappointed either. Breakfast, dinner, and the party at Gram's was fantastic. One of my uncles was in the Navy in the past, and he was amazed that I had made E4 in just 10 months. It took him two years. I didn't tell him how I made E4 early because of my transfer to Vietnam; then I would have had to tell him about what happened, and I wasn't ready to do that.

My leave went by too quickly. It seemed as if I just got home, and I had to go back. Danny had volunteered to drive me back. I didn't take the time to go down in advance; it just wasn't at the top of my list of things to do, and my leave time ran out. I didn't have to be back until Saturday evening at 5 p.m. Danny had the weekend off so he drove me back. He wanted to see the Navy base in Newport, so it was fun for him.

We got to the base around 11 a.m. We pulled up to the guard shack and I showed the marine my orders. He had us park over to the side and told us to go into the office and get a pass so Danny could drive on the base. The gate was about a mile from the pier where the ships were tied up, and it was a long walk carrying a sea bag. Danny was happy he got the pass and was able to drive to the base. We drove around a little before he dropped me off at the pier. There were three piers as wide as a two-lane road and about as long as a football field – all with many kinds of ships tied up. The ships were tied to each other with their gangways going from ship to ship. Some of them were six ships wide. So to get to the outboard ship, you had to cross all six. The ships tied directly to the pier were the repair ships. My ship wasAD27 -- "A" standing for *auxiliary* and "D" standing for *destroyer*. Meaning it was a repair ship for destroyers. We had two types of destroyers: DEs, which were destroyer escorts and DDs which were destroyers.

The base was huge. As we drove around, we saw all kinds of buildings: Movie Theater, bowling alley, PX, Acey Ducey Club, Chief's Club, Officer's Club, and housing for enlisted and officers. On the other side of the base we had the Coast Guard. It was its own entity but shared part of our base.

Danny enjoyed our tour of the base and dropped me off at the end of the pier where my ship was tied up. We said our goodbyes and I told him I would call if I had next weekend off. He said if I did, he would come down Friday night and pick me up.

There were two gangways from the ship to the pier. I knew from my experience in Nam that the forward gangway was for officers, and the After or Aft Gangway was for enlisted. If I didn't know any better, I probably would have walked up the Forward Gangway and got my ass chewed out and sent to the Aft gangway.

I went up the gangway, saluted at the officer of the day, and asked permission to come on board. When I got permission, I told him my name, rank, and that I was reporting for duty. He welcomed me aboard and had the petty officer of the watch bring me to the fire control shop. I met a couple of the guys who were to be my shipmates. We all shook hands and they showed me where my locker was. We had our own locker room on our ship, but I was told to see the master at arms to have him assign me a bunk.

The master at arms shack was on the first deck below the main deck. The main deck had the repair shops for the electronics and upper parts of the ships' equipment. The lower decks contained the bunk rooms, showers, latrines (or head – why they were called heads in the Navy, I don't know to this day). In the middle of the first deck was the mess hall and in the forward part of the ship, the deck Apes, or boatswain's mates, had their bunks and showers and lockers. On the second lower deck were the repair shops for the machinist mates engine men, firemen, and boiler tenders. On the third lower deck were the engines and generators and all the equipment to mechanically run the ship. Below that was the bilge.

Above the main deck is above decks. Just as below the main deck is below deck. The officers' quarters are above decks. As well as the radio room, radar rooms, combat control room and also the bridge where the helmsman steers the ship and the captain does his thing.

The ship is 100 percent self-contained – everything from barbers to doctors, plumbers, electricians, and so forth. It's a whole community that sails across oceans.

After getting checked in at personnel and getting my bunk assignment, I went back to the shop. It was lunchtime and one of the guys was going to chow and asked if I wanted to go with him. I said sure. I was a little hungry, and he would show me the way. We went below decks, headed forward on the first deck, and found the end of the chow line, The sailor I was with was a seaman FTG. The FTG stands for Fire control Technician Gunnery. He told me he was approved to take the test for third class in may. His name was Kenneth Leary, but everyone called him Ken. If you're not rated, which is E4 and above, you're called a striker. So above your three seaman stripes you have an insignia designating the job you're striking for. So Leary was a seaman striking to become a fire control technician Gunnery or FTG3, which is a third class petty officer. He had been on board for nearly a year and was just now taking the test for E4. I didn't tell him how long I had been in. I was in a year less than he, even though I was senior to him. He knew a lot more about the radar systems and attack directors than I did and I figured maybe he could teach me something. He came from Pennsylvania and even though he had the weekend off, it was too far to travel for just 3 days. So once a month, he put in for early liberty, took Friday off and went home, leaving on Thursday evening after work.

 I asked Ken to show me around the ship. He said he would be glad to. We spent the rest of Saturday and most of Sunday going around the ship from the Folksal to the Fantail. From the bridge to the Bilge and everything in between. He also showed the radar systems we used in the ship for fire control. He showed me the attack director and the computer systems we used to direct the gunfire and how we used the radar to aim the guns. Through a series of syncro servo systems, the radar through the attack director and the computers is hooked up to the big guns on board. The alignment of these systems is crucial to the proper operation and aiming of the guns so you can hit the target. Even though the ship is on the ocean with rough seas, the pitch and roll of the ship is controlled with a gyroscope system built into the fire control system.

This was never explained to me in a school. Now that I knew how the system worked; next I had to learn the actual radar system and how it worked. For that I asked Ken if there were any manuals on board I could look over. He told me there was a place on the main deck where I could check out hooks and plans on almost any fire control system in the fleet, including some of the new missile systems. He showed me where it was and it was closed and would be open on Monday.

Monday morning ken and I went to chow then back to the shop for roll call. I met the rest of the sailors in my division – the gunnery division. We had fire control technicians, gunner mates, and sonar men. The gunnery division was just one division that made up the repair department. The officer in charge of the repair department was a full lieutenant. The officers in charge of the divisions ranged from lieutenant junior grade to ensign to warrant officer. The officer in charge of our division was an ensign – Ensign Peters. The person who ran the fire control section was a chief petty officer – Chief Petty Officer Franklin. The fire control men consisted of the chief, two third class petty officers, two seamen and me. From what Ken told me, we were real shorthanded and had multiple jobs lined up on the board.

After roll call and before all the assignments were handed out, I got to meet everyone in our division. Needless to say, I couldn't remember all their names, but eventually I would get to know them. Unknown to me, there was a lot of talk about me and what was going to happen when I got to the ship. Ensign Peters was only a couple years older than me. Fresh out of college ROTC. He was in the middle of his two years of active duty before going into the reserves. Ensign Peters was concerned because of the trouble I got into and what had happened in Vietnam. He also was concerned about me seeing a counselor. He had a little over a year left of active duty and would be up for a promotion to lieutenant junior grade and didn't want to screw that up. He figured that I was a fuck up and could be the one to fuck up his promotion.

Chief Franklin and the first class gunner's mate Johnston both read my record. Chief Franklin couldn't wait to see me. First class Johnston also wanted to meet me. Shooting up the jungle and wounding a Vietnamese whore who I said was a spy was the balls. They also pointed out that I also received a letter of commendation. Ensign Peters wasn't swayed by what they told him. He countered with the fact that I had counseling. They said what do you expect? His best friend was machine gunned to death right in front of him. Nevertheless, Peters came up with a plan to get rid of me. The USS Cole needed a second class petty officer to run the fire control division on board their ship. They're leaving for Vietnam August first and can't leave without a full complement of personnel and the lowest petty officer to be in charge of a division is an E5. Both third class E4 fire control men on board are taking the test for E5. Peters doesn't want to lose either one of them. So he proposed that they pull a few strings, forgo my time in Grade, and recommend I take the test for E5. Chief Franklin was outraged. He said, "That is ridiculous! Elliott hasn't been in the Navy or a year yet – never mind having a year in Grade. Because of his involvement in Vietnam, he lucked into E4. Now you're proposing he take the test for E5 with less than one year total in the Navy? I'm totally opposed to it."

Peters told Franklin, "Look we can't afford to lose our two best men. We're barely keeping up now with all the repairs. If we lose one of them we'll be in deep shit." First class Johnson was privy to all this and told Franklin, "Peters is right. It'll be easier to train Elliott to operate the radar and fire control systems, than to train him to repair the systems at the same level as our two guys. We can't afford to lose him."

Franklin said, "Yeah, I know all that, but he hasn't been in the Navy long enough -- he's too green!" Peters said, "You're so proud of his duty in Vietnam; He wasn't too green for that." Finally Franklin said, "Okay. Do what you have to do."

So Ensign Peters went to the head of the department Lieutenant Commander Mud. After telling Mud all his concerns, he agreed with Peters to talk to personnel and waive time in grade and have me take the test for E5 in May. If I pass the test, I will sew my new stripe on in July and will immediately be transferred to the Cole. Peters will be rid of a potential problem and the Cole with have their E5!

After roll call, all the jobs were handed out. I was going to team up with Seaman Kenneth Leary. Before we left to go to our assignment, Chief Franklin and Gunner Johnston asked us to wait, that they wanted to personally welcome me aboard.

After everyone had picked up their gear and left, Chief Franklin told Ken to wait it out on deck and asked me to step into their office. Gunner Johnston was already in there. When I came in, Chief Franklin closed the door and asked me to sit down. "We want to personally welcome you on board. We read your personnel file and know about your involvement in Vietnam. Your letter of commendation is impressive. I wanted to tell you now because you don't have much time to study before taking the test. Because of your exemplary service and your graduating "A" School in the top of your class, we're recommending you for promotion to E5. The test will be given on May 8; you have just over two weeks to prepare yourself. Do you have any questions?"

RAIN: A Sailor's Story

After dropping a bomb on you, why do they always ask *do you have any questions? Of course I have questions. I am just so astounded that my brain hasn't had time to formulate them.* I didn't really say that, but that is what I was thinking.

Gunner Johnston said, "I know this is a little overwhelming, so for now, go to work with Ken. At the end of the day, I'll be around; you can stop in and see me if you have any questions."

Ken brought me over to the Cole to work on their MK 1A computer. They were having trouble aligning the system. Every time they aligned it, it went out of alignment after only a few practice runs. All the electronic components and servers were tested and were good. I kind of figured if it was not electrical, it was mechanical. We realigned the system and as they made some practice runs, I watched the gears as they were turning the syncros. Then I saw it. One of the gears would slip then catch then slip again, then catch. When we pulled out the syncro and checked the gear, we found that the pin that held the gear to the motor shaft had sheared off. Part of the pin was still sticking out and when we aligned it, it worked fine, but under the pressure of actually working, it would slip, catch, and then slip. By then it was time to roll up the tools, meters, and stuff and go back to the shop. Ken said that the next morning he would show me how to acquisition the parts we need for our repairs, and we'll get a new shear pin.

After that, I went looking for Gunner Johnston. I found him in the first place I looked. He was in the office. The first thing I said was, "Thank you for pulling whatever strings you did to make me eligible for this test. He said that he rarely needs E5s. "The electronics industry is wide open, looking for anyone with a background in electronics. With what they're paying, we can't compete, so all our good men are leaving when their enlistments are up and going to work in the civilian sector. Also we reviewed your record. What you did in Nam is a little controversial, but the letter of commendation speaks for itself." Then he did something that surprised me; he reached over the desk and shook my hand. He said, "Good job, Elliott."

I said, "Thank you. I'm going to need the books to study for the E5 exam. Do you know where I can get them?"

He said, "Check with Belke and Maloof." I gave him a quizzical look. He said, "The other two third-class FTs there are also taking the test. It might be a good idea if you all study together."

When I left the office, I said to myself *Better call Danny and tell him I won't be coming home for a couple weeks.* I figured I had a lot of studying to do. For E4, most of the test was on general electronics knowledge. The test for E5 gets more specific on the actual equipment. I had to wait until the next morning to see Belke and Maloof, as both of them were on liberty for the night.

Next morning before roll call, I met with Belke and Maloof in the shop. They both seemed surprised that I was taking the E5 exam. Maloof said, "Didn't you just get out of "A" school?" I said yes but that I had been in the fleet before going o "A" school. I immediately changed the subject before they could ask any more questions. I didn't want them to know that they were pulling strings for me because of my letter of commendation. I really believed that bullshit story. Later on when I found out the truth, it was too late to do anything about it. Besides making E5 in 13 months was something. That's normally three and a half years minimum. As an E5, they take it for granted you're over 21, simply because no one ever heard of anyone being an E5 under the age of 22, never mind 21. Here I was 19 ½ and only in the Navy for 13 months, and already I was an E5.Belke, Maloof, and I studied every morning before roll call. They were both married and went home every night they didn't have duty.

So they studied at home and I studied in the shop after chow in the evening. In the morning they came back early. I skipped chow in the morning; we had coffee in the shop. That's when we compared notes and asked questions of each other. From the books and the hands-on experience I was getting, I had a good feeling about this exam.

Over the next few weeks, Ken and I worked a lot together. I realized later that it wasn't just coincidence that I worked exclusively on the Cole

The day finally came to take the test. Belke, Maloof, and I went to the mess hall to take the test. The test started at 8 a.m. and you had to be finished by 11 a.m. Maloof left about ten minutes before me, and Belke left about the same time as me. Walking back to the shop, we met Ken along the way. I asked, "How do you think you did?"

He said, "I feel pretty good about it. How about you guys?" Both Belke and I said, "Good." When we got back to the shop, we asked Maloof the same question. He said the technical stuff was a little hard. Belke agreed with Maloof. I really didn't feel that way probably because I had studied military code of justice in "A" school and the military books that I shared with Maloof and Belke I thought I did pretty good.

The next day while working on the Cole, I asked the two third class FTs if they had taken the test for E5. They both said no. One wasn't eligible, didn't have enough time in Grade, and the other one messed up and got back from leave and was AWOL for over a day. Instead of being busted to the next lower pay grade, he was told he wouldn't be recommended for the E5 exam this time.

Over the next few weeks, we repaired all the fire control equipment on the Cole. Our gunner's mates made all the repairs needed on their gun mounts. We worked together on the alignment. We checked the alignment with each of the different radars. Swapping the guns and radars back and forth through the computers and attack director syncro servo system, fine tuning them until we had everything perfect. The last alignment procedure would be done at sea when the pitch and roll Gyroscope would be added to the system. We all believed that the complete fire control and gun systems were in perfect condition. The only thing left was to upgrade their repair parts that may be needed if something wears out.

Over three weeks after we took the test, we finally got the results. They were posted on the wall outside the personnel office. I made E5 on the first increment. There are six increments, one each month, July through December. Maloof and I made it in the first increment, Belke made it on the second. Ken made E4 on the first increment. That night we all went on liberty. In three weeks I would be sewing on my second-class stripes. I was really excited.

The sonar system also uses our attack director to aim their depth charges and hedgehog mount. The sonar is like underwater radar. When the sonar pings on a target, that target is transferred to the attach director. From there, it is aligned to the mount designated by the sonar men as to which weapon they want to use.

I was again going over to the Cole. The sonar man John Slater was going with me. Actually I was going with him, he being a pay grade higher meant he was in charge and I was going with him. The reality of the situation was he did his thing and I did mine. No one pulled rank; we all mostly worked as a team. So our job today was to fine-tune the alignment of the sonar equipment through the attack director to the various anti-submarine weapons on board. That took us most of the week. And on Friday the chief gave us early liberty and let us off at noon. Tom Alpoe, one of the gunner's mates in our shop gave me a ride home. He lived two towns over from mine, so it wasn't much out of his way. He also agreed to pick me up at 6 a.m. on Monday so we would be back on the ship in time for our morning meeting.

Going home on weekends became a regular routine. I didn't mind riding with Tom and mom let me use her car whenever I asked, but I wanted to get my own car. I wanted to get one in high school but never really got around to it. So I figured when I got my new stripe, I would get another pay raise and I could afford to buy a car, so this weekend I decided to look around. It was the last week in June, and I would sew my stripes on the first week in July. I still couldn't believe it – in a little over a year, E5 – amazing.

Dad took me out looking on Saturday, but we didn't find anything. So we decided to go again next weekend. In the meantime, he would keep his eyes open and if he saw something he thought I might like, he would let me know.

Danny and I went to a party that night, had a few beers, and left early. The party was a little on the lame side. We drove to the dance hall but didn't go in. We met some people we knew outside, and they said it was dead. So we went home. Sunday I stayed home with the family. Sunday breakfast, Sunday dinner, the Red Sox ballgame on TV, and before you know it, I was in the car with Tom heading back to the base.

The next weekend I had the duty. I called home and told dad I wouldn't be home so our search for a car would have to be put on hold. Tom also had the duty. I agreed to take his watch on Sunday so he could have the weekend off and be with his family. After all, he did give me a ride back and forth each week.

Wednesday was the big day; July first, the day we got our promotion. At the divisional meeting that morning, Ensign Peters came in and handed Maloof, Leary, and me a packet containing our new stripes. Usually we bought our own, but in this shop it was tradition for the division officer to buy the patches.

We got a big round of applause and were told to go to personnel after our assignments were handed out to sign the paperwork. At the end of the meeting, I still hadn't been given a job. Ensign Peters told me he wanted to see me after the meeting. Before going to the office, I helped Ken get his gear together, let him use my meter, and grabbed a cup of coffee.

When I got to the office, Ensign Peters, Chief Franklin, and Gunner Johnston were sitting there talking. I knocked and they asked me to come in and sit down. Ensign Peters said, "There's no other way to say this, so I'll get right to the point. You're being transferred, effective immediately. You're going over to the Cole." I stood there just looking at him. Finally I said, "What did I do to deserve this? I've only been on board for three months. I've got at least another nine months to go before being transferred. I like it here, made some friends, and am close to home. So tell me, how did I fuck up this time?"

Chief Franklin said, "Rich, you didn't fuck up. The Cole is short on fire control men and needs a second class to run that division. You finding that broken shear pin on that servo system was good work. The system you thought up of hooking up three separate meters to the whole system and reading them all at once sure beats the Hell out of running from radar to attack director to gun and back again. Saves a lot of time and is a lot more accurate. So no, you did not fuck up. Your work and initiative and innovation prove what we though all along. You're a good sailor and we're proud of you. But orders are orders, and you've been ordered to the Cole." I looked from Ensign Peters to Chief Franklin to Gunner Johnston. Not one of them would hold eye contact with me. I knew there was more to it than that. While I was thinking about what to say, it finally came to me. Not all at once, but in bits and pieces. Me being recommended to take the second class test a year early. As I was thinking about this, I also remembered that the only third class on board the Cole that had enough time in grade to take the test for E5 was not recommended because he was late getting back off leave. Normally that would be 30 days restriction to the ship. The punishment, not being recommended for E5, did not fit the crime. So to fill out the fire control division, they needed an E5. By not letting one rise through the ranks on board, they were guaranteed to have one assigned to them. Ensign Peters knew that he would have to supply the Cole with an E5. Not wanting to lose two good men he knew, he chose to arrange for me to advance to that pay grade so he could transfer me to the Cole and keep the men he knew were good instead of the unknown.

As I was standing there figuring all this out, I could see the three of them fidgeting in their seats. Finally Ensign Peters said, "If there's nothing else, I have things to do." I looked at him hard, and he didn't move. I finally told him what I thought. At first he tried to deny it. Ensign Peters was not much older than me, maybe four years. But Chief Franklin had 18 years in the Navy and when he spoke, everyone listened. He was sitting there looking at his hands and finally spoke up. He said, "Rich, put yourself in our shoes. When we were told you were coming on board, we said great – we could use another third class. But when your personnel file came here, Ensign Peters had some reservations. I could tell by reading your file you had to have had something on the ball to have done everything it says in that file and still come out of "A" School tops in your class and an E4 grade petty officer. Your letter of commendation and your time at that crypto lab in Vietnam was impressive, if unorthodox. All that being said, Ensign Peters was worried about you having to see a counselor. I told him it was routine after all you had been through, but he wasn't buying it. And another thing Maloof and Belke are married and Maloof has a kid on the way. We didn't want to take them away from their families.

You, on the other hand, are young and have a lot of time left in your enlistment. This will look good in your file, so after a lot of discussion and some persuading with the Bureau of Personnel, we got you approved to take the test for E5. We had a good idea that you would pass the test; after all, you were in the top three in your class. Our only concern was what increment you would get was a bit of a concern. If need be, the Cole cold have been delayed until the first of October not after that. So when you got rated in the first increment, everything fell into place. Now consider this, you are now a second class petty officer. Some people won't make that in their entire enlistment. You will be in charge of your own division. Again, petty officers with over ten years in don't get that opportunity. So if you look at it realistically, it's a win-win situation for everyone involved."

Was the Cole privy to this information and is that why their third class didn't take the test for second class? Chief Franklin said, "I can't speak for the Cole, but fire control technicians are hard to come by. They're going into a war zone and need a full complement of FTs and gunner's mates. That may be why he wasn't recommended. They naturally would rather get an E5 to fill their roster than a seaman out of "A" school. And the minimum rate one can be to be the head of a division is E5, second class petty officer. Knowing that, they probably pulled some strings of their own to get what they wanted. If you hadn't made E5 until the fifth increment, we would have had to send Maloof. But from where I'm sitting, everything worked out fine."

I asked, "Does the Cole know I'm coming onboard and have they read my personnel file?"

He answered, "Yes, and they are impressed with your work on their fire control system. They would rather have someone with more experience, like Maloof, but what you lack in experience, you more than make up for on ingenuity. And no, they're not worried about you seeing that counselor. So if there are no other questions, you are to go to the personnel and sign your promotion. Prepare to transfer to the Cole on Monday. Oh! Put in a request chit for early liberty. We know you have no leave left, so the best we can do is let you off on Thursday so you can have a long weekend before your transfer. Tom will also have early liberty, so you can go home together. Any other questions?"

I said, "Just one. You said they needed a full complement of fire control technicians because they are going to a war zone. I take it I'm going back to Vietnam?" They all looked at me and just shook their heads. I said, "I would like to take the rest of the day after checking in with Personnel to go over to the Cole and get a feel for what I'm walking into."

"That'll be fine; in fact, take the rest of the day today and tomorrow. And after your long weekend, transfer your belongings to the Cole. As of Monday you will be a sailor on the USS Cole."

I went to Personnel and signed my papers. I was now officially a second class petty officer. I was only a third class for three months. I hadn't sewed my stripes on all my uniforms yet, and now I'm sewing on second class stripes. I was happy when I made third class, but now I'm apprehensive about making second class. Well, at least I'm getting another pay raise. Before going to the Cole, I went down to the laundry with all my uniforms and had my second class stripes sewn on. Then I went back to the personnel office and picked up my new ID. They told me it would be ready in about a half hour. Now I'm ready to go over to the Cole.

CHAPTER 2: The Cole DD 423

I walked over to the Cole as if it were just another day of work. Only today I was wearing my second class stripes. I wanted to talk to my new division officer and the section head to find out what my official role and title would be. I also wanted to talk to my fire control technicians and make sure there were no hard feelings.

When I got to the Cole, everyone was working on their respective equipment. The first person I wanted to see was First Class Petty Officer Lonny Brown. He was a gunner's mate and senior man in our division. Our division officer was Lieutenant Junior Grade Maxwell Cashman; if I couldn't find Gunner Brown, I would look for Lt. JG Cashman. I found Gunnar Brown working on the forward 5-inch guns. When I walked over to him, he said, "Hi Rich. How are you doing?"

I said, "Fine, how are you Gunnar?"

"Pretty good, just realigning this mount. We had to install a new set of brushes in one of the motors that turn the mount. Now we're checking the alignment. The FTS are up in the radar and combat center helping with the alignment."

I said, "I really came over to see you." He looked at me quizzically and then spotted my E5 stripes.

"What's up?" he said.

"Well, I've been told I'm being transferred to the Cole prior to you being deployed to the South China Sea."

He said, "That's news to me; you better check with the division officer."

"Do you have a problem with me coming here," I asked. "You don't seem too happy with what I just told you."

"I'm a little perplexed," he answered. "You just graduated from "A" school a few months ago getting your E4 stripes. How did you make E5 so soon? There's something going on here that I'm not privy to."

I told him, "That's why I'm here; I want everything open and above board. If I can track down Lieutenant JG Max Cashman, will you be able to sit down with us?"

"Sure. In fact, I'm just about done here; I'll help you find him." He answered. We dropped down to the main deck, walked back to the fantail. There we had a small storage locker and a not much larger office. Max was in the office finishing up some paperwork on logistics for the upcoming deployment. Gunnar and I stepped in. I saluted, and Gunnar asked Max, "You got a minute?" I was a little shocked by the lack of protocol, not saluting and calling an officer by his first name. I was to learn that on a ship this sizes that pomp and ceremony was lax to say the least.

Max said, "Sure. What can I do for you?"

Gunnar said, "Rich told me he's being transferred here as of Monday. Do you know anything about that?"

Max told him, "Yes, I found out yesterday. I was waiting for the right time to tell you."

I then said, "Excuse me, gentlemen, but I don't get a real warm and fuzzy feeling about this transfer. Is there something going on here that I should know about?"

Max was the first to speak. He said, "Rich, I have nothing against you, but the way this all transpired was a little unorthodox. You being allowed to take the test a year early for E5 and then sewing it on the first increment. Unorthodox to say the least. We expected to get one of the other E5s."

Gunnar said right out, "Rich, you are not what we expected."

I asked, "Can I speak freely here?" Max looked at Gunnar and then they both looked at me.

Gunnar said, "I'd like to hear what you have to say. It took me fourteen years to make first class, eight years to make second. You haven't been in this man's Navy a year and a month and you're sewing on your second class ranking. Yes, id' like to hear what you have to say!"

"Gunner," I answered, "I'm just as surprised as you are. Max – is it okay if I call you Max?" The Lieutenant shook his head. I went on. "By now, you have probably read my file. You know why I made seaman early and I got my next rate upon graduation from "A" school. Now this is where the plot thickens. I was shocked when Ensign Peters told me I was recommended to take the test for E5. Shocked, but happy. So, I studied hard and passed the test on the first increment. I knew in my gut that something was wrong, but I didn't know what. Why was I working exclusively on the Cole? Meaning no disrespect to you, Max, but not letting Dan take the test for second class because he was late getting back from leave was pretty hard. Normally that would have ten to thirty days restriction. Some games have been played by both parties here, not just on the Grand canyon."

Max went to say something, and I put my hand up and said, "Please let me finish.

The way all this went down was a little deceptive on both sides. Now Ensign Peters, after reading my personnel file, was not really happy about my coming on board. The fact that I had to see a counselor was upsetting to him. I certainly hope that ain't the case here. He also found out that he would be required to transfer one of his second class petty officers to you, provided they both passed the test. He's got two good experienced repairmen in his repair shop, and he doesn't want to lose them. He heard through the grapevine about Danny not being recommended to take the test for E5. If he had and passed it, then he could send me a third class, no problem. Because you need an E5 to be the senior fire control technician in the division, you figured by not promoting Dan, then Ensign Peters would have to send you one of the E5s.

Knowing this, and what you did by not letting Danny take the test, Peters went to the department head and together they put a plan together so as not to lose any of his repairmen and to get me transferred because he didn't want me anyway. Together with the help of the personnel officer, they pulled some strings to get me to take the test early. It didn't hurt that I had already been to Vietnam and you were heading over there."

I really hadn't planned to say all that, but I figured this was going to be my new home and they needed to know. For a few minutes, nobody said anything. Then Max spoke up. He shook his head up and down saying, "Now I see…now I see." Then he looked to Lonnie or Gunnar Brown and back at me and said, "Anything else you want to say?"

I said, "Yes. The one that got screwed in this whole deal was Danny not making E5. Either way, I was the one going to be transferred over here. The difference being now I'm E5 and Danny's E4. I got promoted; he got screwed. This is not my doing. I just did what I was told. Now I'm worried about repercussions and hard feelings. Am I going to be welcome on board your ship?"

Max spoke first. He said, "I realize that right now you feel like you're between a rock and a hard place. But rest assured that you will be a welcome member of this crew. Let's do this. You go back to the Grand Canyon and pack up your things. You're due to transfer over here on Monday. In the meantime, we'll find you a bunk and a locker. I want Lonnie and me to break the news to the fire control team before you get here. Are you going anywhere this weekend?"

"Yes," I said, "I'm going home. In fact, I got early liberty and I'm leaving at noon tomorrow."

Max piped up and said, "That will be good. When you report on board on Monday, come directly to me and Lonnie. We will fill you in on what went down at the meeting within our division. Oh, and welcome aboard. I'm sure things will work out fine. You proved yourself to be an excellent technician, and our radar equipment hasn't worked this well in a long time. Right, Lonnie?"

"That's right, Max. Rich here has done a fine job. It's almost as if he knew it was going to be his gear."

I looked up and said, "Not really, Lonnie. I just always try to do my best. Lonnie, I know I'm new to all this, and I am going to be looking to you for guidance. Can I count on you for your experience to help me through all this? We're heading into war. That should be our priority. Let's put this all behind us. I believe we cleared the slate; now let's prepare for war."

They both looked at me with a little bit of a surprised look on their face. I reached over, stuck out my hand, and shook hands with Max and then Lonnie. As I turned to leave, I said, "See you Monday."

"Welcome aboard," said Lonnie. To hear him say that was music to my ears. He not only said it, but he also meant it.

As I walked over to the Grand Canyon, I was feeling a little better about going to the Cole. And with my long weekend about to begin, I felt pretty good. I'm an E5, second class petty officer. Hot damn!

Next day I left the ship with my new rate on my sleeve; I was walking proud. When I got home, my father noticed my new stripes. He said, "What's this, you got a new stripe?" I said, "Yup, E5 in a little over a year." He told me it took him over two and a half years to make buck sergeant, and that was during the Second World War! I didn't tell him that I got the stripe because the ship I'm being transferred to is going into a war zone. I didn't want to worry him or the family. I told him that the ship I was being transferred to was going on a Pacific cruise and that's why I joined the Navy – to see the world.

The weekend went by uneventfully
. Met my friends, went to the dance, had a few beers, and spent Sunday with the family. I really enjoyed Sunday dinner with the whole family there.

Monday morning I was riding back to the base before I knew it. The weekend went by so fast, it seemed I had just got home and turned around and was heading back. When I got back on board the Grand Canyon, I got all my things together in preparation to moving over to the Cole.

After the morning meeting, everyone said their goodbyes. I went to the personnel office, picked up my orders, and went over to the Cole.

I got to the Cole around 9:20 and went directly to the gunnery division office on the fantail of the ship. Max was there waiting for me. Lonnie had work to do, so it was just Max and I. He said that he informed everyone that I had just gotten out of "A" School and also had just been promoted to E4. Max explained to him that I got my promotion to E5 because of the time I spent at a crypto lab in Vietnam and was needed on this cruise.

After talking to Max, I left my things in the office and went looking for Dan. I found him up at the MK 25 radar system, cleaning up a few things and labeling switches and stuff like that. At first he was a little cool toward me. But my knowing he was a little put out helped me in figuring ahead of time how to get him on my side. I said, "As you know, I've been transferred to the Cole. I've also been promoted to E5. Let me tell you, I'm just as surprised as you. I think the reason I got the promotion and was transferred to the Cole was because of my experience at a crypto lab in Vietnam.

Danny said, "Yeah, I heard something about that from Lonnie and Max." Then he said, "How is it over there?"

That caught me a little off balance, so I just said, "It was rough. This is not a little police action; this is full-blown war. You'll see when we get there. I was wondering if you could find me a locker and a bunk. We can talk more as I get squared away." Danny seemed to warm up to me a little more and said, "I was going to have Al show you around, but I guess I can do it."

"I appreciate that," I said.

Dan led me below decks to the bunk room. There had to be 60 bunks in this one room. There were three tiers high, four to a row. Here was a section against the wall or side of the ship for the gunnery department. He brought me over there and I was in the second row, top bunk. I liked the top bunk – it had a little more space between the bunk and the ceiling. The other two were pretty close together. I guess rate has its privileges.

The lockers were in rows two high, thirty long, back to back. Again, mine was on top. I went back up to the fantail to pick up my sea bag, and I also brought over a multi-meter I was given. It could test one to six circuits at a time. I handed it to Danny. Told him I wanted to put my stuff in my locker and that I would meet him in a little while and we can go over all the gear.

After I got my stuff stowed away, I went up to the fire control radar on the top deck of the ship. This was the unofficial area of the fire control technicians. The radar room was narrow but long. At the far end of the room was an area packed with boxes and test equipment – stuff like that. I don't like clutter. All the FTs were there. We exchanged greetings, and I asked Dan if there was anywhere else we could store this gear that was stuffed into the corner. He said, "These are spare parts and test equipment we needed. We really want it close just in case we need it in a hurry." I also asked him if there was just the four of us. He said, "Yup, just us. When we go to battle stations, we are going to be short-handed. The gunner's mates send us a couple of their seamen to help out. There are two of them that are actually pretty good operators." I asked if they might be willing to change rates and become fire control technicians! He said that he expressed an interest in doing just that but Lonnie said he needed them. He's go twenty-six gunners mates; you'd think he could spare tow of them. I said, "I'll talk to him and Max about it."

Dan said, "These two know that the gunners mate rate is closed. It's hard to make rate as a gunners mate, whereas the fire control technician rate is wide open. Pass the test, get the rate. We have gunner's mates on board with ten years in and are only E4. They're going to look at you and realize how quickly you can make rate as a fire control technician. There's a high demand for electronics technicians on the outside. So fire control men don't normally ship over. They can make a lot more money in the civilian sector."

"But what kind of a job can a gunner's mate get on the outside? Not much, so that is why we have a backlog of gunner's mates and we're hurting for fire control men." I told Dan that I saw a couple of spare lockers leaning against the back wall in our bunk room.

"How about your guys going down and getting them, and bring them up here to store our gear?"

Dan said, "I'll ask the master at arms in charge of the bunk room for them."

I said, "IT might be better just to take them. Sometimes it's better to do it and ask forgiveness then to ask permission. Dan looked at me, smiled, and said, "Okay, but it's on you." I said, "Fine, but let's get this mess cleaned up."

Richard Elliott

On board the ship was painted tow colors: dark gray and light gray. The inside of the radar room was dark gray. The paint was chipped and rust spots were showing through. I figured we could repaint it with the light gray, lighten it up a little, and make it look a lot cleaner.

While the boys were getting the lockers, I went looking for the paint locker. When I got back with the paint and tools to do the job, the guys were just getting back with the lockers. Danny said, "No problems; just walked in and picked them up and walked out. Had to make two trips to get all four, but here we are." He was smiling ear to ear. His joy was catchy, and pretty soon, we were all laughing and joking. We then cleaned out the radar room and started painting. We painted the area where the lockers were going; we put them in right away. Out of sight, out of mind. The work we did, pulling together and fixing up the radar room, cataloguing our parts and putting them in the lockers – all this brought us closer together. I knew I made some new friends and felt accepted.

For the next ten days, we worked together cleaning up the gear, painting our areas and cataloging our spare parts. We ordered whatever parts we may need and even were able to trade some old meters for a complete interchangeable power supply for our attach director. It proved to be large, as we ended up needing it, and kept our gear up and running when we needed it most.

Our division officer Max was impressed and got an *Atta boy* from the Captain. So two weeks after I reported for duty, we're heaving to and heading for sea. First stop: Panama Canal.

Getting underway went a lot smoother than I thought it would. As fire control technicians, we really didn't have much to do. Our seamen had the first watch in after steering. That's where you can steer the ship from if you lose your primary steering.

While underway, the seamen and third class fire control technicians and gunner's mates stood four-hour watches in after steering.

The bosunsmates did most of the work untying us from the ships next to us and pulling on the ropes and bumpers. Before you knew it, we were underway and pulling out to sea. Within a couple hours, you could no longer see land. That's when you realize this big ship you are on isn't so big at all. Actually, it's real small. I guess that the ocean is so big, all ships seem small.

While at sea, you don't feel as if you're moving very fast at all. Looking ahead of the ship, it feels as if you're hardly moving. Two and a half days after pulling out of Newport, I was surprised to see land. We were pulling into Key West, Florida. A one-day layover to double check our gear, fill up on fuel and supplies before heading through the Panama Canal. When we pulled into Key West, we got to have liberty. Because we were only going to be there for one day, we only got four-hour liberty. Half the crew went on liberty from noon to four and the other half from four to eight. I was going over with the second half from four to eight. I had planned on finding a sightseeing bus and touring the city, but as we were leaving, Lonny came to me and asked me to go to the Acey Ducey club with him. I had never been to the first and second class petty officer's club before, so I decided to go to see what it was all about. I was the youngest sailor there. Most second and first class petty officers are 25 years old and up. I was 19 at the time, and the only thing I had in common was my rate. At first I was a little nervous and disappointed. I really wanted to take a tour of Key West. After a few beers, I settled in, relaxed, and started talking to the other guys. I stayed clear of the age thing. A few of the guys talked about going on a tour. I gravitated toward them, agreed with them, and convinced Lonny to go with us. It was interesting; only took about an hour and dropped us back at the Acey Ducey club. It was cool. I got to go on a tour, and I met most of the petty officers on my ship. Again I felt as if I met some more friends. I more or less found a niche where I felt comfortable. The Navy life was coming at me fast, and I had a lot to learn and little time to learn it.

We pulled out at eight the next morning. Once we were safely out to sea, I expanded my comfort zone on the ship. Instead of just hanging around the radar room, I went below decks and met with the other petty officers I went on liberty with. I was starting to get comfortable with my position.

On the third day, Panama came into view. We had to anchor out about a half mile and wait our turn to go through. We found out we were 12th in line to go through, so we would be there for about a day. As we were waiting, a submarine came up out of the ocean a little way away from us. We all ran over to the starboard side of the ship to watch. The starboard lookout was the first to see the mast on the sub. Word traveled fast along the ship, and before you know it, there it was. When I first looked I almost missed it. Then I saw the mast. Then the bow came out of the water. Miraculously the sub seemed to just magically appear. It happened so quickly that you almost could believe your eyes. One moment an empty ocean, next a ship right next to you. Amazing.

Because we were going to be there for awhile, liberty was authorized. I went with the second half of the ship. Danny went with me. We walked around the city taking in the sights and ended up at a bar by the pier called the Beachcomber. It was a big place with a stage, a dance floor, a huge bar, and of course pool tables. There weren't any bands playing, but the juke box was blasting away. Right away we noticed the sub sailors. They were all sitting together at a bunch of tables near the dance floor. They were drinking heavy and telling anyone who would

RAIN: *A Sailor's Story*

listen how they were the best. They could out-drink, out-sail, out-work, out-fuck, and out-fight the sissy surface sailors.

Well, the surface sailors took offense at that. And taunts and threats were yelled back and forth between the group of sub sailors and surface sailors on the other side of the dance floor.

I knew a brawl was imminent, and I grabbed Dan and went over and stood by the door. As we were standing there watching, a sub sailor got up on the stage, grabbed the microphone, and said, "I'm a fucker, I'm a fighter, I'm a submarine rider!! No muff too tough, no thigh too high; I dive for the five – uga uga. I got a wild hair hanging off my ass and I dare anyone to step on it."

That's all it took. Beer bottles started flying, bodies were tumbling and tables were being tipped over. We had to duck a chair that was thrown in our direction. Dan started heading for the brawl. I reached over, grabbed his shoulder, and said, "Danny, you don't want to do that. This is stupid; we're all on the same team. Let's just get the hell out of here." It's a good thing we did. As we were leaving, the mps and shore patrol were pulling up. I just pointed to the door and said, "In there...in there." Dan and I headed to the pier and the liberty launch and got back to the ship.

I headed to the showers, got ready for bed, and hit the rack. Next morning, I could see a bunch of the sailors that stayed at the bar had bumps, bruises, and black eyes. They had been arrested by the shore patrol, put on report, and were waiting to see the captain. Most would be denied liberty for the next couple ports, and then all would be forgotten.

At about 2 p.m., it was our turn to go through the canal. It was exciting going from one lock to the other. When you go in, they shut the doors behind you, fill the lock with water, open the doors in front of you, then you sail into the next lock where the repeat the system. Once you get halfway through, they sail you into a lock and drain the water down so you can go into the next lock. After the first couple times of going from lock to lock, it gets real boring. At the end you just drive out into the Pacific Ocean and off you go. Heading out, it doesn't seem like you're going very fast.

But when you turn around and watch the shoreline disappearing behind you, you realize you're moving pretty good. Next stop, Pearl Harbor.

We pulled into Pearl Harbor on Friday. We were going to spend all weekend there. When we got there, our supplies were waiting on the dock. The boatswain's mates were rigging the holds to take it all on board. The ammo for the guns was sitting out o the dock also. I didn't realize that the five-inch ammo came in two pieces. The projectile and the bras shell casing that shoots the projectile out of the barrel. It had rained the night before, and I was wondering if the ammo should get wet or not. Nobody else was concerned, so I just forgot about it.

We were all looking forward to going on liberty. On Friday we all had to help loading the stuff on the ship. The boatswain's mates were loading everything into the hole. The engineer man and machinist mates were taking on fuel and water. The cooks and mess cooks were stowing away the food. The gunner' mates and FTs were stacking the ammo in forward and aft ammo holds. Everyone was helping in one way or another. We knew if we got it all loaded on board Friday, half the ship would have Liberty Saturday, the other half, Sunday.

I was on the Saturday half, so I was busting hump to finish on Friday. We finally finished by 9:30 Friday night. We were bushed, but a full day's liberty would make up for it.

Lonnie and I had gotten into the habit of going to the Acey Ducey club on liberty. We usually start off there; then I meet up with Dan and he and I try and take a tour of the port we're in.

After the tour, we get something to eat and find the best sailor's bar in town.

So without even saying anything, when I was ready to leave the ship, Lonnie was waiting for me on the after brow (enlisted men's gangway). Dan was heading over with a couple of the other gunner's mates, and we agreed to meet them later. As we were walking down the pier, Lonnie pointed out an English ship that was in port. I wouldn't even have noticed if Lonnie hadn't showed it to me. It was early, one o'clock in the afternoon, but the place was full. We ordered a couple beers, found a place to sit down, and talked to a couple of first class enginemen off the ship. They had already gotten used to me "the youngster" being an E5, so I felt a lot more comfortable around them and was thankful for Lonnie taking me under his wing, so to speak. I enjoyed my time with the older guys. I had a lot to learn, and they were eager to teach me. There were a couple E5s in there that had just got rated same time as I did. Difference was they had been in close to ten years. They were a little standoffish. The more they saw me, the friendlier they got. One thing I had going for me was that I was the only one on board that had been to Vietnam. The information I got from the librarian at Great Lakes came in real useful. I was like the local authority on Vietnam.

In the evening we would sit around a table in the mess hall and drink coffee. The guys would ask questions about Nam. I would tell them what I knew and what I had learned at Great Lakes. We discussed what we thought our role would be. We all kind of agreed we were probably just a deterrent for the Chinese. We learned that that was not the case.

We left the Acey Ducey club, met up with Dan, and took the bus tour of the island. It was interesting seeing all the monuments and sunken ships in Pearl Harbor. There were a couple English sailors on the tour, and we talked to them for awhile. The tour ended back at the pier, and we all walked over to the local bar. Davey Jones Locker was the name of the place – a fitting name for a Navy bar. The place was packed. There were a lot of ships in port, including the British. The English sailors were hot shits. We made fun of their accents, and they made fun of ours.

About once an hour, they made a toast to the Queen, so we would make a toast to the President. It was all cool. A little after midnight, I had had enough and caught the next liberty launch back to the ship. Six a.m. came early and we were getting underway for Okinawa the next day.

We got underway at eight a.m. the next morning. The weather was absolutely gorgeous - a great day to be on the water. The ocean was like glass, and we were steaming along pretty good. After a couple days, the weather was holding and we were a little ahead of schedule on our way to Okinawa. So the Captain decided to slow down a little to have some fun. The gunner's mates set up skeet shoot on the fan tail of the ship. Officers and enlisted men alike took turns shooting skeet; it was a great time. Some of the guys started fishing. We ran into a school of fish – someone said it was Wahoo. Whatever it was, the cooks put it on the menu, and it was the best fish I ever ate.

A week later, we were in Okinawa. Again we took on fresh water, more fuel, and stores. After we leave Okinawa, we will have to refuel and take on stores at sea. We were allowed only a half day leave at port, so Lonnie and I spent the evening at the Acey Ducey club. We talked to sailors from other ships headed to Nam. We were replacing other ships from the Seventh fleet that had been over there for six months and were coming back for repairs and updates to their equipment. It seemed that we just got to Okinawa when we were pulling out. Other ships had pulled out before us, and we could see others pulling out behind us. We were going to Southeast Asia to relieve other ships of the seventh fleet. To see all the ships around sailing together in the same direction was awesome.

At that point I felt invulnerable; it was a powerful feeling. I was also wondering if we would anchor outside the crypto lab at Saigon as we didn't have crypto capability on board. It would be good to stop in and see the guys.

The Tonkin Gulf is part of the South China – Pacific Ocean. It's hard to fathom that I had just sailed from the east coast of New England half way around the world to the east coast of Vietnam. There were some monotonous days in the ocean, but most of it was real interesting. The time flew by. We met up with the aircraft carrier Saratoga which was the Admirals Flag Ship and the heavy cruisers and another aircraft carrier of the seventh fleet. All I could see from horizon to horizon were ships. The whole fleet was heading to Vietnam. Real impressive, whatever our mission, I was super confident that we would get the job done, no problem.

When we pulled into the Tonkin Gulf, we split into two groups. Some of the tankers, cruisers, and destroyers went with the admiral's flagship aircraft carrier; the rest of us went with the other aircraft carrier.

We stayed in the south and headed for Saigon. The larger ships with crypto labs on board stayed with the carrier. The smaller ships, destroyers, and destroyer escorts anchored off my old duty station and waited for orders. I requested permission to go to the lab with the launch when it came with the mail, and return later with the crew from the crypto lab.

My division officer got me the proper clearance so I could go to the top secret area. And when the mail launch got there, I was ready to go. When I got to the lab, little had changed. Most of the guys were out delivering their messages.

Duggy was in the radio room working on deciphering messages. When he saw me, he gave me a big smile and a wave, put up one finger, so I waited for him to complete his latest message. He took the headphones off and walked over to the door to talk to me.

"I see you made E5; how'd you do that?" he asked

"Don't ask," I said, "Because I don't really know."

"Well, I finally made E6 after eleven years."

"How come you're still here and didn't transfer out?" I asked.

"Well, after your shooting that Gook chick, they tightened up security a lot. SO the extra pay is good. It don't cost nothing to live, and I'm banking all my combat pay and more. Oh yeah, since Snowball got killed, we are considered in a combat situation and get combat pay." Just then, Ensign Peers came into the lab.

"Hey Rich. Didn't expect to see you back here."

"In station on the Destroyer Cole," I replied, "and got permission to come here and see you guys. I go back with the mail."

"Won't be any mail going back today, you'll probably have to stay overnight."

"I was kinda hoping you would say that; got an extra bunk."

"Sure, Doug will hook you up."

I said, "Doug, are any of the other guys still here?

"Yeah, Chris Penny, me, Ensign Peers, and the commander."

"Great. Maybe Chris and I can go to the Little America tonight." I said

Doug said, "Come with me. I'll get you a bunk. Chris should be back shortly and you two can reminisce." Doug got me a bunk in a spare room by the head. I didn't realize how good it was to be back. I didn't know what to expect, but now I was glad I came back.

The place was still beautiful like a resort. I felt comfortable there, and the past didn't seem real – more like a nightmare.

After I got settled in, I took a walk around the base. I rushed past the place where Snowball was gunned down and went down back to the dock to wait for Chris. It was calm, and the cove was pristine. It was hard to believe we were in a war zone. It's easy to let your guard down.. About an hour after I sat down, Chris pulled in. He was real surprised to see me. We shook hands and he introduced me to his new mail carrier. I immediately forgot his name mainly because after today, I would probably never see him again.

Chris said, "Hey, new stripes?

I said, "Don't ask. Long story. Think we can go over to the Little America later?"

"Sure, right after chow if you'd like."

"Let me get the boat squared away, and I'll meet you back at the lab," said Chris.

"No. I'll stay here and give you hand, okay?"

"Sure, that'd be great. Can use a little help." When we were finished, we walked back to the lab. I could see that they all wore their flak jackets and carried weapons, even with all the stepped up security. It was good to see that nobody was getting complacent.

After Chris got cleaned up, we went to chow. A couple of the guys came over to say hi. I recognized one but not the other. Chris said, "They're the ones who cooked the pig."

I said, "I thought the Marines got the pig?"

He said, "They didn't want it. Didn't know what to do with it. I'll tell you our cooks knew what to do. I loved the ribs."

After chow we went back to the lab checkout on liberty and walked to the main gate. I was a little nervous wondering how the Marines might react when they saw me. I needn't have worried; most of the Marines that were here had been transferred out including their captain.

We took the Lick Saw to Little America and settled in with a couple of beers. As I was looking around the place, I saw this Gook broad looking at me...staring hard. At first I was thinking maybe she was staring at something behind me. Then I realized she was the one I shot and accused of being a spy. A few minutes later, she must have got her nerve up and walked over to talk to me. I was thinking, *okay, here we go. What is on her mind?* She walked right up to me. "I no spy. I love country. South Vietnam no spy."

"Okay, so you're no spy," I said.

"You shoot me. You think me a spy but me no spy."

"Good," I answered, "You no spy. That's good. Sorry I shoot you."

"Me live in village. VC attack. Burn house. Families run away. Now me work here...support family. No have village. No farm, live in hut not good."

At that point, I reached in my pocket, pulled out a ten dollar bill and handed it to her.

"I no want money from you. You think me spy. You shoot me. I no spy."

"Okay, okay," I said, "You no spy. Here take this for your family. You no spy." She reached out real quick, grabbed the ten and quickly walked away as if I was going to take it back.

When she left, Chris started laughing, and then I started laughing. We laughed so hard we had tears in our eyes. One of the Marines asked Chris what that was all about. Chris told him the story, and he started laughing too. He said, "Yah, I heard something about that. Shot a pig and a monkey too." That made us laugh all the more.

The story spread through the bar, and instead of the Marines being angry with me, they shook my hand. It seems that guarding our lab is prime duty. Better than beating the jungle and getting shot at.

Every once in a while, someone would walk by scratching his sides and acting like a monkey, and the whole bar would break out laughing. Even the girls would laugh. It turned out to be a really good time. Chris and I laughed all night.

Next day, I had to go back to the ship. Chris and I talked to Doug, and Chris got the mail run to my ship so he could drop me off. When I got back on board, I reported in to Max, and he told me to prepare to get underway. "Once the captain gets his orders, we're pulling out." As soon as we got underway, we joined up with our half of the Seventh Fleet. We moved up the coast about fifteen to twenty miles and kind of milled around for awhile.

At seven a.m. the next morning, we were ordered to battle stations. People were running all over the ship. "Battle stations Battle stations!" was going off on all the loud speakers throughout the ship. *Auugha....auugha* sounded the horns. I went up to the second deck just behind the five-inch gun mount, put my headphones on, and waited for orders.

My job was to coordinate the radar, attack director, and the five-inch gun mounts. Through my headphones, I was in constant contact with everyone on the combat system. I relayed orders from the combat center to the radar, from the radar to the attack director, from there to the gun mounts. Depending on the amount of targets, it could be real hectic.

I learned through the headphones that we were engaged in the shore bombardment of a suspected North Vietnamese regiment of Army regulars that took over a hill just south of the DMZ – demilitarized zone.

There were six destroyers in a row. At first I thought we would just sit off the coast and start shooting. But what we did was cruise around in a big circle. As we got close to the coast, we opened up as we pulled away; we ceased firing. It was hard to believe anything or anyone could survive on that hill after the bombardment we were giving the.

We started shooting at nine a.m. We were second in line and had all the five-inch gun mounts fore and aft firing in sequence. The recoil of all that shooting actually rocked the ship. Blasting away from all those gun mounts was real exciting because we were firing at a stationary target, the hill. I had little to do but listen on the phones. The rotation of ships sailing in a circle and taking their turns as they came around to the shore line went on all day.

At around four in the afternoon, it was our turn to start firing. Then I heard it over the headphones – a real excited voice yelling *Misfire Misfire! We need a short charge up here!*

I learned later that one of the shell casings misfired. The primer went off but the powder charge didn't but it had just enough power to push the projectile up the barrel but not enough to fire it out. As the projectile goes up the barrel, the lands and grooves in the barrel spins the projectile and times the fuse. The projectile was still lodged in the barrel and it was timed to go off. The gunner's mates had less than a minute to put in a short charge to push it out the end of the barrel. A regular charge would blow up the barrel because the way the projectile was in the barrel. It caused an obstruction and if a full charge was used it was possible the whole mount could blow up. They didn't get the short charge in time and the whole mount blew up.

The last thing I remember was the yelling, *short charge – hurry – we need a short charge!*

I woke up two days later on a hospital ship. When I awoke, I thought I was back at great Lakes. Staring down at me was Sheila. I could see her talking but I couldn't hear anything. She looked different – older, more serious, frown lines – just different.

I don't believe I fully woke up because when I first saw Sheila, the room was light, like daylight. The next time I saw her was in partial light like a lamp. The timing seemed like only a second, and I was starting to say something to her.

When I woke up the second time I forgot what I was going to say. Sheila had been on station in the South China Sea for about eight months. Her hospital ship was tied up to a pier in Saigon. Every few weeks, the ship pulled out to sea about twenty miles to dump its waste into the Tonkin Gulf. Lucky for us, she was close to where we were and was alongside within a half hour of the accident.

The damage control parties had put the fire out quickly, saving the ship from any more explosions in the magazines. The welders were welding up a few cracks in the seams of the ship's hill.

Other than losing a five-inch mount, the ship was in remarkably good condition. There were six dead and twelve injured. Five seriously, three like me – not as bad, and four ambulatory. The four ambulatory were on their way to an Army hospital in Okinawa, and when I was well enough to be transported, I would be shipped there as well. It was great to see Sheila again. She was sitting in a chair beside my bed reading a magazine. She didn't know I was awake. I was just looking at her trying to collect my thoughts when she looked over and saw that I was awake.

Her face lit up like a Christmas tree. A big smile ear to ear, made her look younger like the old Sheila I knew from Great Lakes. Then the look changed to concern, then from concern to sadness. Sheila had tears in her eyes that started running down her face. Although I wasn't in any real pain, just a real bad headache, I thought there was something seriously wrong with me. I found my voice and asked Sheila, "What's wrong? Am I going to be okay?" She got out of the chair, kneeled on the floor beside my bed, cradled my head in her hands, and kissed me hard and long on the lips. Now I was real worried; she didn't answer me, and I thought she was preparing me for bad news. When she stopped kissing me, she leaned back and looked at me.

"No, nothing more serious than a severe concussion. You've been drifting in and out of consciousness for the last two and a half days. I'm just happy you're alive and that you should probably make a complete recovery." Then she smiled, leaned over, and kissed me again. That's the best recovery medicine I've ever had. A pretty nurse kissing my boo boo. And yes, a kiss does make it feel better.

When we stopped kissing and sat back, she started telling me about all the wounded she was taking care of on the ship. Not only were we nursing American wounded, we were also taking care of Vietnamese soldiers and even the Vietnamese civilians. The children were especially hard on her.

Napalm bun victims were the worst. Little kids with burns over eighty percent of their little bodies was horrifying. She prayed that she was helping and that all her nursing didn't go for nothing. I could see that all the burned, dismembered and shot up people she had to work with were taking their toll on her. In the eight months since I've last seen her, she looks as if she's aged ten years. She's seen the horrors of war close up and it's not what you see in the movies, the Navy nurse that nurses the Navy pilot back to life, they fall in love and lives happily ever after. Doesn't happen. What she sees day in and day out is straight out of a horror movie – one you can't wake up from

My heart ached for Sheila. I'm the one with the concussion and will eventually go to Okinawa. She has to stay here for four more months and live in this nightmare. I held her hand tight as she spoke to me about what she had to face every day.

Once she opened up, it was like she couldn't shut it off. I could see that the telling of the nightmare she was living was lifting a lot of weight off her shoulders. She had no one on the ship that she could offload to because they were all going through the same things.

She talked and talked about this person and that child; this burn victim, that dismembered soldier. After two hours, she slowed and finally stopped.

She stood up, came over to me, laid down beside me, put her head on my shoulder and cried and cried. I didn't realize it at first, but I was crying right along with her. My heartache for her was more painful than my concussion, and there wasn't a damn thing I could do about it.

Sheila did everything she could to keep me on that hospital ship. It was as if me going to Okinawa was something she wasn't ready for.

The day came when I finally had to leave. She walked me out to the helicopter pad. As the helicopter was offloading the wounded, we hugged, kissed, and said our goodbyes. I hitched a ride back to Da Nang and caught a cargo plane to Okinawa.

The hospital in Okinawa was clean, bright, and orderly. Not like the mess on board the ship. Even though the patients were all patched up, the horrors of war were still present.

I wrote Sheila every day trying to lift her spirits up. Trying to be and anchor she could hang onto for support.

After a battery of tests, the general consensus was that I was healing up fine and I would be able to rejoin my ship within a couple of weeks. Trouble was, my ship was in dry dock for repairs and had only a skeleton crew on board. I would need to be reassigned to a new duty station.

I went to the personnel office and asked if I could pick my own duty station. They told me to put in a request form and ask for three places I would like to go for duty and they would do what they could for me. They said where I was injured in combat; I could usually get my first choice.

While deliberating where I would like to go, I received a letter from Vickie Long. She was Sheila's best friend on board the ship. She said that she was sorry but thought that she should be the one to tell me. Sheila was killed in a helicopter accident on the helio pad. She was out there to receive the wounded when the helicopter pitched the wrong way in a gust of wind. One of the blades hit a stanchion and caused the helicopter to crash. Everyone on board was killed along with Sheila and two other medical personnel on board the ship.

I felt like someone hit me in the gut with a bowling ball. I doubled over in pain. I was starting to get real pissed off. First they kill my best friend, now they kill my girlfriend. That did it for me. I finally figured what I wanted for my next duty station: Vietnam.

I wanted to go back and kill Zipper Heads. I had to get out of the hospital and go for a walk and sort things out. When I hurt inside, I get angry – it isn't much later that I let down and cry. As angry as I was now, it would be much later.

I went back to the personnel office and asked the personnel man who I had talked to before – if there was something open for me in Vietnam. He said, "You're an E5 fire control technician. There's really nothing on a land base for you. Maybe I can find you a ship going over there in need of an E5."

I said, "No, I want to be on land. Find out what you can do. I was on a crypto lab before. Please keep on it – find out something."

"Wait a minute, there was something I saw yesterday – let me see. There it is. In Loc Dau on the Mekong River. They

RAIN: A Sailor's Story

need an E4, 5, or 6 gunner's mate to operate a 30-caliber machine gun. Must be machine gun qualified. Are you qualified? I may be able to substitute a fire control tech for a gunner's mate, but you have to be qualified."

I said, "Give me a couple days, and I'll get back to you." I left the personnel office and immediately walked over to the main gate. I asked the marine guard where the outside firing range was and who should I see about getting qualified on a 30-caliber machine gun. He said, "The only person that can get you on that range is Master Sergeant Tom Higgenbottom. If you go over there, he will turn you down on the spot. He don't much like sailors."

I said, "That makes us even. I don't much like Marines. I ain't looking for a friend; I'm looking to get qualified on a machine gun."

He said, "Your best bet is to meet him at the enlistment's club. Buy him a beer; he likes Heineken. Now, I got to get back to work. Let me know how you make out."

All afternoon I thought about what I was going to tell him. Finally I said to myself, *just tell him the truth.*

I went to the enlisted men's club at seven – not so late that I would miss him or too early so as to be one of the few people in there and get noticed.

As people started coming in, I kept a sharp eye on the door. I was looking at stripes, not faces. I didn't know what Higgenbottom looked like, but I did know he was a master sergeant. I was sitting on a stool at the corner of the right end of the bar. I had a good view of the door and the rest of the bar.

At about eight fifteen, Higgenbottom came in. Not only could I tell by his stripes but also the swagger in his walk, his short blonde hair cut high on the sides, and his piercing blue eyes. He wore a chest full of ribbons and a lot of shooting medals. I knew that this was my man. I let him get settled in and then had the bar tender give him a Heineken. He gave me a look, then looked at the beer, then looked at me again. He just turned without as much as a nod of the head. But at least he didn't refuse the beer. Twenty minutes later, sent him over another one. He sat there, picked up the beer, and started drinking it. This time he didn't even look at me. After the fourth beer, curiosity got the best of him. He got out of his seat, walked over to me, and said, "I give up. Why are you buying me all of this beer? I was hoping the beer loosened him up a little.

I said, "I want you to qualify me on a thirty-caliber machine gun."

"Why would I do that? I don't know you, and you're a sailor." He said *sailor* as if it was a dirty word. Then he said, "You want to get qualified, you have to go through the proper channels." He was turning, about to leave, when I said, "I don't have time for that. I need to get qualified right away." He turned back, gave me and gave me a quizzical look.

"May I ask you why?" he said a little sarcastically but more curious now.

I said, "I want to get back to Vietnam, and I don't want to go back on a ship. There's an opening for a machine gunner at a shore base. If I can get qualified, I have a friend in personnel who can pull some strings and get me over there."

"And why," he asked, "do you want to go to Vietnam? Do you know people are getting killed over there?"

I told him, "That's the reason I want to go back. I first went over a year ago; I was attached at a crypto lab outside of Saigon. One day, some VC got onto the base, set up a machine gun, and opened upon me and my best friend. They missed me and killed him. I started doing my own patrols and my superiors thought I was going nuts and sent me home.

I went back on the Cole a Destroyer. During shore bombardment, the after mount blew up, killing six more of my friends. Then on the hospital ship, I met a nurse I knew from Great Lakes training center. I learned yesterday she was killed in a helicopter accident. The Viet Cong are responsible for the death of a lot of my friends. Killing or causing the death of my girlfriend was the last straw.

Now I want payback. I'm asking for your help. Will you qualify me on a machine gun?" For a few minutes he just stood looking at me.

Finally he said, "Are you that crazy motherfucker that killed a monkey and shot a prostitute?"

I said, "How do you know about that?"

"Everyone knows about it," he said. "That story will follow you everywhere you go. So, you're *that* guy. You do know how to take care of yourself. Anyone crazy enough to do what you did is my kind of guy. I don't usually like sailors, but I'm going to make an exception for you. Report to the outside range at 1100 hours tomorrow. I'm letting you know up front, it isn't going to be a cake walk. You will be treated just like one of my Marines. You will get no special treatment because you're a sailor. In fact, I may push you a lot harder because I hate sailors. Now, you still want to qualify?"

I said, "Now more than ever. Finally I meet a real marine and not just a door man at the main gate." As I said that, he gave me a hard look and I eye-fucked him right back.

"Okay, then, he said, "Tomorrow at 1100 hours." As he turned to leave, I could see the beginnings of a smile around the corners of his mouth. I said to myself, *this could be the beginning of a real love-hate relationship.*

I was at the range fifteen minutes early waiting at the gate. Higgenbottom walked up at exactly 1100 hours. By then, there were seven Marines waiting with me. They didn't say much;

they were E3s and E4s, and I was an E5. Even thought they were Marines and I was a sailor, I still outranked them.

We walked through the gate but instead of going to the range, we went to a building off to the right. When we got inside, I could see it was a classroom. I hadn't figured on this, but it makes sense. There is probably a lot of technical information you need to learn before you go to the range and start shooting.

Higgy went right up to the front of the classroom and said, "Pick a seat and let's get started. We have a lot of material to cover before we get the range."

Then he started. "First and foremost is safety. Your safety and the safety of others on the range is our first priority. Never point your weapon anywhere but down range, whether your weapon is loaded or not. Always assume your weapon is loaded. The safety will always be in the safe position until you are directed to fire your weapon. The safety of the men in your squad depends on how safely you handle your weapon. We don't want anyone killed by friendly fire."

Then one of the Marines said, "Yeah, but if we kill the enemy, that ain't friendly." Everyone giggled at that – everyone but Higgy.

He yelled, "Corporal Ryan, you think this is funny?"

"No, Master Sergeant Higgenbottom, I don't."

"Then why the smart comment?"

"Don't know, Master Sergeant. Just came out."

"Then why don't you just come out and give me fifty pushups?" said Higgy. I thought Higgy was a bit excessive about the pushups, but I guess he really wanted to get his point across about safety. I had brought pen and paper with me to take notes. Good thing I did because Higgy didn't hand out any. It was up to me to be prepared. Higgy talked more about safety then got into the nomenclather of the machine gun. He described it and its parts, spread out a large poster of a thirty-caliber with all the parts laid out. Arrows pointed to where the parts belonged on the weapon's frame.

After five straight hours of class, we were dismissed. No lunch break, no coffee break; just straight going. No one complained, not after what happened to Ryan.

When we broke from class, I went back to my room at the hospital and put my notes away and went to chow. After chow I went to the library, asked the librarian if he had anything on the A1 E1 gas operated, air cooled thirty caliber machine gun. He looked at me and said, "Now that's a mouthful. Say it more slowly and we'll take a look."

We found a book on it and I was allowed to take it back to my room. I could check it out for two days, but then I had to bring it back. When I got back to my room, I started reading. I fell asleep studying. I didn't know what time it was, but I learned a lot about the machine gun and figured I was a lot more prepared. I didn't want Higgy making an example out of me. Me being a sailor and all, I wanted to prove myself.

After chow I sat in my room reviewing my notes and referring to my book. At ten forty-five, I was outside the gate at the range, same as the day before. Higgy got there at eleven sharp. When we got into the classroom, I could see someone had been busy setting things up. There were four machineguns set up at the front of the class.

Higgy got to it right away. Didn't say good morning, didn't take roll call – nothing. He took it for granted we were all there and in our seats, which we were. He said, "I'm going to divide you into four teams of two. Each team will stand in front of the machine gun assigned them."

Team 1 got machine gun 1; Team 2 got machine gun 2, Team 3 got machine gun 3, and then came me. He teamed me up with Ryan. Ryan said under his breath, "Why do I get the sailor?" Higgy was in the process of turning to the weapons when he snapped back and said, "What was that, Ryan? You got a problem?"

"I just wanted to know why I gotta team up with the sailor," he answered.

"That sailor has been in battle before, have you? Don't answer that – I already know. No, you have not. He has been shot at, blown up, and has two letters of commendation. That sailor has proved himself in combat and is getting qualified on the thirty cal so he can get back to combat. And right now, I would much rather go into combat with him than you. So teaming up with the sailor is not for his benefit; it is for yours."

Everyone just stood there with their complete attention on Higgy. And from the looks I was getting, I knew I gained a lot more respect from them. If Higgy respected me, then I had to be okay.

I was thinking, so Higgy took the time to go to personnel and read my service record. I was wondering if I would get a purple heart for being wounded. I had a small head wound when I got my concussion. The jury was still out on that.

The rest of the day went by real good and real fast. Before I knew it, we were dismissed and heading for chow. The studying I did the night before helped out a lot. Each team got an ass chewing for not doing something right, but Ryan and I, less than the others. I decided to study harder and be even more prepared tomorrow. With the hands on experience I got today, it brought into perspective the pictures and descriptions in the book. I was enjoying the class and now the Marines were talking to me and treating me as if I was one of them.

Again that evening, I was in my hospital room studying. One of the nurses came in and said, "I see you're going to leave us in a couple of days."

"That's news to me. I'm still waiting for my final evaluation."

"I think you'll be getting that on Friday. How have you been feeling?"

Think quick, I thought. I said, "Sometimes my balance is a little off and I still get headaches."

"Well, make sure you tell the doctors that on Friday."

The next day was Wednesday. I had two more days to get certified. I decided to go to the enlisted men's club and see if Higgy was there. I saw him sitting at the bar as soon as I walked through the door. I signaled the bar tender to give him a beer and sat down beside Higgy. I noticed not too many people sat with him. Maybe because he's a real tight ass, always on point, and never lets his guard down.

He said, "You must want something, Rich, what is it?"

"You have a way of getting right to the point; no *how are you...how you been...nice day...*No small talk with you, Higgy. Maybe you should loosen up a little."

"You're not the first one to say that. Now what do you want?"

"I'm scheduled for my final evaluation on Friday. Will I have my certification by then?"

"If you don't fuck up. I don't see why not, but the paperwork takes a couple days."

"Can you hurry it up a little? If I don't have it, they'll transfer me out to any ship that needs me. All I put in for was a duty station in Vietnam, and without that certificate, I won't get it. Help me out Higgy, will you?"

"I'm Master Sergeant Higgenbottom," he said, "Only my friends call me Higgy."

"You don't have any friends. You sit at the bar drinking beer all by yourself. Right now, I'm the closest thing you have to a friend."

He hesitated for a few minutes and then said, "Okay, Rich, I'll see what I can do to help you out. But I'm not your friend."

I answered, "Maybe I'm not to you, but to me, you are my friend." Again I saw the beginnings of a smile in the corner of his eyes and mouth as he turned away.

I left and went back to my room. More than ever I wanted to be ready for tomorrow. The next morning, I was at the range at 10:45 waiting with the rest of the guys. For the first time, Higgy was ten minutes late. Surprise, surprise, he is usually Mr. Punctuality.

We went into the classroom. Higgy instructed us to head to the range with the machine guns we had been taking apart and putting back together the day before. As we were picking up the weapons, I told Ryan, "Remember, safety first –don't get careless." He tapped me on the shoulder and said, "Good heads up – I'll remember. Let's watch the other guys."

"No, I'll just whisper in their ear and have them tell each other. We don't need Higgy getting pissed off before we even get started."

Everyone was extremely careful getting to the range, safeties on, guns pointed at the ground away from everyone, and the Breach Block open and clear.

We got to the range and took turns firing the thirty-cal machine gun. I thought the Thompson was bad, but this thing was awesome. Again, I had that invincible feeling. Short bursts – short bursts – the weapons no good if you overheat and jam that barrel and they cost $840 each, so remember, short bursts. One guy would shoot and the other would load. Then the loader would shoot and the shooter would load. We all took turns and practiced shooting, loading, aiming, and foremost – safety. By two o'clock, we were out of ammo and done shooting for the day. We took the weapons back o the classroom where we took them apart and cleaned and oiled them.

RAIN: A Sailor's Story

Higgy then told us we all passed, shook our hands, and handed out our qualifying certificates. I guess he couldn't give me mine without giving them theirs. That's why he was ten minutes late – he was getting the certificates.

I said, "Thank you, Master Sergeant Higgenbottom. Thank you very much."

"Don't thank me, sailor – you earned it. You all earned it. You all did a fine job on the range. I was impressed on how safe you handled your weapons. Good job. Take tomorrow off." I expected more, but that was that.

I hurried over to the personnel office and got there just in time. They were about to leave for the day. I turned in my qualification certificate on the thirty and was told it would be entered in my file and to come back tomorrow.

After chow I went to the club. I didn't want to sit in my room all night and I was hoping to see Higgy and buy him a beer. when I got there, Higgy wasn't there, so I ordered a beer and talked to the bar maid. She was a cute little Japanese girl, looked about 18 years old but found out she was closer to thirty. She spoke real good English and worked Thursday, Friday and Saturday nights. Most clubs are run by the military but hire mostly civilians to work them. The reason being that once you train them, they usually stay, whereas a military person could be transferred out at anytime. As I was talking to Lisa – her American name because no one could pronounce her Japanese name – the bar maid brought me over another beer. I said, "I didn't order that." She pointed to my left and said, "He order it." I looked over and there was Higgy with a smile on his face. It was the first time I saw him smile. He looked different, kinda young and mischievous. That's probably why he didn't smile much.

He said, "I beat you to it. That's for getting qualified. You did a real good job. Maybe you should have become a marine."

I said, "Maybe." We sat and talked for a couple hours. I found out that Higgy was human after all. A couple hours later I told him I had to go. I had the doctor's evaluation in the morning, and I had to go to personnel in the afternoon. We stood, said our goodbyes, and shook hands. He sat down and I headed for the door.

Next morning the nurse came into my room. She told me I needed to get ready to see the doctor at nine o'clock. So at nine a.m. I went up to the second floor and checked in at the window. I was told to take a seat and the doctor would see me in a minute. A half hour later, I was called in to his cubicle. He asked me how I was feeling and to sit on the edge of the examining table. I told him I still had some dizziness and headaches. He took a light, checked my eyes, ears, throat, and had me follow his finger with my eyes. Then he checked my blood pressure, heart, and lungs. He said, "Rich, you look fine. I'm going to say that you are fit for active duty. Any questions?"

I said, "No. Well, just one. When do you think I'll be leaving?"

He said, "Take this evaluation report over to personnel. The rest is up to them." I buttoned up my shirt, grabbed my white hat, and left. I had my medical evaluation report; the personnel office had my machine gun qualification certificate; now we had to work some magic so to speak.

When I got to the personnel office, they were waiting for me. "Were you found medically fit for duty? Have you got the evaluation?"

"Yes," I said, "I'm all set."

"How did you make out?"

"I'm going to get into trouble if I don't get a machine gunner over to Loc Dow right away. I just couldn't find anyone qualified until now." As he said this, he gave me a wink. That means I'm it. I'm back to Nam.

"Yup, I'm processing your orders as we speak. I knew you would pass your physical and be declared ready for duty, so I started the process yesterday. I was just waiting for the eval report before cutting your orders. How soon can you be ready to leave?"

"Almost immediately," I said. "I've been living out of my sea bag since I got here. Cut my orders, find me some transportation, and I'll go grab my things."

"You might want to see the pay master on your way. It shows here you got some back pay coming. I'm not sure if you're going to need it, but it's nice to have if you do."

"Thanks, I'll do that. Didn't need much in the hospital, and for a while, I was out of it."

I went down the hall, talked to the pay master and picked up my pay. I had three months' pay coming. I just realized I had been recovering for six weeks. The time on the hospital ship I had kind of blanked out of my mind.

I picked up my things at the hospital, checked out, but instead of heading to personnel, there was something I had to do first.

I went over to the range to see Higgy. He didn't have a class going on right now. The next one started on Monday. So he was just hanging around the classroom getting things set up for the next class. When I walked in, he looked up and said, "How'd you make out, Rich?"

"Good!" I answered, "I'm heading to Nam right away; I got my orders. I'm going to Loc Dow on the Mekong Delta. I came by to thank you again. You didn't have to help me. I was curious as to why you did, me being a sailor and all."

"Rich, I liked the way you asked, and those beers didn't hurt either." We both laughed at that. He continued, "I don't know if I did you a favor or not. You're going into combat and there's a good chance you'll get killed. Rich, you're right. I don't have many friends. Reason being, it hurts too much when they get killed. So take care of yourself. I got to liking you even though I tried not to."

"I'll do my best to stay alive. I got a lot of payback to deliver." With that, we shook hands and I went back to the hospital to pick up my things.

Chapter 3: Loc Dau, Vietnam

With all the personnel flying back and forth between Da Nang and Okinawa, you'd think they would get a regular airplane. The ride in those cargo planes sucks out loud. When I finally landed in Da Nang, it reminded me of the first time I was there. The newly repaired craters in the runway stood out like puddles in a parking lot.

Walking across the tarmac toward the admin building was like De javu The smell, heat, and humidity brought back memories. Just as the first time, I didn't make it to the admin building. A jeep pulled up beside me. The driver, a marine corporal, called over, "Richard Elliott?"

"Yeah, that's me. What's up?"

"I'm your transportation; you're my priority. I've got to get you all the way down to the Loc Dow, pronto." I threw my sea bag in the back of the jeep and hopped in beside the driver. As soon as my ass hit the seat, he sped off. When he said *pronto*, he meant *pronto*.

"Hey, what's the hurry?" I asked.

"I don't know. I was told to get you down there *most skoshie*."

"What's *most skoshie*?"

"That's Vietnamese for *pronto*."

I was surprised to see how beautiful the countryside was. As he sped along, I watched the jungle, rice patties, and little hamlets. It was peaceful; you wouldn't know there was a war going on – until we started getting shot at. I was sitting there daydreaming but lucky for me, my driver was paying attention. He drove into a ditch, jumped out of the jeep, and ducked down behind it. I followed his lead, and we were both trying to burrow down into the ground as quick as possible. He said, "Can you reach up and grab my rifle?" I started to but as soon as I moved up a little, my white hat stood out like a beacon. A hail of bullets almost took my head off. I ducked down really quick. I looked around and spotted a stick on the ground.

"Hand me that stick over there, will ya?"

"What are you going to do, club your way outta here? Guns beats clubs all the time."

"No, I'm going to put my hat on it, lift it in the air, and while they're shooting at my hat, I'm going to get your gun."

"In that case, grab the radio too so we can call for help." I grabbed the stick, put my hat on it, and wedged it between the back bumper and the tailgate. The shooting started as soon as they saw my hat. I quickly reached into the back seat of the jeep, grabbed his rifle, web belt full of ammo, and the radio. He handed me his M14 and told me to shoot back.

"As long as I'm shooting back, they won't charge us. Let them know we're armed."

"What are you going to do?"

"Use the radio and call for help."

"Luckily we have some ammo, but try not to be wasteful; we don't know how long we'll have to hold them off. So I fitted some rounds in the general direction they were shooting from. Then I got an idea. I got my hat, now full of bullet holes, back on the stick. I lifted it up, watching for where the bullets were coming from. That gave me a better location of where to shoot. There was a group of bamboo that the bullets seemed to be coming out of. So I took aim in the center of the bamboo patch and shot off three, well-aimed shots. Next I moved a little left and shot three more. I picked up my hat on the stick and got some more bullet holes in it. Watching where the bullets were coming from. I aimed more left and emptied the clip. I heard some yelling – then all quiet. The driver said, "Hey, I think you hit one of them."

"Yeah, it sounds like it. That hat trick worked pretty good."

"that should keep them back for awhile."

The shooting went back and forth for awhile and then they stopped. I was wondering if that was a ploy to lure us out. Then I heard it – a big truck coming down the road. I was looking for Marines, but instead it was the South Vietnamese Army with a machine gun and a dozen soldiers. The relief I saw on my driver's face must have been the same look on mine.

The truck pulled up next to us and stopped. I started yelling, "Over there! Over there!" The driver just sat there. The petty officer in charge calmly climbed out of the passenger side of the truck and walked over to us. I said, "Why ain't you going after them?" He told me, "They are long gone, faded back into the jungle, and it would be futile to give chase." He asked, "Is our jeep ok?" After a careful inspection, my driver said, "She seems okay. Nothing leaking out. Let's see if she starts."

The jeep started right up. The truck gave us an escort until we were back into what was considered a safe area. They turned around and went back and we traveled on to Loc Dow.

When we finally go to Loc Dow, it was getting dark. We checked in at personnel. The personnel officer came out and said, "You're late. You were supposed to be here two hours ago. The patrol boat had to pull out without a competent machine gunner."

My driver told him about the ambush and our subsequent truck escort. With that, the driver turned and said, "I gotta get back. I can get up to the next post before too late and that'll get me a good start for tomorrow morning."

The personnel officer took my orders, handed them to a personnel and told him to sign me in, find me a bunk, and I was to report back to him in the morning.

The personnel man took my orders and said follow me. I grabbed my sea bag and headed for the door. I don't know what I expected, but this sure wasn't it. He took me over to a six-man tent. Six bunks and six footlockers. At the moment the tent was empty. The men that lived here were on the patrol boat and would be gone three days. Of the six bunks, only four were occupied, so I had my choice of two. I picked one, put my sea bag on top of the foot locker and asked where the head was. I was told that this is basically a marine base and here they're called latrines, and it's right out back. The chow hall is in the second Quonset hut to the left. After breakfast, report to the personnel office. I asked if I could get something to eat now. He told me, "There are some MREs just inside the door to the mess hall. They're not bad and will hold you over till morning." I walked to the latrine, took care of business, and then went to the chow hall and picked up three. I was hungry! I hadn't eaten all day. As I was going back to my tent, I looked around the base. Mostly tents, sand bags, and Quonset huts. There were about six Quonset huts in all and it looked like they were building three more. The largest of the bunch was the chow hall. I figured I would find out the rest tomorrow when I had a chance to look around. As for now I was really tired and my bunk was calling my name.

    In the morning I went to the latrine then to the showers and over to the chow hall. The base may have been a marine base, but the chow hall was definitely Navy. I knew I was hungry but I didn't know how hungry. I ate enough breakfast for a whole squad.

    After breakfast, I checked in at the personnel office. I was told that I was to be attached to a coastal patrol boat. It was a converted P.T. boat. The depth charge racks and torpedo tubes were removed and replaced with thirty caliber machine guns. It would be gone for two more days. While I'm waiting for it to come back, I should get acquainted with the base.

    "Oh! The personnel officer wants to see you. He's in the office up the hall." I rapped on the door and was told to come in. I saluted and said, "Richard Elliott, ETG2 reporting as ordered."

"At ease, sailor. I understand your patrol boat won't be back for two days. I was reading your personnel file and apparently you like to go on patrol. So while you are waiting for your boat to come back, you will be required to go on patrol with a squad of Marines. If you're all checked in, report to Sergeant Wade over at marine side. Any questions?"

"Yes, how often is this going to jump and bite me on the ass?!"

"I don't know, but I want to know if you are as tough as you think you are. Dismissed."

After walking out of his office, I asked the personnel man, "Where is marine side?"

"Third Quonset hut on the right."

"Thanks."

By the time I checked in and got over to marine side, it was a little after nine a.m.

I walked up to the third Quonset hut on the right. There was a private standing guard duty at the door. I asked, "Where's Sergeant Wade?"

He looked me over and I could see he was wondering why I wanted to see Sergeant Wade. But after seeing I out-ranked him by two pay grades, he decided not to give me any shit and told me he was out behind the Quonset training his squad. So I walked out back and could see the whole squad doing P.T. When Sergeant Wade saw me, he came walking over. "You, Elliott?"

"Yes, that's me."

"I was told to expect you."

"So you want to go on patrol with me tomorrow, right?"

"No, I was ordered to go on patrol with you."

"Did your captain tell you why he is sending me out with you?"

"No, only that he heard that you've been over here before and that you like going out on patrol so much, you went out every night by yourself." I was thinking that the bullshit from the crypto lab will follow me forever.

He said, "I suggest you take today to get acquainted with the base and oh, go to the PX and pick up some camofatigues and bush hat – you'll need them tomorrow. Also, stop at the armory and pick up a weapon. We'll be moving out with first light. Meet me here at O-four-thirty tomorrow morning, ready to go."

So that's that. I walked away and wandered around the base. I found the PX and picked up some fatigues and a bush hat. Then I found the armory and checked out a Thompson sub machine gun. I got familiar with it back at the crypto lab and liked it. By the time I got that done, I was almost late for chow. After chow I went to a section of the base to try out my Thompson. It was called a range, but it was just a cleared area where you shot at stumps and rocks out into the jungle.

The range officer issued me some ammo and I fired off a couple of clips. Everything seemed to work okay so I picked up my stuff and started walking away.

The range officer came up to me and said, "You might want to go back to the armory and pick up a couple more clips. A forty-five Colt hand gun might come in handy also. Tell them sergeant Big Joe said to give you what you want. Can't have you going out without enough fire power."

"Thanks, I'll do that." So it was back to the armory. I told them I wanted two more thirty-round Magazines for the Thompson, and a forty-five pistol. I didn't have to say Big Joe sent me, the guy in charge of the armory just started handing me stuff. First I got two more magazines for the Thompson, a forty-five caliber hand gun, a web belt with a holster on one side, and a clip holder on the other with two clips in it. Then he handed me four fifty-round boxes of ammo. The Thompson and the pistol both took the same ammo forty-five cal ball ammo. I took everything back to my tent. There I cleaned my Thompson and loaded all the magazines. Then I checked out the forty-five pistol. Dry fired it a couple times and loaded all the clips. Two in the clip holder on the web belt, and one in the pistol. Next I tried on my fatigues and bush hat. I figured I was as ready as I would ever be. How much trouble can I get in – I'll be with a whole squad of Marines, after all.

Fear, so scared you can't breathe, your heart racing, tunnel vision, the swet under your armpits, dripping down to your waist.

I was sitting under a bush waiting for a VC patrol to come around the corner on a trail we had been on the other way just five minutes earlier.

What was I doing here? I'm a sailor, not a marine.

The sergeant leading our patrol handed me a twelve-gauge Ithaca pump shot gun. He said, "Rich, I want you to sit under this bush and hold your fire until the first Dink sees you."

I asked, "Why me? I'm a sailor – I haven't been trained for this shit."

He said, "My patrol is pretty green and you're older than they are. I think I can depend on you not to freeze up and not to shoot too early."

I was waiting, sweating, shaking, heart pounding – it seemed like forever. Then I saw him coming around the corner. Their point man, looking left and right. I froze. He kept walking closer and closer. At one point I thought he would walk right by me. That wasn't part of the plan. I didn't really want to shoot him. I didn't even know him. So I just said, "Hey you." He jumped as if he was stung by a bee. I was thinking, shoot, shoot, but I just sat there. Then he saw me, started to bring his gun up, and I realized I had to do something or I was going to be killed.

I was already aiming the shotgun at him, so I pulled the trigger. The blast hit him in the chest. He fell over backward. But like the clown punching bag that you knock down and bounces back up, he bounced back up. I pulled the trigger again. This time the blast blew his face off. Next thing I knew his whole patrol was shooting at me. I shot back until the shotgun was empty. Everything was in slow motion except my brain was in overdrive. I was wondering why ain't my guys shooting back? Did they run away and leave me, am I gonna die? I pulled my forty-five from its holster and started shooting in the direction of the enemy patrol.

Then everything came into real time. I could hear my guys shooting back. We had them surrounded. It was a real turkey shoot. Within minutes, it was all over. We killed them all and not one of us was even wounded.

I was shaking so bad I could hardly pick my gun up. I thought, *now I've gone and done it – I killed somebody. I'll spend the rest of my life in jail.* I stayed under my bush, loading my guns, trying to calm down. I was thinking about what my captain was going to say.

The sergeant walked up to me and said, "Great job, Rich. I knew you could do it. You did real good."

I said, "I killed that guy."

Sarge said, "Yeah, I saw you. You waited till the last second – it was perfect. I'm putting you in for a letter of commendation."

I couldn't believe it. Instead of being punished for killing, I'm getting a letter of commendation. At that point, I stopped being scared. I knew then that sometime in the future I would get killed over here. I didn't worry anymore about being killed – I knew it. Worrying about being killed and knowing you're going to be killed are two different things. I had nightmares about that patrol for the next seventeen years. In my dreams I could still feel the fear.

We stripped all the bodies of anything useful. We didn't leave anything for the VC to salvage and use against us. The bodies we just left figuring that some other VC will come get them or maybe the animals will get to them. Either way, nobody seemed to care. We brought back all the stuff we collected. Guns, ammo, food, water, papers, shoes or sandals; I guess shoes were in short supply to the VC and we didn't want to leave them any. One of the VC had a pair of jungle boots on. We figured he had to get them from a dead GI. That really pissed these Marines off. They shot a bunch more holes in him. Me, I thought what's the use, he's already dead. But I guess it made them feel better and release a little anger.

When we got back up to base, everyone knew what had happened. The radio man had radioed ahead and we had a bunch of people waiting for us when we got back. We had a body count of eleven VC without one of us getting a scratch. I found out that this was the first bunch of VC that had been spotted in this area in months. Just my luck I had to be there. Why couldn't it have happened when I was on my patrol boat? Well, I came here for payback; I guess you call this payback. It was only the beginning.

After we dropped off all the stuff we collected from the BC, we all just went back to our tents or the Marines went to their Quonset hut, and I went back to my tent. It was late afternoon, and I hadn't had anything to eat since four a.m. this morning. Chow hall opened at four thirty, so I had about an hour's wait. Back at my tent, I changed out of my fatigues and into my Navy dungarees and white hat. After all, I am a sailor and proud of it.

At the chow hall, I was sitting alone eating like a horse. A long hike in the woods – or more appropriately jungle –makes you real hungry.

I saw Sergeant Wade come in. he filled up his tray and came walking over and sat with me. I was more than a little surprised knowing how sailors and Marines feel about one another. I said, "Ain't you afraid of what people might say, you sitting with me?"

"No, I could care less. I talked to Captain Palmer and told him I was putting you in for a letter of commendation. But before he approves it, he wants to talk to you."

"Why's that?" I asked.

"He wants to hear your version. That still don't mean you're going to get it. Your division officer still has to approve it, and he won't be back from Saigon for two more weeks."

"You mean there's an officer on base in charge of the Navy section?"

"Yeah," he answered, "You didn't know that?"

"No."

"The personnel files are all in one spot, but each side of the base has its own officer in charge. The Navy side has a good contingent of sailors, but right now they're all out on patrol. Some of them are providing escort for your division officer to Saigon. It's faster and safer than going by jeep."

"I wonder," I said, "Why they didn't pick me up while I was up there?"

"You were supposed to be here in time to go with them. If you hadn't been ambushed on the way, you'd be with them now. Lucky for me you got here late; you did a hell of a job out there on patrol. I just wanted to tell you that. That second VC you shot with that shot gun almost landed on the guy behind him. They didn't know where to go. You were shooting like a madman. After emptying your shot gun, it was like John Wayne

– you pulled that forty-five and kept the lead flying. We opened up as they tried to run away. We had them trapped – they had no way to turn. You sitting there shooting like that, made them think there was a whole Army in front of them. You did a great job—thanks."

I didn't want to tell him I was scared shitless and that I kept shooting not because of him but because I didn't want to be killed. But all I did was say, "No problem. I'm glad everything worked out the way it did."

He said, "When you're done eating, stop over and see Captain Palmer for a debriefing."

So after eating, it was back over to the personnel office. I was thinking *okay, what now?*

Captain Palmer was waiting for me; I didn't have to wait outside his office. I stood at attention, sounded off, and was told, "At ease, sailor – take a seat. Sergeant Wade told me you did a good job yesterday, so good in fact, he's putting you in for a commendation."

I just sat there; that wasn't a question and I didn't know what to say. Next he walked over to me and shook my hand.

"You're the real deal and it's something I wanted you to know. I know it was hard on you not being there for more than a few days and being sent in to combat right away. But tomorrow you'll be on your patrol boat, and I wanted to find out about you while you were still under my command."

Finally I had to say something. "You took a big chance sending me out on patrol with no training. What would have happened if I froze – or worse yet – ran? People's lives were at stake, and you just wanted to test me! Well, I hope you're satisfied. It could have turned out differently and the lives of the whole squad were at stake."

"I read your service record, Elliott." He answered. "You think I didn't know what I was doing? The information in your record combined with what I saw in you when I first met you and what I heard from Master Sergeant Higgenbottom, I basically knew what would happen, but I had to be sure."

"How did you know about Higgy…"

"He knows everything that goes on in Okinawa and he and I have known each other for a long time. So when he heard you were coming here, he gave me a heads up. Oh, and that letter of commendation I'm going to recommend it – you deserve it. Keep up the good work. Dismissed." The meeting ended so abruptly that I just stood there a few seconds. Finally I saluted, about faced, and walked out.

My boat would be back either late that day or early the next morning. I couldn't wait. I wanted to get checked in and learn what my duties would be and who my shipmates were.

I walked down to the docks. There were two of them, both about the same length – maybe 100 feet long and 20 feet wide. They were fifty or so feet apart and right now they were empty. We had nine patrol boats, and all of them were either on patrol or escorting the captain's launch to Saigon. I'd find out which patrol boat I was assigned to when it got back.

I sat on the dock and looked out into the mouth of the Mekong River. We were right on the corner of the river where it meets the ocean. To my left I could see some rocky beachfront and to my right was the river. The water in the river was brownish as compared to the blue waters of the ocean. It felt quite tranquil at that moment. I sat for a long while, enjoying the ocean breeze and just let my mind wander. Later, I went back to my tent, checked out my guns, made sure they were ready to go and the safeties were on. Couldn't be too careful. I laid on my bunk, took a nap, and waited for evening chow.

Just before four p.m. PBC (Patrol Boat Coastal)18 came in. I heard the commotion, jumped to my feet, and ran to the pier. I didn't realize there were other sailors still on the base; I thought they were all out in the boats. There were probably twenty-five or thirty sailors waiting for the PBCs to pull in. I found out that they were cooks and supply personnel and lived in the Quonset hut next to the chow hall. There was no apparent uniform of the day. Most were wearing cut-down white pants, sneakers with no socks, and t shirts with the sleeves cut off.

I was in my work uniform Navy issue dungarees, shirt, and pats, and my boondockers and white hat. I stood out from the crowd, needless to say.

The boat had just finished tying up when I got there. The crew was jumping off and carrying boxes of contraband they had taken from Sampans and junk boats they had searched during the three days on patrol.

When the captain of the boat stepped off, I wasn't sure if that wasn't my boat or not, but when I saw him walking toward me, I figured it probably was.

The captain was a black man, a chief warrant officer C4. He was originally a chief bosunsmate and had gone to warrant officer school. There are four grades C4, C3, C2, C1 – C1 being the highest. So he hadn't been out of school that long before being sent over here. And as a bosunsmate, he was the perfect choice to run a coastal patrol boat. Or as everyone called them, just plain patrol boat. When he got to me, I saluted name and rank. He saluted back and told me to relax.

"We ain't real formal around here. So, you're my new thirty-cal machine gunner. I'm Maurice Livingston – you can call me Cap. I asked the crew to call me Maurice, but they all just call me Cap. What do they call you?"

"They call me Rich or if they want to get formal, Richard. I like Rich."

"Okay, Rich – step over here and I'll introduce you to the rest of the crew. That big red-headed guy over there is our cook and he'll be your loader, Bill Cooper – we call him Coop. Coop, come over here. This is Rich, our new machine gunner. I've got to run over to report in. Show him the ropes and introduce him around."

Coop came walking over. "Hi Rich. I'm Cooper. Everyone calls me Coop. I guess you and I will be working pretty close. Hop on board and I'll show you around."

First we went forward to where there was a pair of thirty-cal machine guns set on a swivel mount and mounted side by side. At first I thought how could two people fit on those machine guns? Then I realized that one man fired both guns. I looked at Coop and asked, "Are those my guns?"

"Yup and I'm your loader. We're going to have a lot of fun together." I started liking Coop right then and there.

Next we started aft when a radio man was coming out of the pilot house. Coop said, "Hey Big Mouth, I want you to meet our new thirty-cal man. Rich, this is our radio man Pete Maloni. Everyone calls him Big Mouth."

"Hi, I'm Rich."

"Call me Big Mouth – everyone else does."

"Okay, Big Mouth it is."

Then we headed aft. We stopped in the middle of the rear deck. A fifty-cal machine gun was on a mount similar to my 30s, one on each side.

"These here are our 50s. Gunner's mate second class Tommy Souza is on the port gun; that's him with the big arms and tattoos over there We call him Tommy Gun."

I looked to where he was pointing and saw Tommy going through the boxes they took off the boat.

"Next to him is George Lane second class bosunsmate and our other fifty-cal gunner. We call him Night Train."

The two seamen with them are our bosunsmates and their loaders. The shorter, stocker one is Rob Perry. We just call him Rob and the other one is Shaun Davison. We call him Fish. He

RAIN: A Sailor's Story

can swim a mile under water without coming up for a breath." I gave Coop an unbelieving look and he said, "Well, almost. Any time we need someone to swim after something; he is in the water without a second's hesitation. Everyone can swim, but Fish is unbelievable – the best of any one on base."

The engine compartment was open so we walked over there and I saw two men working on the engines. When I looked down, I was surprised to see three motors. I figured maybe two.

"This here's Tony Sheehan Engine Man Second class and his striker Fireman E three Marion James, affectionately called Monkey. He can almost scratch his ankles without bending over his arms are so long."

I said, "Hi guys. I'm rich." They stood up and said, "Hi, Rich. I'm Tony and this is Monkey."

Tony was an average looking guy with deep blue eyes, kind of piercing. Monkey was a young kid, maybe nineteen years old, short blond hair, thin with big ears and long arms – and I do mean long! Now I know why they call him Monkey.

Monkey looked up and said, "Hi, Rich...ooh ooh!"

Coop said, "That's Monkey talk for *welcome aboard*."

I asked Coop, "Can we go back up forward and look at them 30s again?"

"Sure, after all, as of now, they belong to you."

I looked them over real good, sliding the bolts back, checking the loading ramp and barrels, and then decided to take them apart and give them a good cleaning. I asked Coop, "Where is the cleaning equipment? I want to tear these guns down, clean them up, and oil everything before I put them back together."

"Rich, let's wait till after chow. We've been living on C rations and for three days, and I could use a good meal." So we headed to the chow hall and without saying anything, the rest of the guys fell in behind us. Coop, although he was only an E4, was the oldest guy on the boat. He had seventeen years in the Navy and was the unofficial leader.

We all sat together in the mess hall, and it felt good to get back to a group of guys. To be part of the team. The camaraderie was there. The way they picked on each other, the good natured ball busting made me feel right at home. I started feeling better about my new duty station.

After chow we all went back to the boat. Everyone had something to catch up on. Coop and I started dismantling the local machine guns, cleaning and oiling and putting them back together. I noticed against the pilot house were six extra barrels. I asked Coop bout them. He said, "In case you overheat, one we have new one to replace it. We can't afford to have a gun down, period."

"I thought that if you use short bursts, the barrels wouldn't overheat?"

"Sometimes there's so much shit going on, you can't afford short bursts. You just pour the coal to 'em until they're all gone or until the barrel wears out; then I'll crank you in a new one. We can't risk someone's life for an $840 barrel."

I loved hearing that. That short burst bullshit I didn't like from the beginning. *Yeah, baby, turn me loose on them puppies!*

While we were cleaning the guns, Maurice came on board and walked over to Coop. Coop looked up and said, "what's up, Cap?"

"We're pulling out at 0-800 tomorrow. Load up the boat with everything we need and have the engine men get it ready. Oh, make sure they top off the fuel tanks."

"Cap, we just got back. Why are we going back out?"

"There's been a lot of activity just north of Saigon, and we have to make sure the Dinks ain't getting any supplies from the junk boats and sampans in that area. Also, we are being separated into two teams, six boats each. Instead of all of us going it together, we're going out in teams of six. Three days out and three days back. That way, we'll always have a presence along the coast."

"That's going to spread us a little thin, don't ya think?"

"Better to be a little thin than not to have any presence at all." With that, Cap left, and Coop told everyone what was going on and what we had to do.

I went back to work and played with my 30s, checked on the ammo, and got general feel of the boat. I was ready to go.

There was a certain table in the chow hall that our team usually sat at. So the next morning after filling my tray with chow, I went to that table. Coop and Monkey were already there. Big Mouth and Tommy Gun and Night Train came in next. Right behind them were Tony, Fish, and Rob. We were all early, so we just sat and talked about the mission over a second cup of coffee. A few minutes after seven, we all got up and walked down to the pier. I didn't notice anyone standing pier sentry before, but now with the patrol boats back in, we had a marine on each pier guarding them

It was a comforting feeling knowing they were there. I didn't know their names, but I saw them around, so I said hi. They said, *hi, Rich*, waved, and continued their watch. I walked to the boat. Coop said, "How do you know them?" I told him about the patrol I went on with the Marines. He was amazed. He never heard of a sailor going on patrol with a squad of Marines. He probably would have been a little more amazed if I had told him about my recommendation for a letter of commendation in my service record.

When we got to the boat, everyone went about their business like it was second nature to them. Nobody had to be told what to do; they had done it so many times in the past.

By the time Cap walked up and climbed on board, everything was ready to go. The guns were all checked out and loaded, the engines were started and idling, nicely warming up, and Big Mouth ha all the electronics up and running. As soon as Cap took the wheel in the pilot house, the two bosunsmates untied the boat and pushed off.

Cap popped us in reverse, backed us out into the river, and off we went. I loved it. You could feel the power of them three motors. How effortlessly they pushed us through the water. The wind in my face, and the machine guns in my hands, gave me an awesome feeling of power.

As we were motoring up the coast, I could see the other boats pulling out behind us. Also, I could see other boats coming back. As we got close to each other, we would blow our horn, and they would do the same. I was enjoying this.

It's hard to explain the feeling of freedom I had out there on the ocean. Combine that with the secure feeling you get from the camaraderie of your shipmates and the other group of patrol boats all part of the same team. Shipmates, teammates – all with the same purpose and being a part of that felt good. The feeling of power you get from the twin machine guns in the palms of your hands simply adds to that feeling. This was all new to me, but like most things, after awhile, It became business as usual.

I had no idea where we were going. I could hear Big Mouth talking on the radio, but I couldn't' hear what he was saying. Combine with the wind in my face and the noise of the motors; I couldn't make out the words. Coop sat on an ammo box beside me. I was standing on my foot stand that goes around the bottom of the tripod my machine guns were on. This gives me the mobility to swing my machine guns around in any direction while moving around on this platform. I also had a large belt that I could use to strap me to the tripod to help me keep my balance in rough water. So I stood there strapped into my machine guns, moving a little left and right on that platform as the boat pitched and rolled as we motored ups the coast. I really didn't care where we were going; I figured I'd find out when we got there.

We were only about one mile off the coast, traveling at about sixty miles per hour. I saw off to the right a speck on the horizon. I pointed it out to Coop, who in turned pointed it out to Cap. We turned that way, and in a few minutes were alongside a Chinese junk boat with the big square sail. It felt like stepping back in time about two hundred years.

We tied up to the junk and had Rob go on board and check for contraband. The Chinese on board were affable enough and didn't give us any trouble. After a few minutes, rob came back on deck, gave Cap the thumbs up, and untied us from the junk They went on their way and we went on ours.

This stopping and searching junks went on the rest of the day. As we got closer to Saigon, we not only searched junks but also started seeing and searching sampans. Sampans are a smaller version of the junk boat. Some had motors and some just sails. No matter, we searched them all. Later in the afternoon, we saw a junk heading toward the beach. We quickly gave chase and headed them off before they could get to shallow water. They were acting a little hinky. So instead of Rob going on alone, Tommy picked up his M16 and went with him. Then Coop saw them throw something over the side. Almost before he got the word Fish out of his mouth, Fish was over the side, going after it. I started to get worried when after a minute I didn't see Fish come up for air. After two minutes, I was starting to take my flak jacket off to go in after him. Coop put his hand on my shoulder and held up one finger. Sure enough, a few seconds later, Fish surfaced just off our port side. Monkey with his long arms was helping Fish get a box on board. Luckily, the box was made of wood so that it gave a little buoyancy. Without Fish's swimming ability and strength, it would have landed on the bottom. With the help of Monkey, we got it on board.

Cap looked inside the box and ordered everybody off the sampan. There were three Asian men on board along with Rob and Tommy Gun. As soon as they were all on board our patrol boat, Cap told me to sink it. I looked at Coop for a little help, not knowing exactly what to do. Coop had taken the tracers out of the ammo belts. Normally, every sixth round is a tracer. That's so you can see where your bullets are going. But also the enemy can see where they're coming from. So Coop fills belts of ammo with tracers only, or regular ammo only. Then we can't use the tracers to get on target, take them out of the gun, put regular ammo on, and keep on shooting. Today was tracer day. Tracers actually burn. They're made out of an alloy that starts on fire from the friction of the barrel when the bullet passes through it. Then keeps on burning, even under water.

Coop loaded up both guns with tracers. Then he told me to shot up the sampan, starting at the water line. I swung the guns around and fired away. Within minutes, the whole thing was ablaze. Cap had the motors in reverse and we were backing away. It's a good thing he did. Cap knew what he was doing. After starting on fire, the whole sampan blew up. I learned later that the Captain had seen explosives in the box Fish and Monkey brought on board. That's why he had me fire the boat and why he backed way off.

The three Asian men were on the deck I the back of the boat. I could see the fear in their eyes. They didn't know what was going to happen to them. They were caught red-handed, smuggling explosives and their sampan had been blown up.

I asked Coop, "What now?"

"Well," he said, "Now we take then to Saigon and turn them over to the military authorities there. Then it's up to them as to what happens to them."

As we shifted into forward and started heading toward Saigon, I could hear Big Mouth on the radio; I still couldn't make out the words but knew he was calling ahead and figured he was letting someone in Saigon know we were bringing in some prisoners.

Tommy Gunn sat with his back against the pilot house and kept them covered with his M16. The rest of us stayed o the lookout for other boats carrying contraband.

By the time we got to Saigon, it was early evening. After dropping of the prisoners and filling out reports, it was late evening and dark out. The captain decided to stay in port for the night and allowed us to go to the chow hall and scrounge up some food. Usually the chow hall was open all night and had leftovers. Anything was better than the C and K rations we've been eating. We even managed to find some beer at the enlisted men's club.

After eating our fill and packing a few sandwiches to take back to the boat, Monkey and Tony showed up with the beer. It was real relaxing after being on patrol all day. You don't realize how stressful it is to be constantly on the lookout for smugglers and being ready to shoot if you have to. So a good meal and a few beers really hit the spot, to say the least. We took turns standing watch that night and pulled out at first light to resume our patrol.

We were headed up the coast just passed the DMZ (demilitarized zone). The first suspicious junk we saw was in late morning. Things had actually been a little peaceful and serene up until then.

I was enjoying the ride, but Monkey and Rob were a little bored, so they volunteered to check out the junk boat. I had a funny feeling about this one, the way the men were moving behind the mast and boxes on board. It was as if they were hiding something. When we were to close to rotate the 30s low enough to cover the junk, I picked up my Thompson. Coop seeing me do this picked up his also.

I stepped off the 30s and walked to the side of the boat. We pulled up beside the junk and were tying up. Monkey and Rob were jumping over when two of the men turned and opened fire with AK47 sub machine guns. Rob was hit and went down. Monkey dove into the ocean and swam underwater to the other side of the boat. Coop and I opened up with the Thompsons. The slugs from our guns tore the shit out of that junk. I kept shooting. Both Zipper Heads were killed. The third that was trying to cut loose from us was also killed. I just kept shooting into the junk from stem to stern. I emptied all three of my magazines into that boat. Fish was in the water helping Monkey, and Tony was on the junk checking out Rob. I grabbed a magazine from Coop and he boarded the junk with Tommy's M16. After checking everything out, Coop said that everyone on board was dead.

Rob had a hole in his upper left arm. He was bleeding pretty good and needed immediate medical attention. Tommy laid him down on the deck and was tending his wound. Cap looked to me and Coop, "Sink that fucking junk." I never saw Cap so pissed.

Coop said, "what about the stuff on board? The contraband?"

"Send it to the bottom, Rich. Light 'em up burn the bastard." He was already backing off and as soon as I was far enough away to angle my 30s down low enough to shoot into the junk, I opened up. The tracers were doing their job. Within minutes, the junk was burning.

The captain wasn't the only one pissed. Tommy Gun and Night Train were on the 50s and opened up as soon as we were far enough away so they could angle their guns on it too.

When those 50s opened up, the wood was being shot to bits. The fire power from the 50s was awesome. Normally we wouldn't waste the ammo, but now they wanted payback for shooting Rob.

We waited until the junk disappeared below the water. There was shit all over the ocean – stuff floating everywhere. Cap turned the boat around and headed back to Saigon. The hospital ship was there, and we needed to get Rob some medical attention. Tommy was doing a good job stemming the flow of blood. He had a battle dressing on the wound and a tourniquet that he would loosen every once in a while to keep blood flow to the rest of his arm.

Cao had all three engines going full bore. We were flying. These boats do about seventy miles an hour, but Monkey had this set up perfectly. We were doing closer to eighty.

Lucky for Rob the ocean was dead calm and we could open up. We had a triple rooster tail coming up the back of the boat about eight feet high. We were spraying water like you read about.

We were heading up the coast all day. We stopped a few boats and checked them out. Admittedly we were only at half throttle. I was amazed at how fast we got to the hospital ship back at Saigon. Didn't seem more than an hour and we were there. Tommy Gun and Monkey brought Rob up the gangway of the hospital ship. We were tied off at the landing down below. About a half hour later, Monkey came back.

Cap asked, "How's Rob?"

"Don't know yet. We're still trying to get someone to look at him."

"You got to be shitting me."

"Rich, didn't you say you knew somebody on this ship?"

"Yeah, I know Vickie – one of the nurses."

"Well, get your ass up there and see if you can get her to look at Rob."

I jumped over the side onto the landing and climbed the ladder two steps at a time. When I got on board, I had Monkey show me where Tommy Gun and Rob were. Rob was laying on a gurney in the emergency medical area on the main deck just aft of the gangway.

Tommy Gun was standing next to him working the tourniquet. I asked if a doctor had seen Rob and was told not really. Some nurse had seen him and said someone would get back to him as soon as they could. So I went looking for Vickie. She was usually over by the helicopter landing pad receiving incoming. Sure enough she was there in that emergency room. She was working on a wounded marine and looked as if she was just finishing up. I walked over and said, "Vickie – it's Rich."

Surprised, she looked up and said, "What are you doing here? I thought you were in Okinawa?"

"It's a long story, but right now I've got an emergency. One of my guys is wounded and I can't get anyone to look at him. When you finish with this guy, can you look at him?"

"For you, Rich – anything. It's the least I can do after what happened to Sheila."

For a few seconds we just looked at each other and I wondered if the sadness I saw in her eyes matched the sadness I was feeling at the mention of her name.

"I'll be finished here in a minute. You over in the aft emergency area?"

"Yes. Two of my guys are with him. I'll wait here for you and walk over with ya."

"Okay, give me a second."

With that she finished bandaging the marine, gave him a shot of something, and said, "Okay, let's go."

RAIN: A Sailor's Story

We walked together without talking. I imagined she was thinking about Sheila as was I. that's the one thing we had in common. When we got over to Rob, Monkey had gone back to the boat. Tommy Gun was standing there talking to Rob, helping him relax.

Vickie took the battle dressing off, looked at the wound, and said, "It looks worse than it is. The bullet missed the bone but hit the main blood vessel. Have you given him any morphine?"

Tommy Gun said, "No."

"Well, I'm going to give him a shot to relieve the pain while I sew him up." While she was working on Rob, I told Tommy Gun to back to the ship and tell the cap that Rob was in good hands. Tell him, "I'll wait here with Rob and let him know when she's finished?"

When Vickie finished sewing up Rob and dressing his wound, I asked if he had to stay here or could we take him back to base? She told me that everything went back together real well, but the main thing was the loss of blood and to watch out for infection. I told her we have pretty good medical facilities back on base.

I asked Rob if was able to walk.

He said, "Yeah – the morphine worked good and I feel pretty good." He started to get up, felt woozy, and laid back down. A minute later he got up, was still a little unsteady on his feet. I put my arm around his waist, held him next to me, and guided him out onto the main deck.

When the boys saw us coming, Big Mouth and Night Train were the first two over the side and up the gangway to help us down to the boat. When we got on board, Cap asked us, "So how is he?"

"He's okay. No broken bones but a pretty bad wound. Vickie said to get him plenty of rest and watch for infection. She gave me a ten-day supply of penicillin to give him."

"Good to hear, Rich. Let's get him back to base. Night Train – you, Monkey, and Tommy gun make Rob comfortable. The rest of you get ready to get underway."

When we got back to Loc Dau, it was pitch black out. We helped Rob back to his bunk and went to scrounge up some food and beer. We decided not to bring rob to the medical building until tomorrow. He was resting comfortably and he said he wanted to be with us.

As we were sitting around outside our tents, I noticed Monkey seemed a little down. I got up and walked over to where he was sitting, kind of off by himself. I sat down beside him and said, "Monkey, are you alright? You seem a little out of it."

"Rich, I feel like shit. When those Dinks on that sampan opened up, I panicked, dove into the water, and left Rob. I should have helped him."

"Monkey, you did just the right thing. By diving into the ocean, you got out of the way so we could open up on them without worrying about you. Then you stuck with Rob all the way to the hospital ship. Monkey, we're your shipmates. We were watching your back. You have nothing to be sorry about. Being afraid in a situation like that is normal. Instinctively you did the right thing and let your shipmates take care of business, okay?"

"Thanks for that, Rich, I feel a lot better."

After that, he joined in the conversation, had a few beers, and lightened up.

Next morning Rob was feeling pretty good. The morphine had worn off and his arm hurt like hell, but he was able to go to chow with us. Monkey got him a tray of food and we all sat together. After chow, monkey walked with rob over to the medical building. At the last minute, Fish decided to go with them just in case.

The rest of us went down to the pier to check out the boat. We didn't have to, considering we had three days in port, but we all felt like we needed something to do so down to the boat we went. I cleaned and oiled the machine guns, including the Thompsons. The rest of the guys were all busy doing their thing.

A little while later to our surprise, Cap showed up.

"Can't you guys stay away from the boat? You got three days off; relax, go play cards or something."

Coop yelled back, "What are you doing here then? Can't you stay away?"

"I got some paperwork to fill out, and I wanted to check the gauges. ...you know, the hour meter and things like that."

"Yeah, right; you got three days to do that. You're just like us. You can't stay away either. We may sleep on base, but this boat is our real home."

I heard the guys saying things like *right on* and *Amen, brother* and *you got that right*. I looked over at Cap and he had a sheepish grin on his face, and I knew he felt the same way.

When we were out on patrol for three days, we didn't sleep a whole lot. At night, Coop and I would take turns sleeping on our may west life preservers against the pilot house. With the hum of the motors and the rocking of the boat, it was easy to fall asleep. One guy watched, while the other slept. There was no time limit – we just took turns. We had some bunks below decks, and I knew they took turns going down below for naps. There were always three or four of us sleeping at night, but during the day, from dawn till dark, we were all up and ready to go.

Later that evening, we all went to the enlisted men's club for a few beers and to shoot some pool. I heard Tony was pretty good and I wanted to play him a few games. I can hold my own on most pool tables, but Tony was in a league all by himself. To say he was good was an understatement. After he beat me a half dozen times, I sat down to talk to the guys. We all joked around, busted each other, and generally had a good time. Later we all stumbled back to our tents together. We lived with each other, partied with each other, cared about each other, and generally liked each other. That is a great feeling.

You would think that we wanted to stay on base. Just the opposite – we were itching to get back on the boat and out on the ocean. Base time was good to relieve the tension, fix equipment, or in Rob's case, heal your wounds, but we all would rather be out to sea.

Morning of the fourth day, we all got to the boat early. The chow hall opens at five a.m.; we were in line at four-forty-five and on the boat at five twenty. As soon as Tony saw Cap coming over the hill, he started the engines. Cap came on board, asked everyone how they were doing, ran through his check points, and said, "Okay, let's get to it!" Ron wasn't coming, so Fish and Monkey cast off the lines and pushed off. By five thirty a.m., we were underway.

This morning the ocean was dead calm. Cap decided to take advantage of it and run up to the DMZ and work back to Saigon. We were booking at about fifty-five miles per hour. I was strapped into my 30s, enjoying the ride. Coop was in his usual seat on the top of the pilot house, scanning the horizon for anything suspicious. About two hours out, we saw a sampan off to our right, way off on the horizon. Cap turned right and headed out to take a look.

When we came upon the sampan, there was an old Chinaman running the boat. The guys started smiling – they knew him.

"Hey Charrie," Tony yelled over, "What's up?"

"Working going Saigon. Got load food stuff."

I saw a young Chinese girl trying to get my attention. Before Tony could tell him he could go, I said, "Hey Tony – hold on. I want to look at his stuff." Because I had never said anything before, and never boarded another boat before, everyone gave me a funny look.

Coop had his Thompson held loosely in his hands. But when he saw me hand Tony my Thompson and jump onto the sampan, he came to the ready.

As soon as I came on board, Charrie walked over to me. "Hi. You new. I no see you. You new. Me Charrie – everyone know Charrie."

"Well, Charrie. I don't know you and I want to inspect your cargo."

"Okay. You want look at cargo. Me show you."

I casually looked at the stuff in the hold and got closer to the girl.

She said, "Me slave you help." I instantly went on alert.

I walked over and asked her, "What did you say?" Charrie came over.

"She no speak American. She can't speak you," he said.

I said, "Stand back over there where you were." He backed up and glared at the girl. Again I asked, "What did you say?"

"Me slave you help me. Charrie make me work no let go home."

"You want to come with me?"

"Yes, me and Ling Ling go you."

"Ling Ling, who's Ling Ling?"

"Ling Ling my baby." Just then a little girl came out from below in an old sail cloth.

"Are you both slaves?"

"We slaves we go you."

I made a decision. Right or wrong, she was going with me. The blisters on her hands, bruises on her arms, and her general disarray helped me make up my mind. I helped them onto our patrol boat, under heavy protest from Charrie.

"She no go. She work for me. She stay - she no go!" I just took her on the boat, told Charrie to shut the fuck up before I beat him like he did her.

When I got on board, I said, "Untie the son-of-a-bitch and turn him loose."

Cap came over, "Rich, what are you doing?"

"Cap, she's a slave. Look at her. Bruises all over her, blisters on her hands, busted fingernails, and a little girl. That's enough for me. She's coming with us."

"What the hell do you think we're going to do with her?"

"I don't know, but she's not staying with him. There must be something for refugees in Saigon."

"We're not going to Saigon; we're past that."

"We can stop on our way back."

"No, we can't. We have orders to get back to base."

"Well I heard about a refugee camp across the river in Cambodia. Maybe she can go there?"

"Okay, Rich. She's your responsibility. Any problems, it's on you."

I brought them below, pointed to a bunk they could use, and gave them some food. Mre's all we had, but the way they ate, it was like a five-course meal.

I left them there and went back to my machine guns. Ten minutes later, they came up on deck and walked over to where I was and stood by me. I said, "You can't stay here. I have work to do. You should go below."

"We stay you. We stay here."

"No, it's not safe here."

I knew they didn't want to stay below, so I found a place on deck where they could sit.

Later she came back with a canteen of water. "You want drink." I was a little thirsty, so I took a drink. She handed it to Coop and he took a drink. She went around and gave everyone a drink. She even got cap to take a drink.

Next she started handing out crackers, chocolate, Chiclets, and cigarettes. All stuff she found below in the C and K rations. I'm thinking she wants to be useful and make us like her. And I liked that about her. After I took a few crackers and a cigarette, I felt something on my leg. I looked down and saw little Ling Ling standing there. She had one arm around my leg and her thumb in her mouth. She was staring up at me with these big brown eyes.

I thought to myself, *what did I get myself into?* I realized the responsibility I took on. Now the lives of these two people are in my hands. I had a small panic attack, but looking down at this innocent little girl and over at her battered mother, I made a resolve right then to take care of them. If they're my responsibility, then so bit it. I will do my best.

All the way back, she made herself useful. If someone wanted a drink of water, she ran and got it. Cigarette, she ran and got it. Soon everyone started calling her Run Run instead of Wein Wein. Of course little Ling Ling stole everyone's heart. Looking up at you with those big brown eyes, you just couldn't help yourself. Everyone felt like a big brother to little Ling Ling.

I saw Cap holding little Ling Ling and showing her how to steer the boat. I felt better knowing my ship mates felt the same way I did.

When we got back, we had to find something to do with them. Rob was standing on the pier waiting for us. He was still wearing a sling on his right arm but looked good otherwise.

We all off-loaded on the pier. When Rob saw Run Run and Ling Ling, he said, "What's this?"

I told him about Charrie and her being a slave and how we brought her back with us. I told him, "She can have my bunk until we find something to do with her – a refugee camp or something."

We started up the hill toward the base when cap said, "Hey, where you going?"

"We got a mission to go on."

"Refuel the boat, get more rations, and water check your weapons."

"I'll get our orders; we're heading out right away."

I brought Run Run and Ling Ling up to our tent and showed her my bunk. I told her that I had to go back out and she was to stay here with Rob and that Rob would take care of her.

She said, "I want go you."

"No. You and Ling Ling stay here with Rob. I'll be back in awhile."

"I go you get water cigarettes. I help."

"No! You stay here. Understand? You stay here. Rob will take care of you." She went to protest and I stomped my foot and pointed at the tent.

"You will stay here. I will be back. You wait here for me." I turned to Rob and told him to see about getting her, her own tent. By the time I got that settled, Cap was back with his orders.

"Mount up; we're heading out." We all jogged back to the boat. As I was getting Run Run settled in, the rest of the guys refitted the boat and we were ready to go,.

Instead of heading out to sea, this time we headed up river. I looked at Coop and asked him to find out what's up. Coop went into the pilot house and talked to Cap. When he came back, he said, "Rich, we're heading up river to pick up some 82nd Airborne. They were to be picked up by helicopter, but the LZ was way too hot."

"What's an LZ?"

"Landing zone."

"So, it's going to be hot when we pick them up?"

"Not necessarily. They've been able to evade the Dinks and are heading for an area on the river where we can pick them up. Charlie owns this river, so stay on your toes. Rich, we may need these machine guns at any moment."

That brought my attention level up a notch or two. I reached down, picked up my flak jacket and put it on. Seeing me do it, one by one, everyone else followed suit.

The ride up river was uneventful. We didn't normally go up river so Charlie wasn't looking for us. I figured someone was watching and would report to the VC what they saw, and the ride back might be a little more exciting.

When we got to the extraction point, I could hear Big Mouth on the radio. He was in contact with the soldiers. Then I heard the shooting off to our left about a half mile ahead.

Big Mouth yelled, "Rich, fire some tracers in the direction of that gun fire." I swung my guns around. The left barrel was full of tracers. I fired off a couple bursts. Big Mouth said, "A little more right." So I swung right, lit off a couple more bursts. Then Big Mouth said, "A little lower." I brought it down a little lower. Then Big Mouth said, "a little more left."

Finally I told Coop, "Get me those ear phones and mouthpiece. I have to talk to them directly." Coop got me what I wanted and I immediately heard their radio man asking for more fire power. I told him, "I'm the gunner – walk me in." I lit off a long burst of tracers.

"Come left a little and down a little." I moved slightly left and a little down. "Okay, a little more left." I moved left and immediately heard, "Right on – make it rain!" So I started shooting from both barrels. "You still on, Rain – make it rain! Make it rain!' I kept the triggers pulled back and raked the jungle up ahead of us. "Okay, Rain – a little more left and down a little. Keep pouring it on." As I moved the barrels a little, I heard him come on again, "That's it, Rain, pour the lead into them – keep it coming."

The left barrel was empty within a second. Coop had it reloaded and I was back shooting both barrels without missing a beat. "Keep it coming, Rain! Keep it coming. You've got them running for cover." As we got closer to the extraction area, the shooting got louder and the excitement level was in overdrive. Then we saw the first of the airborne come out of the jungle, slide down the bank of the river, turn and help give cover fire. Within seconds, the other three airborne were sliding down the bank and waiving us in.

With them laying on the bank shooting back into the jungle, the 50 cal machine guns opened up. I didn't expect it, and I almost jumped out of y skin. With my twin 30s and our 50s, we were tearing that jungle up.

The soldiers walked out into the river and we pulled up beside them, still shooting into the jungle.

Fish and Monkey were helping them into the boat. As each one got in, he would turn and give cover fire with his M16. When all four were in, Cap turned the boat around and kicked it in the ass and got the fuck out of Dodge.

On the way back down river, I kept a wary eye on the jungle. Cap swung the boat into the middle, keeping as far away from land as possible. Most times we were three- to four-hundred yards from the river's edge. But on the occasions when we had to get close, everyone went on high alert – sailors and soldiers alike.

During the times when the river was real wide and we were gliding along real comfortable, the guys started giving me shit.

"Hey, Rich, what's this *Rain* stuff all about? You tell us your name's Rich and these guys call you Rain – is there something you ain't telling us?" I didn't have an answer for that, so I just gave dirty looks and swung my machine guns back and forth.

Finally one of the soldiers spoke up, "We didn't know his name, and he was in charge of raining lead on the enemy. So we called him Rain. As long as he's running those machine guns, people are going to call him Rain, so he better get used to it."

Coop was sitting in front of the pilot house prepping ammo when he looked up at me and said, "Well, Rain, I think you finally got your nickname. Monkey, Fish, Tommy Gun, Night train, and now Rain. You know, I kind of like it."

I thought about it for awhile. At first I thought it was kind of girly. Then I started thinking, *what do I do? I rain lead on the enemy. That's it. From now on, I'm Rain.* I looked back at the crew and said, "Okay, you can call me Rain. But the first one that calls me Rain Rain will get kicked in the balls." Everyone laughed like hell. The soldiers didn't really understand; they hadn't met Run Run or Ling Ling yet.

When we got back to the base, there were a lot of people waiting for us. The soldiers from the Army corps of engineers whose base was attached to ours had people there to pick up the airborne rangers we brought back. Some Marines were there basically out of curiosity, and Rob, Run Run, and Ling Ling were standing on the pier. Our division officers, with a couple other sailors, were standing on the hill.

The soldiers got off the boat first then we got off. As soon as I got on the dock, Run Run and Ling Ling came running over to me. Run Run put her arm around my waist and hugged me, and Ling Ling put her arm around my leg. When I looked down, she was sucking her thumb, looking up at me with those big brown eyes. It felt good to have someone waiting for me when I got back, but it was also a little strange and uncomfortable. It would definitely take some getting used to.

Rob came up to me and told me he managed to get them a tent this morning and it was all set up. They now had their own bunks and tent. Last night, they slept in my bunk. He also told me that they badgered him all day as to when I was coming back.

By now it was late evening and starting to get dark. We were all hungry and heading for the chow hall. Run Run and Ling Ling went with me, still holding on to me all the way. Run Run with her arm around me waist, and Ling Ling holding onto my pant leg with her little hand.

While we were eating, Rob and Monkey went and got us some beer. Back at the tents, we sat around and drank a few beers, relaxing before hitting the bunks. I walked Run Run and Ling Ling into their tent, checked it out, and decided it needed a little fixing up. I would get on that the next day. I went back to my tent, hopped into my bunk, and fell fast asleep.

Next morning, I woke up and found Run Run and Ling Ling sleeping on the floor beside my bunk. I woke them up and told them they couldn't sleep there, that they would have to go back to their own tent. Grumpily, they went back.

I went to the latrine, over to the showers, and by the time I was ready to go to chow, Run Run and Ling Ling were waiting for me. Rob must have squared things away at the chow hall because they let them in without a problem.

The guys, most of them anyway, were sitting at our usual table. I asked Rob, Monkey, and Fish if they would help us get the girls set up in the tent. "Let's scrounge up things like a lamp, extension cord, something to sit on, a table – you know all the comforts of home." Big Mouth said he could get an extension cord with a plug for us. Fish, monkey, and Rob said they would help and headed off to see what they could find.

After chow, I went back to the girls' tent to check out their belongings. They didn't have much – a few pair of the pajamas they had, a brush for their hair, and Run Run had flip-flops, but Ling Ling was barefoot. It was heart wrenching to see what little they had. I asked where they were showering and what latrine they used. Run Run said, "me not know shower; just wash in river. Go in latrine in back; hold Ling Ling – she go."

I said, "Come with me." I took them to the showers. At this time in the morning, they were empty. I showed her how to turn the water on and regulate hot and cold. Then I went to my foot locker, got a couple towels and a bar of soap and told her to take a shower and wash little Ling Ling.

She made me stay so nobody would come in. She took her clothes off so fast, it took me by surprise. She seemed not the least uncomfortable being naked in front of me. I quickly turned around as she undressed Ling Ling and they got into the shower. They were in there giggling and speaking Chinese. I couldn't' understand a word they were saying, but they were obviously having a good time. When they finished, I gave them the towels and their clothes and waited for them to get dressed.

While they were showering, I was making a mental list of what they needed. I would take them to the PX and order things for them out of the catalogues and get them soap, towels, and anything else that might fit.

Over at the PX, I bought Run Run a pair of white sneakers, men's size 5. They were a little big but not bad. I got her some small t-shirts, still a little big, but not bad. The smallest pants I could get were a size 28 waist. I got her three pair of dungarees with a blue belt to hold them up. Also, I got her some new shower shoes. I ordered underwear, bras, shorts, and blouses through a catalogue. Then came little Ling Ling. Nothing fit her. I bought the smallest shower shoes I could find and figured I would cut them down. Then I bought a sewing kit, hoping Run Run knew how to sew and could make something for Ling Ling. I ordered some sneakers and clothes for Ling Ling through the catalogue and was told it would take anywhere from one week to one month to get here.

We brought the stuff back to her tent. I remembered there was an extra foot locker in our tent, so I brought that over for them. Run Run was so happy; you'd think I gave her a million dollars. She put her new sneakers on and paraded them around the tent. She was so cute, it was funny.

I stepped out of the tent looking for Big Mouth and the extension cord when I saw Fish, Rob, and Monkey coming with all kinds of things. They had these round spools that the wire came on. One was about eighteen inches around and two feet high, and the other was three feet around and three feet high. They had a broken office chair that Monkey said he could fix, no problem, and Fish told me that the Army corps of engineering had a junk track and would gladly give us the front seat out of it after what we did to bring back their troops. He said it would make a great couch. Then I heard a whistle. It was Big Mouth. He wanted a hand stringing out the extension cord and three-way plug. He also managed to find a lamp and a florescent light.

I asked Monkey if there were any more wine spools, the small ones. He said, "Sure – lots."

I said, "If we could get three more, we could use them for chairs around the big spool and the big spool could be our table."

"Good thinking. I'll go grab some." As Big Mouth and Rob were hooking up the lights, the florescent on the ceiling with a pull chain, and the lamp on the little spool beside Run Run's bunk, Fish and I went over to Army side to get the truck seat.

The Army had it all set up. It was four and a half feet long with blocks bolted to the frame so that it sat back about fifteen inches off the ground. Perfect height for a couch. They even loaded it into a truck and drove it over to our tent for us. I thanked then profusely, and they said, "You're Rain, right? We heard about you and the way you laid down cover fire for our troops. Anything you need, you let us know."

I thought for a second and said, "Yes, there is one thing. Can you come out back for a minute?" When we got out back, I took him to the latrine and asked if he could section off an end for the girls and make a special seat for Ling Ling. "Also, can you section off an entrance and shower unit for them?"

"Absolutely, no problem. We'll have it done in no time. Like I said, we owe you – anything you need."

By the end of the day, we had everything set up pretty good. The lights were working; the round table and chairs were set up; the truck seat couch was in place; and monkey had fixed the office chair. The tent was transformed into a pretty nice little home considering what we had to work with, and the Army corps had done their thing. Now the girls had their own latrine and shower. And little Ling Ling had her own little toilet seat.

I really appreciated what the guys did and told them so. They all said not to worry about it and that they enjoyed doing it and it gave them something to do. To have a place like that and Run Run and Ling Ling to take care of it gave us a sense of having a home. Little Ling Ling was so cute; everybody loved her. She got more piggyback and pony rides than you could count. Everyone was happy; me too.

That night as we sat outside the tents drinking beer, Fish and Monkey took off. They came back with some more small wine spools. Now we had some seats to sit on. The place was beginning to feel homier.

The next morning, I woke up to Run Run and Ling Ling sleeping on the floor beside me again. I started to scold her but saw the pain in her eyes and knew it wouldn't do any good.

"You come stay in tent me and Ling Ling. You come."

"It's not right. I can't live with you."

"Yes, you live me Ling Ling."

"I can't. It wouldn't' be right." Finally, Tommy Gun spoke up.

"Rain, just go and live with them. Nothing's right over here and besides, they're your responsibility. Now go and let us sleep." So that settled it. After chow, I went to the Army corps, had them make me a bunk, two mattresses wide. By mid afternoon, I had moved in with Run Run and Ling Ling. The office chair was more or less mine, Ling Ling bounced around from her bunk to Run Run and my bed, and Run Run sat on the truck couch.

That night after the evening meal as we were sitting outside the tent, an Army sergeant pulled up, got out of his jeep and walked over. I recognized him as the one who got us the seat. I said, "Hi Sarge – would you like a beer?"

"No thanks – can only stay a minute. Look, my men got together and made you this radio. They took it out of the truck, hooked it up to a converter, and asked me if I would give it to you.""

"Why are you doing all this for me? I appreciate it, believe me, but you really don't owe me. I was just doing my job."

"It's not just for you; we heard how these girls were slaves and how you saved them. That's honorable, and we like it. And we want the girls to have a radio to keep them company when you're out on patrol. It only gets the military station, but it's better than nothing."

To hear him say that, and to know that these people care about m y girls brought a tear to my eyes.

"Thank you very much, Sarge. I'm sure the girls will really like it. Are you sure you won't have a beer?"

"Well, maybe a quick one."

"I'm Rain, by the way, and this here's Monkey, Tommy Gun, Night Train, Rob, Fish, and Big Mouth."

"Hi guys. They call me Pole."

I looked quizzically and said, "Pole?"

"Yeah, I'm Polish. First it was Joe the Polack, then Joe the Pole. Now it's just plain Pole." We all laughed, picked up our beers and said, "Here's to Pole" and drank a toast. Pole drank his beer and had to leave. I walked him over to his jeep.

"Thanks again, Sergeant Pole."

"Just glad I could help. Keep up the good work, Rain." We shook hands and off he went. That night I slept with Run Run. We didn't have sex, even though I was aroused, to say the least. But I'll tell you, she fit up against me real good, whether I was hugging her back or she was hugging mine. In the morning, I was surprised to find Ling Ling in bed with us. I told her she should sleep in her own bed, so she got up and went over to her own bed.

Later that morning, we got the word we had to pull out. One of the other coastal patrol boats, the Number 6, was going with us. We were to leave at 1300 hours.

So we did our thing and got the boat ready to go. Right after lunch, we started the engines and cruised into the middle of the river. The other boat, the 6, pulled up next to us. I heard

Tony yell over, "Hey – those motors sound like shit, slowpoke!"

Someone yelled back, "Oh yeah? You want to race?"

Monkey ran up to Cap and said, "What do you think, Cap, want to give them a go?" The water was real calm, not even a slight chop. So the Cap said, "Sure, let's do it."

Tony gave the thumbs up, and they took off, got the jump on us. I was thinking, not fair. But I need not have worried. Cap put the power to it and we started flying. Most of the patrol boats can go between sixty-five to seventy miles per hour. Ours on a calm day could do eighty to eighty-five. Needless to say, we smoked them, blew by them in no time at all. After we passed them, we slowed down so they could catch up. When they came along side, their engineman yelled over, "What you got in that thing?"

Tony said, "Monkey motors!"

"What the hell are Monkey motors?"

"Motors that Monkey built!"

"Then, I'll just have to call you the Monkey Boat." And with that, we drove off. We all looked at each other. We hadn't thought to name our boat; now it's got a name. Later when we got back to base, Big Mouth, who is a pretty good artist, painted a picture of a monkey on each side of the boat. From that day on, we were known as the Monkey boat.

Our first encounter of the day was late afternoon about thirty miles southeast of Saigon. There was a sampan with two motors on it heading toward shore about ten miles off the coast. When they saw us, they gave it all they had and started trying to out-run us to the beach. Even though they had the angle on us and were way ahead, they couldn't out-run the Monkey. We cut them off and pulled up beside them. We all were on high alert because of the two motors and the fact that they decided to run. When we got so close that the 30s were ineffective, I reached

RAIN: A Sailor's Story

down and picked up my Thompson. Coop did the same. As we were pulling up alongside of them, Fish and Monkey were preparing to board them and tie off. Just then I saw something like a baseball fly through the air. I heard Night Train yell, "Hand grenade!!" Luckily the grenade bounced off the deck and flipped over the side of our boat. At the same time, Coop and I opened up with our Thompsons. There were four men on board. With the first round of fire, we killed two of them. The third guy managed to get a few rounds off with an AK47 before Coop nearly cut him in half with his Thompson. The guy threw his gun down and surrendered. No one on our boat was injured.

Fish and Monkey boarded the sampan and tied off to us. Then they started clocking the boat out as Tony with his M16 and me with my Thompson climbed on board, all the while keeping the one guy left covered. Tony went over to the guy and ushered him over to our boat. Night Train helped tie his hands behind him and made him stand in the back of the boat. Fish came from down below and said, "Rain, you've got to see this." I went below and couldn't believe my eyes. The boat was full of munitions. I saw hand grenades, AK47s, cases of bullets. I also saw some land mines. Then Monkey pulled something out of a box. "Hey Rain, look at this." I was further amazed to see the barrel of a mortar.

"Are there any rounds for that thing?"

"Yeah, a couple boxes of them. Looks like they're made in China."

"Fish, go get Cap – he's got to see this. Monkey, you wait here for them; I'm going to check on the dead."

As I as coming upon deck, Cap was coming over with Big Mouth. I said, "Cap, wait till you see that stuff. This is by far the most contraband one has recovered."

Cap went below as I checked the dead. I asked Tony to help me move them to the back of the boat and put a sail cloth over them. When the Cap came up, he told Fish, "You and Monkey hook a tow line up. We're towing her back with us. Big Mouth, get on the horn, call the base, get a hold of the lieutenant, and tell him what we got. Tell him we're twenty miles south of Saigon – should we tow it to Saigon or home?" Cap already knew that the lieutenant would want us to bring it home so that he could take credit for it. Asking was just a formality. By the time the tow line was hooked up and we were ready to get underway, the Captain got his answer – *Home, James.* He told Fish and Tony to stay on board the sampan and steer and told Fish to keep the line taught and don't let it get down into the props.

So off we went. At first, the going was smooth and easy. But by the time we got to the river, the wind had picked up and we had a pretty good chop going into the mouth of the river. Have to give Fish a lot of credit – he was pulling on the tow line at the right moment to get us over a wave and to keep from capsizing. It took a couple tries to get us heeled around and in a position to tow the over weighted sampan through the rip and up the river.

When we finally got to the dock, the river was calm and we slid alongside the pier, nice and easy. I think the whole base came out to see what we got. Marines, Army, Navy – everyone. When we pulled up, they all started clapping and cheering. I didn't know what the big deal was until Sergeant Pole said, "Rain, you may not know it, but by grabbing that boat, you just saved a lot of lives."

I said, "It was Cap that did it – chased his ass down!"

Then Cap said, "Yeah, but Rain did most of the shooting. Let's just say it was a team effort." We were all smiling, Monkey was doing his monkey walk, scratching his sides going, *ooh ooh oooh*, making monkey sounds. That got everyone laughing. Then I saw Run Run and Ling Ling standing on the pier. When she saw me looking at her, she walked over to me. She said, "That wong boat."

"What do you mean wrong boat?"

"Not wrong boat. That Lee Wong boat."

I said, "You know this boat?"

"Yah, that Lee Wong boat. He bad bad man."

I called the Captain over and said, "Cap, she knows this boat. Run Run, tell the cap what you know."

"This Lee Wong boat. He bad man." He comes down China. He kills sometimes. He bad man."

Cap said, "How do you know this boat?"

"I see him when I slave."

"Rain, take her back to your tent. I may want to talk to her later."

"Okay, Cap."

"Fish, you and Monkey take care of our boat and see if the Army Corps will bury the dead. Night Train, you and Tony untie the tow line and secrure that sampan to the dock until we decide what to do with it."

Cap went up tot alk to the lieutenant, and the rest of us went about our business. The marines and soldiers all took turns going on the sampan and checking out the cargo. I took Run Run and Ling Ling back to the tent.

Run Run held me tight. I said, "Hey, why are you holding on so tight?"

"Me afraid you no come back."

"Don't you worry, Run Run – I will always come back for you."

When we got to the tent, she brought me a sandwich and a cold beer. She had been busy since I'd been gone. She fixed up the tent real nice. She put a curtain between Ling Ling's cot and ours. She put our couch and chair at the other end of the tent against one wall, and our round table and chairs were against the other wall. She also managed to scrounge up a cooler and some ice. She saved the beer we had left over from the other night and brought back some sandwiches from the chow hall. She also had some cake that the pastry cook gave her and little Ling Ling. It felt good to be home.

Run Run and Ling Ling were real happy. The guy at the PX gave Ling Ling candy; the pastry chef gave them cakes and sweets. They had their own shower and latrine, and even though we lived in a tent, it was the best home she ever had. She had a nice home, all the food she wanted and wasn't forced in to labor. To say she was happy was an understatement; she was ecstatic.

As everyone finished their assignements, they came walking up to the tents. Sargeant Pole and a couple of his guys came up carrying a case of beer. Marine Sargeant wade and some of his guys came over also, carrying some beer. I looked around and said, "IT looks like the beginning of a party." I brought the radio out, got the military station on, and heard the Rolling Stones playing "Can't Get No Satisfaction."

We all started drinking beer and telling the story of how we ran down that sampan and the thing about the grenade and shooting and finding all the munitions. Monkey was doing his monkey walk, and Fish made up his new Fish walk where he moved his arms like he was swimming and wagged his head back and forth, puckering up his lips in a fish face. Between the two of them, they had us all roaring with laughter. One thing that sargent Wade said made sense to me. He said, "Go get qualified with the hand grenades so you can keep some on board. You never know when you may need one." I told myself to talk to Cap about that tomorrow.

The party lasted to a little after midnight. Even Cap came over and had a few beers. Before he left, he made a point to come over to me and shake my hand. "Good work today, Rain.

RAIN: A Sailor's Story

The men look up to you. You've done a real good job since coming on board. Keep it up. The Lieutenant's putting the whole boat in for a letter of commondation. Oh, and you were approved for that other letter of commondation. It's now official and in your service record."

    I said, "Cool. And Cap? I need to talk to you tomorrow about something."

    "Okay, Rain, anytime."

    After Cap left, the Army and Marines left. They said their goodbyes all around and wished us all luck.

    Earlier Ling Ling had fallen asleep on my lap and Run Run ahd put her to bed. So after everyone had gone, I said goodnight to my guys and Run Run and I went to bed. With a curtain between Run Run and Ling Ling, Run Run took off her clothes, then took off mine. She pulled me down on the bed and pulled me to her. At first we made love real slow and as her excitement level picked up, so did the tempo. Her arms came around my neck, crushing my face to hers; her mouth open, kissing me, nibbling on my lips, trying to devour me. Then her legs came up around my back and locked on to me. She was matching me thrust for thrust. We were no longer making love. We were in the heat of passion so intense, we threw caution to the wind; we didn't care if we woke the whole world up. I was pounding away like a crazy man, and she was pounding right bck. For such a little woman, she sure was strong. Harder, faster, harder, faster, faster, harder. She exploded in a split second before me. My orgasm was so intense it was like nothing I felt before. And I knew she was feeling the same thing. What started off as a tender, gentle love making ended up as thrusting, pounding,and rutting fornication.

    When we were finished, we just laid there holding each other. I fell asleep like that. The next morning, I woke up hugging her back with Ling Ling lying alseep behind me. I couldn't get up because I had no clothes on, so I had to wake Run Run up and have her put Ling Ling back in her own bed. When she came back to bed, I took her into my arms and kissed her hard and deep. It's amazing what a couple of weeks of good food and rest can do to a person. Run Run went from looking like a ragamuffin to a beautiful young lady. Some new clothes, good shower, and home is all she really needed. Every day her English got better. Not just a little but a lot better. Ling Ling was speaking English almost without an accent. She picked it up real quick.

I got up, went to the latrine, took a shower, and headed to the chow hall. I didn't eat last night and I was famished. Before I got there, Run Run and Ling Ling caught up to me. I was surprised – I thought I left them home sleeping.

After breakfast, they went back to the tent and I went to see cap. Cap was sitting there having a cup of coffee.

"Ya got a minute, Cap?"

"Sure, Rain, what's up."

"I think we should have hand grenades on baord the boat. After what happened yesterday, I'd feel a lot better if I had a few grenades to throw back."

"You must have read my mind because I was thinking the same thing."

"How do you suggest we go about it?"

"Well, there's a case of grenades on that sampan we confiscated. I say we keep them. And just so there's no one to pull red tape and say we ain't qualified, I think a couple of us should go over to Army side and take the course and get qualified in the use of hand grenades."

"I need your permission to see who wants to go and to contact Seargant Pole and have him set it up."

"It looks like you've thought this out pretty good, Rain. Okay, go for it." Said Cap, "Oh, and keep me informed how you make out."

I went back to the tents to talk to the guys. Most were there and a couple were on the boat. I asked who wanted to go over to Army side and get qualified with the hand grenade. To a man they all wanted to go. Fish ran down to the boat to talk to Coop and Big Mouth. And sure enough, they wanted to go too.

I went over to Army side and talked to Sergeant Pole. He took me to see Sergeant Calhoun. He was probably the darkest black man I ever had seen.

"So's yous wants to throws the grenades, right?"

"Yes. Counting me, there are nine of us."

"Okay, yous come back here in one hour, and I shows you how to throws the genade."

An hour later, we were all there. Sergeant Calhoun took us out to a clearing near the Jungle. There was a semi-circle of sand bags at one side of the clearing and some stumps and logs on the other side. We all walked over behind the sand bags.

Sergeant Calhoun started off by saying, "One of yous at a time lobs the genade. Everyone else gets down behind the sand bags, unnerstan?"

We all shook our heads up and down.

"Now yous don't throws the genade. Yous lobs the genade. Yous takes the genade like so, holds it like this, puts your hand down behinds yous, and then yous lobs the genade likes this." With that, he lobbed the hand grenade toward the pile of stumps. We were all down behind the sand bags when we heard it go off. He taught us how to pull the pin lob grenade, and that was pretty much it. So then it was our turn. Fish first, Monkey, me, and so on and so on.

After I lobbed my grenade, I decided to peek out around the end of the sand bags so I could see it go off. When Tommy Gun lobbed his grenade, I peeked out the end of the sand bags to watch. Sergeant Calhoun said, "Hey Rain! Did you sees the genade?"

"Yeah, I saw it."

"Well, remember. If yous can sees the genade, the genade can sees you."

Needless to say, I didn't peek at the grenades any more. When we got back to the tent, Cap was there. "How did you make out?"

"Good. We all learned how to lob a grenade. We'll have our paperwork in a couple days. Then I'll go to personnel and have him put it in our records."

"Where's the case of grenades?"

"I had Tommy Gun stash them away on the boat."

"So, we're all set?"

"Yup. All set."

"Good. We'll get the boat ready. We're pulling out tomorrow."

Now usually the Cap told Coop all this and Coop told us. Lately the Cap's been telling me. I didn't want any hard feelings between me and Coop, even though I out-ranked him.

So I flat out asked him, "Coop, does it bother you that the Cap comes to me to pass on the orders instead of you?"

"No, Rain, not really. To me, it was a pain in the ass anyway. I'm not the senior man on the boat, and it made me a little uncomfortable. So actually I'm glad I don't have to do it anymore."

At our table in the chow hall, I told everyone we were pulling out in the morning. "Any last-minute adjustments get them done. Big Mouth, did you get me my own set of ear phones and mouthpiece?"

"Yah, I did, Rain. But we still have to adjust them to your melon."

"My melon! You saying I got a big head?"

"No just shaped like a melon." Everyone started snickering, and thumping the side of their heads saying, "is it ripe yet?" They even had me laughing.

At first light, we were on the river again. Instead of heading down river out to sea, we were heading up. I looked at Coop and said, "Find out what's going on." Coop goes into the pilot house, comes back, and tells me.

"Some Australians are up river and need an extraction. They've been out for three days and need us to pick them up."

I said, "Are the helicopters broken?"

"No, they're in Cambodia and we're not supposed to go in there. A helicopter if shot down would be a big political problem. But us on the river, that's a different story. There are no real boundaries on the river."

I just shook my head and said, "Here we go again. The Monkey boat to the rescue. You'd think we're the only boat in the fleet."

"No, it's not that. It's because the Monkey boat has done it before. You know we got the experience."

"Okay, Coop, I got it. It's like when you do your job too good, they pile more work on you."

For the rest of the ride, we kept a sharp eye out for Charlie. As we turned a corner in the river, we saw a motor launch coming at us. It was a North Vietnamese patrol boat. It was a real surprise. When I recognized there were Dinks on board, I opened up with my 30s. We were coming at each other head to head. So we couldn't open up with our 50s, but they couldn't open up with all their machine guns either.

At the moment I had them out-gunned with my twins. They turned to my left so they could bring more fire power to bear down on us. Big mistake by turning; they opened themselves up to our 50s. The 50s opened up and blistered them up real good.

We were all firing away, me at the pilot house trying to take out their captain and the 50s directly in the middle of the boat trying to cut it in half.

Suddenly, I felt like I got punched in the stomach. It hurt like hell. A stream of bullets came across our bow, one of them hit me. I moved my gun to the right, aiming at the machine gun. I had tracers in my left barrel, so I could see where my bullets were going,. I walked them right into their guns.

The 50s had done their job; their boat was sinking. My 30s shot out most, if not all, their fire power. Now we were just cleaning up the mess. Shooting anything and anyone that moved. We were lucky; we were in alert mode, and they were sitting around relaxed. They didn't expect to see us that far up the river. Surprise, surprise!

I had my flak jacket on, and it stopped the bullet, but it still felt like someone punched me in the guts. When I looked down, I could see the bullet hole in my flak jacket and wondered if the bullet was still in there.

Later when we got back to base and I took my flak jacket and t-shirt off, I could see a bruise the size of a softball on my lower left rib cage.

When we got to the extraction point, the Australians were already there waiting for us. We drove right in to pick them up. They were taking on sporadic gunfire from across a rice paddy off to the right. I watched the high grass from where the gunfire was coming from and sent a couple of long bursts of machine gunfire at them. That stopped the gunfire, and we got the Aussies in the boat and were back on the river in no time at all.

To us it was all in a day's work, but the Aussies thanked us profusely. They called us Yanks. That was strange, sounding with their accents. They told us if we needed anything, just ask. Tony said, "What have you got to eat?"

RAIN: A Sailor's Story

"Nothing with us right now, Yank, but back at the base we have a lot of hams. It seems they made a mistake and put an extra zero on our ham order so we got ten times as many as needed."

Tony said, "Rain, maybe you and I can get a truck from Sergeant Pole and go get some hams. Being a Polack, he must like ham."

Not really thinking, I said, "Okay."

Sure enough, next time we had three days' base time, we went to see Sergeant Pole, got a truck, and went south to the Australian base camp and filled it with ham. When we got back, we have half to Sergeant Pole and half to our own chow hall. We all soon got tired of ham sandwiches.

We were back on coastal patrol duty, and things were pretty quiet. We had only a few minor incidents over the next few weeks. Run Run and Ling Ling were the light of my life. We were in a routine: three days on; three days off. I was liking it. I made arrangements on base to give Run Run anything she wanted, and I would take care of it when I got back. Run Run had fixed our tent up real nice. She braided a rug out of rags she found on the base. She was able to keep a cooler full of ice for cold drinks and things and even added a few knick knacks like sea shells and such. The place felt real homey. There wasn't much for a little girl to do on the base, but Ling Ling found something to do every day. She went everywhere. Everybody knew Ling Ling. She got candy at the PX, cake and cookies from the pastry cook; when some of the guys went fishing, she went too. Everyone loved little Ling Ling. She spoke English better now than Run Run. She even picked up a few swear words, which I had to explain to her were not nice words. Considering our circumstances, it was a happy time; I would go back in a second if I could.

The afternoon of the second day back, we were on the dock, some of us in the boat and the others carrying supplies. Run Run and Ling Ling were with us. One of the other coastal patrol boats pulled up in the slip next to ours. "Back a little early?" Coop yelled over.

"Yeah." One of their guys said. "Got a prisoner and some contraband."

As they were taking the prisoner off the boat, he looked over at our boat with a look of sheer fright on his face. He started yelling in Chinese and pointing at the boat. I asked Run Run, "What's he saying?"

"He say that Monkey boat. That bad boat. Go up river shoot everything. Go Saigon burn sampan shoot everyone. Monkey boat evil. Monkey boat go all over shoot fire. Monkey boat no good."

We all started grinning. I guess everyone knows about the Monkey boat. Monkey was walking up and down the pier doing his monkey walk. Then Fish had to get into it with his fish face and walk. It was real funny. The Chinese prisoner didn't know what to think. Even the guys on the other boat couldn't help laughing at Monkey and fish. The more they laughed, the more Monkey and Fish acted up.

We finished up, then helped them unload their contraband. The Marines came over, took charge of the prisoner, and picked up the contraband. I managed to grab another case of hand grenades. I was thinking, *If yous can sees the genade, the genade can sees you.* Afterward, we all met up at the chow hall, ate, talked, and drank coffee. Later, we sent Monkey and Rob for beer, went back to the tents and drank beer, hung out, and talked about where we might go tomorrow.

Later on Cap stopped by. It wasn't too late because it was still light out. To our surprise, he even grabbed a beer and sat down.

"Look guys, we're not pulling out tomorrow. Big doings going on. An LSD is coming in tomorrow, bringing with it a contingent of Navy Seals and nine swift boats. Before you say anything, a swift boat is a little smaller than our boat and is made out of steel, which offers a lot more protection. They also have a lot more fire power. In addition to the twin 30s and the two 50s, it has a 20-millimeter canon on the left side and a mortar tube in the center of the deck surrounded by sandbags. We will be assigned two marines to operate the mortar. Also the twelve patrol craft are being turned over to the South Vietnamese Navy. With only nine swift boats coming, three captains won't have boats. These men will stay with the coastal patrol and train the South Vietnamese in how to operate these boats. Also some of the engine men and radar slash radio mane will stay to help out also. The rest of the men from those three boats will be distributed among us to work the 20-millimeter cannons.

Tomorrow we've been assigned to check the river for the enemy to see if they have a surprise for the new ship. Also we will drop off a contingent of Marines on each side of the river about a mile and a half up. They will work their way back down, checking the make sure that Charlie has nothing up his sleeve. We will stay in the river treading water just in case either of these teams need our help. Oh, and Big Mouth, paint over the *Monkeys* on our boat. That logo stays with us."

When he said *that logo says with us*, it made me believe that our crew was to be one of the crews to get a new boat. I was thinking about the new boat being made out of steel. That'll give the crew more protection from machine gun fire. Our coastal boats were made out of plywood, and the bullets went right through it. Fish and Rob were constantly fiber glassing over bullet holes in the hull. Wonder what the new boats are like. Can Monkey jazz up those diesels? Guess I'll just have to wait and see.

The next day everyone was on the pier at 0700. The crew and two squads of marines, twenty more people to squeeze on the boat. Good thing they only have to go a couple miles upriver. Run Run packed me a bunch of sandwiches, ham of course, and some of Ling Ling's cupcakes. God bless the pastry chef. I was as ready as I'd ever be.

At 07:30, off we went. Coop was already eating one of my sandwiches, sitting there prepping ammo.

The Marines were in the middle of the boat, sitting on their helmets. Usually they wore bush hats, but for some reason today they wore their helmets. When we got a couple miles upriver, we found a good place to drop off the first squad. They all put their bush hats on and asked if they could leave their helmet with us. Monkey stowed them below. Same with the second squad. They only brought their helmets so they would have something to sit on. The rest of the morning we slowly cruised up and back down the river. Boring! Back and forth, around and around. A little after noon we got a call; the first squad was back, and the second squad was ready for a pickup and to be brought back to base. By then coop and I ate all the sandwiches and cupcakes and were hoping we would get back in time for noon meal at the chow hall. We were both getting tired of ham sandwiches. We picked up the second squad of Marines and headed back to base. Cap wanted to make the noon meal also and had the Monkey boat flying. We came around an island in the river, and there I was: This huge ship sitting in the middle of the river. When we got close, we could see the name on it: The USS Danforth LSD 23. I knew it had to be big to have nine swift boats inside her hull, but when you see it sitting in the river, it was a little overwhelming.

Cap cruised right up to it, circled it a couple of times, and then pulled into our pier. The ship was less than one quarter mile off our base. Anyone of us could swim to it if we had to. Being that close to the base, it was in the lea side of the river where the current wasn't so strong.

When we got back to base, we all jumped off the boat and raced to the chow hall. With all that was going on, the chow hall stayed open and would stay open all day. As usual, we all stayed at our table after finishing our lunch and drank coffee, discussing what we thought might happen next. When will we get our new boat? What does it look like? I for one will miss the Monkey boat. Monkey said he would miss it too, and everyone agreed. But the idea of a brand new boat was intriguing.

Coop asked Monkey, "What do you know about diesels? can you soup them up?"

"I know a little if I can get into the machine shop at the motor pool over to the Army corps of engineers. I may be able to fabricate a blower. Put a blower on a diesel, and you can increase horse power by twenty percent or more."

I said, "Let me talk to Sergeant Pole; I'm sure we can work something out."

I saw Cap come through the door and pointed at him with my head. When the guys saw my head bob, they looked over and saw Cap. We all sat up expectantly.

Cap came up and said, "Finish up; we're going over to look at our new boat. Monkey, check the engines, and pick out a good one." Tony Sheehan was senior to Monkey but knew that Monkey was the man when it came to motors. And on the boats, seniority didn't mean shit. The best man for the job did the job. Really the only one on the boat that was considered senior was Cap. Everyone else was basically treated equally.

We hustled out of the chow hall, hopped on the Monkey boat, and headed to the Danforth. On the way by the tent, I hollered up to Run Run, "I'll be back in awhile!" she waved and returned to what she was doing.

We pulled up to the landing beside the Danforth and climbed the ladder to the main deck. Cap requested and received permission to come on board. When we got on board, the officer of the day came over and talked to cap. He had us wait while he got a petty officer to show us around. Give us the grand tour, so to speak.

The landing ship dock is just that – a dock. The back of the ship is shaped like a horse shoe. It has big gates on the back that when open, give clear passage to the sea. The inside of the horse shoe is full of water and had the swift boats tied up to both sides of the interior of the ship. It was a real impressive sight. The swift boats would drive right inside the ship and tie up directly to the main deck.

After looking at the boats, we were taken below decks and shown to our living quarters. Not only were we to tie up to the ship, we were going to live on it. When I learned that, I had a slight panic attack. What am I going to do with Run Run and Ling Ling? I said to myself, *no matter what, they come first. I'll find a way.*

On one side of the horse shoe, inside the hull of the ship was the Navy quarters. On the other side was where the Seals were quartered. Even though we were all in the same Navy, they kept us separated. The Seals liked to be by themselves. While we were there, the guys were picking out bunks and lockers. I just picked one beside Coop but knew somehow I'd be living on base.

Then we went back up on the main deck and finally boarded the swift boats. We were the first team on the ship, so we got first choice. Monkey was like a kid in the candy store. He was running from boat to boat, checking this and checking that. And finally between him and Big Mouth, they picked the boat they wanted. Monkey, Tony, Big Mouth, and Fish were to stay on board and get our new boat ready, so to speak. It was already ready, but we wanted to fine tune it to our special needs.

Back on the Monkey boat on the way back to base, I went into the pilot house and talked to Cap. "Cap, I want to stay on base and live in my tent with Run Run and Ling Ling."

"I was wondering about that myself. I'll talk to Big Mouth and see about a radio for you so we can keep in contact. You have to be ready to go on a second's notice. Officially you will be on the Danforth; unofficially, you can stay here. I'll tell the crew; you can tell Run Run.

We had three tents that we lived in. Now that the men were moving onto the Danforth, we decided to move the tents end to end, giving me three tents to live in. On one end, I put our bunks, Ling Ling on one side; Run Run and me on the other. In the center tent, we put the cooker and the wire spool table and chairs. And the third tent was like our living room. With the truck seat couch and the office chair, wire spool end table and radio. Run Run was all excited, moving this and moving that. Setting up our foot lockers, her knick knacks, planning this and that. I thought that this would work out fine. I would miss not having chow or hanging out with the guys, but I'd still have Run Run and Ling Ling.

While I was getting set up, the rest of the guys were moving foot lockers and personal stuff over to the Danforth. Rob was painting over the Monkey logo on the Monkey boat with some battle-ship gray paint.

Later that evening, the guys were on the ship and Run Run, Ling Ling, and I were in our new home. The change happened quickly and suddenly our whole world changed. The next day, the guys came over on our new swift boat. They came to pick me up. We were heading up the coast for a shakedown cruise. Our old patrol boat was picked up earlier this morning. so within two days, we went from living in tents on a Marine base, patrolling the coast in an old converted PT boat to living on a ship and traveling the river in a brand new iron-clad swift boat.

The shakedown cruise was a big disappointment. Calling it a swift boat was somebody's idea of a joke. The "tub" was slow, didn't maneuver very well, and my machine guns were on top of the pilot house. If felt like a sitting duck up there. Well, one good thing – the rest of the crew had the protection of the steel hull. It would be interesting to see if Monkey could get those motors to run any faster.

we were getting a guy named Hal and a guy named Doug off one of the other boats to man the 20-millimeter cannon. At the moment, they were taking a class on how to operate the thing. So far, we haven't been assigned any Marines to set up and operate the mortar. Maybe I'll talk to Sergeant Wade to see if he's heard anything about who they might send. Also, I want to talk to Sergeant Pole and get Monkey started on the motors.

Sergeant Pole gave Monkey the go ahead to use his machine shop. He also managed to get Monkey almost everything he needed. What they didn't have, they made. I met with Wade and asked if he heard about our mortar and if he knew who was to be assigned to our boat. He said he requested the assignment himself and Private Rogers also requested it too.

I was surprised and asked, "Who's going to take over your squad?"

"Corporal Grimaldi; he's due for his sergeant stripes. It'll be good for him and the squad likes him." I was thinking cool, Wade's a good man, although I don't remember Rodgers. With nine swift boats, we're going to need 18 Marines. They will live on the LSD with the Navy. I'm sure they will get their own section.

The crew left to go back to the Danforth and I stayed with my girls. It was a little sad not having the guys around, but little

Ling Ling sitting on my lap and Run Run chatting about our new home made up for it.

To my surprise, I saw the swift boat pull up to the dock. I figured there was some emergency and they were there to pick me up. They came for a visit. They missed sitting out by the tents talking and drinking beer. I was smiling from ear to ear. Monkey and Rob ran to get some beer, and we all rounded up our spool seats and sat around talking. later that evening, they went back to the ship. From then on, when we were back from a patrol, we would hang out and drink beer.

Two days later, we got our first assignment. Wade and Rodgers, our Marine mortar crew, and Doug, our 20-millimeter cannon operators, met us on the pier.

I guess this was it. We were to take a Seal team up river to an island that had a Viet Cong village on it. There were hundreds of islands in the river and Charlie controlled them all. This was about to change. The Seals were here and we were about to take over.

The swift boat picked us up at 0730. Introductions were mad all around. The Marines got acquainted with their mortar and Hal and Doug, the 20mm. The Seal team kept to themselves, not really talking to any of us. I guess they were too elite to talk to lowly sailors. The team consisted of ten Seals. We were to drop them off at an inlet on the south end of the island. It was a perfect hiding spot for the swift boat. We backed into this small inlet that had jungle foliage overhanging the whole thing like the roof on a garage. We decided it would be a good place to hide while waiting for our Seal team to get back.

Sergeant Wade and Corporal Rogers were going to patrol our immediate area and make sure we were unobserved. They came back in about two hours and told us the whole area was secure. There was one main trail and two smaller ones heading in toward us, and he asked Cap if he and Rodgers should guard the trails as we waited for the Seals. Cap told them, "That's a good idea. As soon as you see the Seals, get back as quick as possible." While waiting, the rest of the crew cut shooting lanes through the foliate. I was on top of the pilot house and only needed to cut a couple of large fern type jungle plants so I could see. If I had to start shooting, the machine guns could cut down the rest of the bushes in front of me.

We could hear the shooting way off in the distance. We knew it had to be our Seal team. They were on their way back, and it sounds like they stirred up a hornet's nest. From the sound of it, the Seals were moving fast. I put my headphones on and waited, my guns pointing in the direction of the noise. The voice on the earphones was calm, to say the least. Unlike other military pickups, this guy was calm and matter-of-fact.

"We are returning to the rally point. We have a casualty and are taking heavy fire. We are west of your position. We request cover fire."

"How far out are you? I will start shooting high; watch for tracers and walk me in."

"We are five to six hundred yards out. Start shooting." I had already turned west so I started shooting. As usual, the left barrel was full of tracers. After a second or two, I heard, "Come lower and left." I lowered my barrels and swung left.

"Back right, one click and still lower." I moved slightly right coming lower.

"A little lower. Okay Rain, you're on." Now I hear a little excitement in his voice. "Keep it coming, rain; you're on. Make it rain! You're still on; make it rain!" I had both barrels going, standard ammunition. A tracer every sixth round. When they got close enough to shoot back, we would take the tracers out completely. The Seals could watch the tracers and keep me on the enemy.

"Little lower, little left; you're right on, Rain. Keep it coming; make it rain." Wade and Rodgers were back on the boat. They were at the ready with their M14s waiting to give cover fire when the Seals came in sight.

The first of the team to break through the jungle were moving fast, half-carrying and half-dragging a wounded Seal. From where I was sitting, I could see some of the others coming in. Now I could see the VC chasing them. They were more spread out than I thought running hard right toward us. I lowered my aim and started raking the jungle left to right and back again. Now that I could see them, I could give more effective cover fire. Charlie slowed down a little but was still coming fast and there was a shit house full of them.

Monkey and Fish were helping the wounded Seal on board. The other two Seals backed into the jungle a little way to give cover fire for the rest of their team. Wade and Rodgers jumped off the boat and went with them. A second later, the 50s opened up. That slowed the advancing VC almost to a stop. I could see the moving from tree to tree instead of coming head on.

When the rest of the Seal team got close, Wade and Rodgers got back on board and took up a position on the mortar tube. We all wanted to see what the 20-millimeter could do. So Cap gave the order, *Light it up!* That's all that Hal needed to hear. With a big smile on his face, he lit it up. What a rush; he was blowing shit up all over the place. Hal firing, Doug loading. The 20 was used mainly for helicopters or enemy patrol boats. We weren't supposed to waste ammo shooting at people; that's what the machine guns were for. But when the 20s opened up, it stopped Charlie right in his tracks. My 30s were bad; the 50s were worse, but when the 20s opened up, Charlie was horrified. Then to make matters worse, Wade dumped a few mortars on the bastards. "Ha ha! How do you like me now!?" he yelled. I could see the Dinks turn and start running. All the shit we were throwing at them; they had enough.

Fish and Monkey were helping our Seals on board and Wade dumped a few more mortars on Charlie just for good measure. Everyone was grinning from ear to ear. It was like scoring a touchdown and winning the game. That was the first time I saw any emotion out of the Seals even they were smiling and patting one another on the back.

Their team leader looked around the boat and said, "You guys were awesome. We didn't know what kind of support we could depend on from you; now we know. No doubt you guys are good. And Rain, you sure can handle those 30s. Thanks, great job."

I believe the whole ship felt good. The Seals are the elite of the elite. To get a compliment from them really means something.

Cap was moving the boat out into the river, and we all got back to our positions, figuring Charlie now knew we were there and might have a surprise waiting for us.

Seal's a good name for this team. They're more at home in the muddy waters of the Mekong Delta. The operate most effectively in the monsoon jungle rain. The wetter it is, the more they seem to like it.

Me, I hate the rain. It might be my name, but sitting out in the open on top of the pilot house on my machine guns taught me to dislike the rain, a lot. My feet were soaked all the time, so wet they were wrinkled up. There are two things about the jungle rains that makes them tolerable – number one, they are not too cold; number two, and most important, they give us good cover. That's probably why the Seals like it so much. Me? I still hate it.

After we got back from our first mission and the other teams from theirs, we had to change strategies. All the teams had problems and most had wounded. Even though we had the element of surprise, we were so out-numbered we were lucky to get out alive. If the VC had been properly trained, the outcome could have been a lot worse.

While the top echelon were figuring out a new strategy, Monkey and Tony were souping up the motors on our swift boat. The rest of us were getting our weapons ready. Wade was able to secure more ammo for his mortars and helped Hal get more 20 mil ammo. The 20mm cannon was becoming the weapon of choice in the delta. So there was less of that ammo to go around. Everyone had orders to conserve, but when lives are at stake, we all fire away and scrounge up whatever ammo we can. I still had some contacts with the destroyers I used to deliver messages to, so I had Big Mouth get them on the horn and see if they could spare some 20mm ammo. If they could, I'd tell cap and we would make a special trip up the coast and pick it up. Sometimes if they were pulling out, they would leave it at the crypto lab for us. It made for a good trip and a little down time.

Most nights the crew would sit outside the tents, drink beer, and joke around. On one of these occasions, Night Train and Tommy Gun actually talked some of the Seals into coming over. Introductions ere made all around, and soon they were comfortable enough to relax and let their hair down. Soon they too were joking and laughing. They started coming more often after that.

Ling Ling as always was everyone's favorite. You couldn't help but love her. And Run Run was the perfect hostess. I don't know where she got it, but she always had something for the boys to eat. These were good days. But good things must come to an end.

The upper echelon figured it would be best to go on night missions. The cover of darkness when Charlie was asleep. The

Seals were the perfect weapon for this strategy. We had some French maps of the delta that were fairly accurate, so even in the darkest nights, the Cap could find his way around. Even though Monkey and Tony had the diesels pumped up, they were still able to muffle the noise and we were pretty quiet.

Our first night mission went off without a hitch. We pulled out at 1200 hours exactly. The Seals had their usual green face paint on and were itching to go. The last five days with nothing to do was boring. Me and the rest of the crew were looking forward to the mission also. This was our first night run upriver and this could prove interesting.

The island we dropped them at was a lot closer than any of us thought. Less than an hour up river, and we were going slow on quiet ode. After they left the boat, we pulled out away from the island and parked against the jungle on the other side of the river. The jungle grows right up to the river's edge. We learned in the past that here are usually places where we can slip under the canopy and hide. We picked out a good spot, slowly coasted in, and waited for a call from our team to let us know they were on their way back, and we would go back to the island and pick them up.

Tonight's mission went off without a hitch; no shots fired. When the Seals got back, they told us that the Dinks didn't even have any sentries posted. they snuck into the village and booby-trapped the whole place. They told of how they even slipped into some of their huts and slit the throats of some of them while they were sleeping.

Hearing them talk about it made me a little queasy. Shooting them from a distance is one thing, but killing them up close and personal is another thing all together.

The other teams on the other boats had the same good luck – in and out, no problem. After tonight, it wouldn't be so easy;

Charlie would know we're there and will start posting sentries and be on alert.

We were getting three or four missions a week. Some were easy and some a little more difficult. The Seal teams were specialists in stealth tactics. They were like ghosts in and out before anyone knew they were there. Kill the sentries; kill some of the Dinks in their huts; and booby-trap their villages.

Coming back from one of the missions, the Seals were talking about one Seal in particular They called him Indian Joe, like in the book Tom Sawyer. He had a cross bow sent to him from home. It was extremely accurate ad powerful. It actually had a fancy pulley system used to load it. He took it with him on all his missions. It hardly made a sound when he shot someone with it. And he was adept at head shots. He practiced with it all the time. Soon instead of calling him Indian Joe, they just called him the injun or just plain Injun. Between missions, we hung out at the tents, cleaned our weapons, and generally prepared for the next mission.

We were sent on a mission up the Tiger River. So instead of heading up river toward Cambodia, we went right, deep into the heart of South Vietnam. This was the area where most of the jungle warfare was going on. Our mission was to drop the Seals in an area known for a strong hold of the Viet Cong. The Seals were to go in scout the area, and try and capture a high ranking officer and bring him back for interrogation.

We dropped the Seals at dusk and expected to extract them at dawn. After dropping them, we found a hiding spot and waited for their call. As dawn was coming up, we had to find a better hiding spot. Cap was starting to worry; the team should have been back a long time ago. We found a spot where the jungle canopy overhung the river and backed under it. Big Mouth was monitoring the radio, checking all the different frequencies we used, hoping to make the contact. I had my headphones on, tuned to the frequency that the team and I checked before they left the boat. My headphones were dead silent. All I could hear was the trickle of the river going by the boat. The sun was staring to rise, and it was coming up big and red. They had a small rice paddy to get through before they got to the pickup location, and they were supposed to get there in the dark. To cross it in the bright morning sunlight was going to be hairy to say the least. Then I got the call to say they were coming in, and hot was to put it mildly. They were screaming over the phones; you could hear the machine gun fire in the background. Cap had the boat going instantaneously. Coop was putting straight tracers into both barrels and I was swinging the guns in the direction of the rice paddies. They told us that they were coming to the river two clicks north of the paddies and needed support immediately. We were already a little north of the paddies, so Cap swung the boat around and headed north. I swung the guns to the other side of the boat and as cap swung the boat around, I started shooting. I heard, "Left, Rain – more left!" I swung left they were more north than I thought. Cap saw me move the tracers to the left and kept heading up river. Then I heard, "Lower, Rain –lower – and a little left. Move left a little lower; little left, left, lower…okay, you on, you on! Make it rain, Rain. Rain, make it rain!" Knowing how much trouble they were in, and with the big sunrise, I told Coop to leave the tracers in. they needed to see where I was firing to keep me on target. "More right, lower, little right, lower, keep em coming, Rain. Make it Rain." My left barrel was heating up fast. Then it jammed completely. Coop reached down, picked up another barrel from the front of the pilot house and within seconds had it changed. I was back shooting almost without stopping. Practice makes perfect. Time well spent. Coop gave Sergeant Wade the sign to get the motor going; he waved at the men on the 50s to be ready, and as he was doing this, the men on the

20mm rotated their cannons into position. Big Mouth was now on the proper channel and was listening to everything that was going on. He put it on the speakers so everyone on the boat could hear also. Cap was wagging his head up and down as he watched Coop giving everyone the signal to get ready. Then cap pointed at Wade and gave the thumbs up. Wade dropped in the mortar and waited. You could hear the kathump of the mortar shooting out and seconds later, the explosion in the jungle. Then on the speakers, "too far..too far, come back 200 yards!" Another kathump and explosion. "Come back 50 yards!" Another kathump and explosion. "Okay, keep 'em coming. Rain, a little lower." The mortar explosions weren't that far off. And the 50s were sending out sporadic fire, waiting for feedback from the team. The guys on the 20s were itching to get into it.

I kept on shooting, the voice in my earphones constantly directing my fire. I was shooting so low that my tracers were streaming straight into the jungle. I thought to myself, *I hope the guys are coming in low; I don't want any friendly casualties.* Coop was the first to see them coming through the jungle. He tapped me on the shoulder and pointed. They were coming in slightly to my left. I turned left to give cover fire and saw the Dinks right behind them; way too close for comfort. Coop was already picking up his Thompson. Now everyone was shooting. The 50s were right on. The 20s were covering the right flank. The mortars were still kathumping away. Everyone was into it. With all this fire power coming at them, Charlie slowed down, giving the Seals a little breathing room. Cap brought the boat right up close to the bank of the river, and Rob and Monkey were preparing to help the Seals back on board. As they got back to the boat, they laid on the bank, giving cover fire to the rest of the team that was still coming in. We had one wounded that Monkey, with his long arms, was helping on board. Rob was busy helping a couple Seals bring their prisoner on board. The rest of us kept firing, keeping the VC down so we could load up the rest of the team and boogie on out of there.

Now we would find out if Monkey's blowers would work. Cap poured the power to it, and the blowers kicked in, leaving little doubt that Monkey knew his shit. The boat almost leapt out of the water. Within seconds, we were safely out into the middle of the river leading home.

The Seal team looked like shit. They were soaked to the skin. Their face paint was all smeared, their fatigues were torn, eyes sunken in their heads. I don't know what they went through, but from the looks of things, it wasn't any fun.

Later we found out that the team had been surrounded and spent an hour under water breathing through bamboo straws, waiting for Charlie to pass by. When clear, they had to figure how to break through their lines to get back to the boat. The only way back was through a swamp. To keep their prisoner quiet, they had to knock him out and take turns carrying him back. When they broke out of the swamp, Charlie spotted them and the chase was on. Thankfully, they were close enough so I could give cover fire.

As I was watching the edges of the river, watching out for snipers, the Seals were stripping down and burning leaches off one another. Watching them do that and seeing the big red sores they left behind made me glad I wasn't a Seal. But on the other hand, watching the camaraderie and how they took care of one another made me proud to be a small part of the team.

The wounded Seal was being taken care of by his teammates with Rob handing them battle dressings, sulfur, and morphine. The prisoner was awake and tied up, sitting on the rear deck of the boat.

We pulled out of the Tiger River and into the Mekong River right where the gulf begins. Where the two rivers meet, it opens up into a huge gulf. With islands, tributaries, swamps, mud flats, rice paddies – everything. Cap knew where the channel was and swung into deep water almost without slowing down. The new Monkey boat was earning its name. It was by far the fastest swift boat on the river – nowhere near as fast as the old Monkey but, but faster than the rest of the swift boats.

We drove inside the Danforth, tied up to our regular spot on the left side, and offloaded the Seals and their prisoner. The wounded Seal was taken to sick bay to get checked out, and the prisoner was left standing on the deck.

We were mulling around the monkey boat, cleaning up mud and leaches that the Seal team left behind. Tony was checking the oil and fuel levels. Coop and I were cleaning up our spent brass. Everyone was doing something, basically just to keep busy.

Cap was up on the Danforth talking to the officer of the day waiting for orders. Normally they would turn us loose until they had another mission for us. Today, we had to deliver the prisoner and two passengers to Saigon. The two passengers were a Navy captain and a major in the South Vietnamese Army.

Tony and Monkey had finished checking the motors and refueling the boat. The rest of us had finished our cleanup. The men got on board and off we went. No fanfare; just get the job done.

The Navy captain was impressed with how the Monkey boat ran. The monkeys painted on the sides were far from regulation, but nobody said anything. When we got out into the ocean and kicked in the blowers, we even impressed ourselves. Monkey had them engines tuned to perfection.

When we got to Saigon, we offloaded the prisoner and the officers and were told to hang tight. The captain that came with us would return with us the next day. Cap told us we could go to the base on liberty but leave a couple guys to watch the boat. I decided to stay on board and clean my guns while it was still light out and would go over to the Acey Ducey club when someone came back to relieve me.

Next morning we all went to the chow hall, then back to the boat and waited for the captain. Hal and Doug managed to obtain some more 20 mm ammo. How, I don't know; don't ask – don't tell. The captain came back on board, talked to Cap and off we went back down the coast to the Danforth. As usual, the Monkey boat ran beautifully.

When we got back, we dropped off the Navy captain and checked to see if we had a mission to go on. We were told nothing right now; they would get back to us.

So with nothing scheduled, Cap and the boys came back to the base with me. We were getting into the habit of staying on base most of the time, unless we had a mission. Cap usually hung out with us except chow time. He ate at the officers' mess while we ate at the chow hall. After sitting around the camp fire in front of my tents, I went to bed with Run Run and they went back to the Danforth. To me, it was like going to work, then coming home to my wife and daughter – difference being my job was warfare and my home was a tent. Never the less, I was fairly happy. I loved Run Run – she was perfect – always happy, great hostess, liked my shipmates, and was a fabulous mother to Ling Ling. And little Ling Ling was spoiled rotten. Everybody loved her. How could you help it? The way she looked up at you with those big, brown eyes, her happy outgoing nature; she stole everybody's heart. Everyone had little treats for her, and found, bought, or made toys for her. She had a doll house that the soldiers made. She had dolls, stuffed animals – even a pair of roller skates. Although we were at war, it was a happy time.

RAIN: A Sailor's Story

Thanksgiving was only a few days away when we were sent up river with our Seal team. We were at the point where we were now getting the same Seal team on all our missions and we got to know them fairly well. And they started hanging around the tent with us.

The prisoner that the Seal team captured was a wealth of information. Important to us was the fact that they had a bounty on the "green faces." That's their name for the Seals. Also, he told us of an upcoming offensive by the NVA (North Vietnamese Army). It was planned for their new year – that was just after our Christmas.

We were going on three or four missions a week. Although each one was different, it was becoming routine. With Thanksgiving a few days away, and Christmas around the corner, there was talk of a temporary cease fire. And according to the information we got, that's when the NVA planned to move their troops in place for their Tet offensive.

The Monkey boat was still the most effective and fastest boat on the river. We were all proud of that fact. Even the Seal team bragged about being on the Monkey.

Nights, while not on a mission, we still hung out in front of my tents. With Christmas right around the corner, the military station on the radio started playing Christmas songs. That's when Ling Ling surprised all of us. Somehow she got hold of some fake reindeer antlers, a red ping pong ball nose, and she would wear her sneakers inside my boondockers for hooves. Every time it played "Rudolph the Red Nosed Reindeer," she would put her reindeer costume on and hippy-hop around the campfire. The first time she did it, everyone just busted out laughing. I never saw Run Run laugh so hard. Being Christmas and all, they played that song a lot. Each time they played, Ling Ling did her thing. We all laughed and laughed; watching her was heartwarming to say the least. My heart swelled up in my chest and I was thinking what an awesome little girl she was. At only three and a half years old, she was loved by everyone. Any one of us would defend her to the death.

The Seals had been coming over more and more. The night Ling Ling did her Rudolph impersonation, they just happened to be there. It was amazing to me at first to see these hard core elite military personnel sitting there taking turns giving Ling Ling pony rides. I guess we all have a human side!

Between missions we got ready for Christmas. Run Run, after hearing about the Christmas tree, wanted to have one. SO Coop and I went into the jungle and picked out this jungle swamp fern that most resembled a Christmas tree. Big Mouth contacted everyone and had them all order spare indicator lights for their electronic equipment. They only came in red, yellow, orange, and green. But with nine sift boats and the help of the Danforth, he was able to string together an impressive array of Christmas lights. The Army core of engineers even got into the act with some homemade ornaments. Run Run strung beads together and with the help of sick bay, got a bunch of cotton to put under the tree to look like snow. Ling Ling was jumping around looking at everything we did to trim this 'Christmas" tree and when we finally turned the lights on, she went wild. She was laughing, smiling from ear to ear, and hopping up and down. She could hardly contain herself. Her excitement and happiness was contagious. All the guys had big grins on their faces and were real happy to be part of Ling Ling and Run Run's first Christmas. They all were talking at once, let's do this and let's do that.

Everyone bought Ling Ling and Run Run presents to put under the tree. We kept them hidden in the stern of the Danforth till Christmas morning. We even talked Hal into playing Santa Claus. He was short and chunky, and with a red fireman's jacket and pants, his boondockers, red beret fashioned into a Santa's hat, and of course some of the cotton from sick bay, he made an impressive Santa Claus.

We had big plans for Christmas morning. Everyone on base knew about our tree and came by occasionally to see it. Gus the pastry chef that made treats for Ling Ling was in on the plans. He was going to get up early and bring over coffee and breakfast for the crew – Seals included. No small job. Rob and Monkey, after sneaking the presents under the tree, were going to help Gus. The rest of the guys were going to set up our chairs and tables for the big occasion.

Run Run and I woke up early, snuck out back to the latrine and showers. We quickly dressed, making sure we didn't wake up Ling Ling. Then we moved into the living room and waited for the guys. I had ordered new sneakers for the guys. The old were pretty stinky and worn. For the Seal team, I had ordered Swiss army knives. They probably wouldn't use them, but it was the thought that counted. Even Cap got into the swing of things and somehow had gotten a tricycle delivered.

When we finally got everyone ready and all the presents were under the tree, we woke up Ling Ling. I had ordered her pajamas a while back, the ones with the feet in them. And when she walked out of the tent in her PJs, rubbing the sleep out of her eyes, everyone yelled, "Merry Christmas!"

Her whole face lit up; she was grinning and hopping around. And when she saw Santa Claus, she screamed, "Santa Claus!!" She ran right over to Hal and jumped up onto his lap. Hal played his role perfectly. "Have you been a good little girl?" All she could do was nod her head up and down. She had stopped smiling and stared at Santa. Everyone was quiet, waiting to see what was going to happen next. Santa said, "Let me see if it says here you have been a good little girl. Let's see what Santa has for you." Ling Ling started opening up gifts, one right after another. She was amazed. When she was finished opening all her gifts, Cap brought out her tricycle. She was beside herself. I have never seen anyone so happy. The look on her face will be etched in my memory bank forever.

While she was playing with her toys, everyone else was eating breakfast and opening their gifts. I knew the guys liked their new sneaks, and the Seals said the liked their knives. Run Run opened hers. I had ordered her some jeans and new sneakers. The guys had gotten her some blouses, some a little bit dressy, which naturally she loved, and she also got some things for the house. Where they found a toaster and toaster oven, I'll never know. I think Pole had something to do with that.

Gus wasn't finished yet. Unknown to me, he had arranged with Cap and Big Mouth to have Christmas dinner delivered to our tent. Cap, Big Mouth, Monkey, Rob, and some of the Seals went to the mess hall and packed it up and brought home turkey and all the fixings. Gus also made Ling Ling's favorite cupcakes, and there were pies for everyone and a huge chocolate cake. He later came over and joined the festivities.

Later that night as things were winding down, Ling Ling fell asleep on Cap's lap. Cap had a few beers in him, and the look in his eyes said what everyone else was feeling. Being away from home, this was the best Christmas anyone ever had. We talked about it for the next week. When Run Run and I went to bed, she snuggled up to me and said this was the happiest she ever was. "I like this Christmas a lot. It make me so happy. I love you, Rain. A lot. you good person and Ling Ling call you daddy." That was the best Christmas present I've ever had. We made love real slow, kissing and cuddling each other, hoping the moment could last forever.

Next day as I was cleaning up, I got a call on my radio to be on the pier. The boat was on its way over to pick me up. BY the time I got to the end of the pier, the Monkey boat was already there waiting. I hopped on and we pulled out immediately and headed back to the Danforth for a briefing.

The Army Rangers had a recon team in the area where our Seals had captured the VC officer. We were to go back up the Tiger River and be ready for an extraction. The Army had a helicopter extraction planned, and we were to be the backup in case things went wrong.

We were to leave at first light. Slip up the river and hide wherever possible. Next morning we went up the river, got close to where we were supposed to be, and hid under the jungle canopy. Waiting and listening is always boring. Today was no different. Hour after hour, waiting and listening.

Big Mouth as usual was switching channels while I stayed on the channel we were assigned. Big Mouth heard a call on one of the other channels. He held up four fingers meaning I should go to channel four on my received. I then heard the gunfire. The Army Ranger team was in a gun fight. The LZ was hot and they were going to have to repel out of there.

The first Ranger was on board and the second one was halfway up the rope. The two Rangers on the ground were giving cover fire. Cap started to motors and headed up river. Coop was scanning the shoreline with binoculars, looking for anything that might help us locate the team. Around the bend, up ahead we saw the ass end of the helicopter. Then it disappeared back into the jungle. Cap increased speed into that direction. As we got closer, we could hear the gunfire. Now the second team member was on the helicopter and the third was on the way up. The fourth Ranger was still on the ground giving cover fire. The machine gunner on the chopper was also shooting and as we came upon the scene, the third was in and the fourth was on his way up. Even though he wasn't in the chopper yet, the pilot was pulling up and back toward the river, trying to get out of range of the Dinks. We could see them on shore shooting up at the helicopter. Even though we were pretty far out and closing in, I decided to open up. Maybe distract their attention so our guy could get into the chopper.

When my guys on the 50s saw me open up, they opened up also. We were closing fast and I could see my tracers spraying everything around them.

Then the Ranger let go of the rope and fell into the river. Cap headed in between the VC and the wounded soldier. Before you could say the word *Fish*, he was in the water. If you didn't' see it, you wouldn't' believe how fast that boy can go. In no time, he had his arm around the soldier and was swimming back to the boat.

Tony was loading the 50 for Fish and Monkey was waiting to help Fish get the man on board. ME and the two 50s were tearing up the jungle. Wade was dropping mortars in the jungle just behind the shoreline. Hal and Doug were in position with the 20s and started firing. The Dinks didn't know what hit them. Then we could see the Dinks pointing at the boat. A look for terror on their faces. I started to look around…was there a sea monster or something in the river? Then I remembered the paintings on the monkeys on the bow of the boat. The reputation of the monkey boat preceded us. The VC had had enough. They were running back through the jungle like their pants were on fire. By now, Fish and Monkey had our wounded on board and we were turning and heading for home.

The Ranger looked around in amazement. "I haven't seen so much firepower in such a small area all the time I've been over here. You guys are something else."

Big Mouth was on the horn telling the chopper pilot that we had his man and he could pick him up later at the medical building at Loc Dau.

We got back without any problems and dropped our wounded at sick bay on the Danforth. The wound was not that serious; he'd heal up just fine.

What he told us on the way back made us take notice. The recon team was there specifically to check on our intel reports about the NVA planned attack. Tet was the start of their new year, and according to intel, they were going to mount a major offensive on Tet.

We had negotiated a cease fire over Christmas. During the case fire, the NVA took advantage of it and moved a full battalion of North Vietnamese regulars into South Vietnam.

During that same period of time, we moved the fifth armored cavalry into the Nugean Valley on the other side of the Tiger River. South and east of their position, we moved in two companies of Marines and a company of Army regulars. Not only did we have them out-flanked, we had them outnumbered. Further south along the Mekong River, the South Vietnamese regulars were gearing up to join the Fray.

After our stop off at the Danforth, we went over to the base. Because of the success of Monkey boat and our solid reputation, when not out on a mission, we did basically whatever we wanted to do.

When we got back over to Loc Dau, I checked on the girls. Run Run had done a beautiful job on the tent house. She braded rugs from rags she had found on the base. With the help of Joe the Pole, she had transformed lockers into kitchen cabinets and counter tops. Now with the toaster and toaster oven, she could cook. We had the nicest home on the base.

Ling Ling was out back riding her tricycle. Just a normal day at home. Some of the guys were going fishing and asked if I wanted to go. I told them that I wanted to stay with Run Run and wait for Ling Ling to come home. Cap went over to officers' quarters where he still kept a room to see if anyone had heard anything about the Tet offensive.

After the evening meal, the guys came back to the tent. They caught some fish and gave them to Run Run. You'd think they gave her a million dollars. She went right away and cleaned them. The cooler was low on ice so Run Run got her two buckets out and was going to the chow hall for more. Fish took the buckets from her and went and got the ice. She told Fish that she should get ice because it's her place to go. Fish pooh-poohed her and took the buckets. I knew Run Run would make us a great meal with fish and rice. She would also add some wild plants and vegetables she found in the jungle around the base. She never ceased to amaze me.

We were all looking forward to dinner tomorrow afternoon. After drinking a few beers, everyone was tired; it had been a long day. They went back to the LSD and Run Run and Ling Ling and I went to bed. I knew it wasn't good to plan too far ahead, but when I rotated out and went back to the States, I would find a way to take Run Run and Ling Ling with me.

In the morning I went to chow with Ling Ling and Run Run. The guys for some reason didn't come over and it was just the girls and me. After breakfast, we picked up more ice and went back to the tent. I cleaned up around the outside with the help of Ling Ling. I think it was a little more play time than cleanup but it was fun. Run Run was cleaning the house and getting ready for the fish dinner she planned for that afternoon. I was still looking for the guys to show up and was wondering what was going on.

Early that afternoon, the guys finally showed up. I knew Run Run was as worried I was and seemed to relax as we saw the Monkey boat pull in. Everyone was there – the whole crew. Two members of our Seal team were with them. These guys were regulars at our tent. They became basically part of the family. There are a lot of men that you get introduced to. So many, in fact, that it's hard to remember names. Funny nicknames are easier like Monkey, Fish, Tommy Gun, and so on. But these two Seals hung with us so much that we remembered their names. Lenny Franklin was about five foot, nine inches and one hundred and seventy-five pounds. He had red hair and freckled face. If it wasn't for his uniform, you'd think he was in high school. Ronny Noyles was similar in size with the exception of blonde hair. Both were in extremely good condition and had skills that were not common to most people.

we all have a sixth sense. Did you ever have a feeling that someone was looking at you and turned around and there was someone looking at you? Well these guys had premonitions about people being close to you in the jungle. Their instincts were honed to the ultra sharpness. They could outrun, lift more weight, and do more pushups than anyone on the Monkey boat.

The only thing that we could beat them at was swimming. Fish could swim circles around them. They couldn't' believe how fast he could swim. They went through training with a lot of other Seals and they said that never saw anyone that could swim like Fish. Under water, on top of the water – not matter, Fish was the man. It made us feel good and Fish took it all in stride.

Fish, Monkey, Rob, and the two Seals kind of hung together. Cap and Big Mouth, the same thing. Tommy Gun, Tony, Night Train, Coop, and I kind of sat together. Night Train was the quiet type – didn't say much but was real solid in a pinch and was excellent on the 50s. As a team we all knew one another's strengths and weaknesses and adjusted accordingly.

Run Run came out with the fish and rice. The vegetables and plants she got from the jungle were really good. We all ate our fill, and everyone complemented the cook. Run Run was the perfect hostess and did a great job. As usual, Ling Ling was on

Cap's lap. Cap didn't have to say anything, but we knew he looked at Ling Ling as if she was his own daughter – in fact, we all did.

After dinner, Cap took me aside and told me he wanted to tell me why they were late coming over. It seemed that the NVA were on the move. Tet had started and so had their offensive. The fifth armored cavalry was holding back, as were the Marines. The army was engaging and falling back, then reengaging. Our intentions are to lure them down along the Tiger River toward the Mekong. When they are past the Nugean Valley, the Fifth armored cavalry will cross the river and cut off any retreat. The Marines will move in from the east and cut off their left flank. Our job, with the rest of the swift boats, is to monitor everyone's position and keep the NVA from crossing the river, effectively cutting off their right flank. We will have them surrounded and plan to wipe out their whole battalion. Say goodbye the girls; we'll be leaving at 1800 hours.

That gave me about an hour to get ready. The plan sounded good but the old saying "the best laid plans of mice and men often go astray" popped into my mind. I told the girls I had a mission to go on and would be back later.

We got on the Monkey boat, dropped Ronny and Lenny off on the Danforth, and headed up river. Because we had been up the Tiger before, we took the lead. Six of us moved up the Tiger, the rest stayed in the Mekong. As the battle progressed, we would move along blocking any escape across the river, effectively blocking them in.

It was late by the time we got into position. We wanted to get there at night under the cover of darkness. Surprise was on our side; they didn't have any idea we knew about the upcoming invasion.

The next afternoon around 1400 hours – or two p.m. civilian time – we heard our first gunfire. Actually I think it

RAIN: A Sailor's Story

might have been artillery fire. For the next three hours, we moved up and down the Tiger River, depending on where we heard the most firepower coming from The scope of the battle was unbelievable. Fifty thousand North Vietnamese regulars were a lot of people. We had the fifth armored cavalry pushing them from behind; the Army's third infantry brigade blocking them in from the east; the swift boats on the river to the west; and the Marine corps at the junction of the Tiger and Mekong rivers. The battle was stretched out over ten miles along the jungle, paralleling the Tiger River. At one point, some of the NVA started moving into the river looking for a place to cross. We were a little too far north to get into the fight, but three of our boats opened up with everything. The NVA made a hasty retreat back into the jungle. That was the only action we saw.

As we were pushing the enemy into the box that the Marines had set up, word came back for the Marines to step down. IT seemed that the decision was made to let the South Vietnamese army close the trap. Finishing off the NVA would give them more experience and confidence. That turned out to be a big mistake.

When the battle started, the better trained North Vietnamese held their own against a poorly trained South Vietnamese army. Officers and enlistment alike dropped their weapons and ran, opening the door to the whole of South Vietnam along the Mekong River all the way to the sea.

The North Vietnamese were quick to take advantage of this and overran every military base and village along the river. When we got word that the North was heading down river, I told Cap, "Let's get back – we got to protect our base." I was really thinking about Run Run and Ling Ling. Cap said he had orders to stay and monitor the advance.

Preparations were in place to shore up the South Vietnamese army and plan a counter attack. The South

Vietnamese regulars were in such disarray that the retreat could not be stopped and no such counter attack was mounted. The North continued down river and crossed into Cambodia. On the way, they overran every base along the river. Most of the bases had time to evacuate. I was hoping our base at Loc Dau had time to go and that the girls were safe.

When they finally turned us loose and let us come down river, it was too late. The North Vietnamese soldiers that were left behind to cover their retreat were quickly wiped out. That took something and by the time we got back to base what we saw made my heart drop.

The Danforth had raised anchor and pulled out into the ocean and was supposedly on the way back. The base was still burning and completely destroyed. Our piers were still intact and that's where we all tied up. Most all of us lived on the base. When were on the coastal patrol boats and still considered it home. We were all appalled by the destruction we saw. This made us hate the enemy even more, but also we disrespected our South Vietnamese allies because of their cowardess in the face of the enemy. If our fathers had turned and ran during our Revolutionary War, we would still be part of England.

We wandered through the base and as we were going through the side where the Army corps of engineers were stationed, we saw the men that evacuated the camp coming back. They managed to salvage truck loads of supplies and were as horrified as we were at what was left of the place.

I found Pole and asked about the girls. he said he didn't know anything – the Marines were in charge of evacuating that part of the base.

Some of the guys went back to the base with Pole and his men to help with whatever needed to be done. Cap, Big Mouth, Coop and I kept going up the dirt road, looking for the rest of the people from the base. Me, I was looking for my girls.

A short ways up the path, we saw the Marines heading back. I asked the first one I came to about my family. He said he hadn't seen them and to ask Sergeant Grimaldi who was overseeing the evacuation. I spotted Grimaldi and asked where the girls were. He said he didn't know.

"Weren't you in charge of the evacuation?" I asked.

"Yes. At first, she refused to leave. She said you would come back for her and she wanted to wait for you."

"So she left with you?"

"Yes, but a little while later, I looked around and she was gone. "

"You didn't go back and check to see if she went back?!"

"Look, Rain, I had my hands full – we were moving the whole base, salvaging anything we could. I did my best."

"Your best apparently wasn't good enough." I was sick to my stomach the girls went back to wait for me and I didn't come for them. I let them down. I wanted to smash something, preferably Sergeant Grimaldi, but it wasn't his fault – it was mine. All I knew was I had to find them. Coop said, "Don't worry, Rain – we'll find them." I knew from his voice he was as worried as I was. I turned and looked at Cap. He had this stricken look on his face. I knew how much he loved Ling Ling; it was as if she was his own flesh and blood.

He reached out and put his hand on my shoulder. "Rain, whatever you need, you got. I'll help you find them any way I can. That's a promise."

That made me feel a tiny bit better; I just shook my head up and down and headed back to the base. Coop was talking to Grimaldi and I could tell he was reaming him a new ass. Coop doesn't normally get angry, but seeing him this mad said a lot about how he felt about Run Run and Ling Ling. Wait till the rest of the crew finds out.

When we got back to the base, Cap and I went back to the boat. Coop rounded up the rest of the guys and met us on board. We told them about the girls and that we wanted them to help us find them. Cap started up the boat and we headed to the Danforth. It had returned and was anchored back in its original location. From then on, we would stay on the Danforth.

Gus the cook, who was back at the base, promised to contact me if anyone heard anything. From all over the base, people were wanting to help. Everyone knew Run Run and Ling Ling and liked them.

Once on the Danforth, we went down to the mess hall, got something to eat, and planned on how to go about our search. Cap sent Fish back to the ship to get his maps. We decided to split up into teams so we could search a large area faster.

The teams were assigned villages, bases, and refugee camps to search. While the military bases along the river were being rebuilt, our missions were cut down by about half of what they were. The Seals were a lot more ruthless in their attacks. By now we had cleaned up close to half of the islands and were building military bases on strategic ones.

When we weren't out on a mission, we were searching for the girls. We had a night mission where we joined up with some Australian scouts. They were going to lead our Seal team to a Vietcong supply base on the Cambodian border. Wade and Rogers volunteered to go with them. While we were waiting for them to come back, we talked about the search and how frustrating it was. When you thought you got a lead, it turned out to be false or the wrong person.

When the team got back, Wade came over to me and told me that the Australian scouts heard about a prisoner that was captured when the NVA crossed the river. He had said something about taking a woman and her child from one of the bases they overran. The prisoner was turned over to the South

Vietnamese Army intelligence unit for interrogation. He was transported to Saigon three days ago. I went to Cap and told him. I said, "Can you make up some excuse to get us to Saigon?"

"Let me see what I can do when we get back to the ship."

The sun was just coming up when we got back to the Danforth. As soon as we tied up, Cap was headed topside to get permission to go to Saigon. When he got back, he told me that he couldn't go directly to Saigon, but we could tie up to the crypto lab on the pretext of picking up more 20mm ammo. We had three days, four if we left immediately.

I said, "What are we waiting for? Let's go."

"Tony, start her up – we're pulling out." Cap was as anxious as I was to get up there.

Monkey had those diesel engines cooking. We made real good time getting there. We pulled in a little after three p.m. Big Mouth was on the radio to the Marine base in Saigon to find out where the prisoner was and how I could get in to talk to him. When we got to the lab, Dougy was on the radios finding out where the prisoner was. Big Mouth had called him to give him a heads up that we were on the way and what we wanted.

With his crypto status, he was privileged to information that Big Mouth was denied access to. Dougy was talking fast and writing down information on a grease board in front of him. He often used a grease pencil because it was faster and he could erase it afterward.

We hung around the lab waiting for him to finish up. It seemed like just yesterday that Snowball got killed – even though it was over a year ago. I still got that sad feeling in my guts.

Dougy had the information I needed and the contact person we had to see when we got there. The prisoner was being held at the Army headquarters on the north side of Saigon. We were to meet a Lieutenant North in the U.S. Army, check in at the gate, and someone would bring us in.

I thought Cap would be going with me, but he didn't want to leave the boat. So we decided Coop should go. While the guys waited, they would try and scrounge up some 20mm ammo – after all, that's the so-called reason we came here.

Cap wished us luck and Coop and I walked the half mile up to the main gate and caught a cab. The cab was a yellow VW with gray primed doors. The driver was Vietnamese with some French blood. He had a black goatee and spoke four languages – Vietnamese, English, French, and Chinese.

He and Coop carried on a conversation – small talk about weather, food, beer, this and that. As we got close to Saigon, which was only about twenty minutes to the outskirts of the city, the traffic picked up and we had to slow down. I was in a hurry to get to the Army base and this traffic was annoying. I was staring up ahead, looking to see if it was loosening up a little and didn't' see this Vietnamese kid walk up to Coop's side of the cab. Because of the lack of air conditioning, all the windows were open. When I saw the kid out of the corner of my eye, I yelled, "Coop, look out!" Coop looked up just as the kid dropped a hand grenade into the cab at Coop's feet. The kid made a big mistake. The hand grenade was the old style commonly called the pineapple. It was a seven-second grenade, meaning it took seven seconds to explode. The newer grenades were round and a lot smaller and go off in three seconds. If it had been a new grenade, Coop and I would have been killed instantly. Instead, Coop reached down, picked up the grenade and threw it back at the kid. He was just standing there waiting to see the grenade go off. But when the saw Coop throw it back at him, he turned to run. It was too late. The hand grenade went off and blew the kid up. I jumped out of the cab and could see the boy was hurt real bad. He was still breathing but I knew if he didn't get medical help soon, he would die.

I told Coop to help me get him in the cab. I asked the cabbie if there was a first aid station around. He said he knew of one just ahead two streets over. He cut through an alley and got us to the medical facility.

The boy couldn't be more than twelve or thirteen years old. His breathing was labored and he was unconscious. Coop and I carried him to a gurney and laid him down. A doctor came over and we stepped back to give him room. After looking at the kid, he said, "He's dead."

I said, "He was alive a second ago."

"Well, he's dead now. There's some paperwork that has to be filled out, so please go into the office and fill out a report."

Coop and I went into the office. On the way, I signaled the cabbie to wait for us. There was a deep sink in the back of the office where we washed the blood off our hands. We filled out the reports and got back into the cab.

When we finally got to the Army base, I was still on my adrenaline rush. After almost being killed, I was a little pumped up. Coop and the cabbie were feeling the same way, talking to each other all the way to the base. The cabbie thanked us over and over, saying we saved his life. Truth be told, we were just trying to save ourselves.

We stopped at the gate, walked over to the guard and told him who we were and we were there to see Lieutenant North. We made a phone call and a private came out and escorted us into the building. Just inside the door, Lieutenant North was waiting for us. He walked with us and asked us what we wanted to learn from his prisoner. I told him about Run Run and Ling Ling and what the Aussies had told us about what the prisoner had told them. Now I wanted to know where the girls are.

He said, "Okay, you got one half hour, then he goes back to his cell. We have an interpreter there with him." He brought us to an interrogation room. The prisoner was sitting in a metal chair that was bolted to the floor. His arms were strapped to the arms of the chair and his legs were strapped to the legs. He was wearing an orange jumpsuit with Navy issue shower shoes.

Coop and I walked in and sat at the table. North and the interpreter stood. The prisoner looked at Coop and I and said, "Me no talk. Who yous. I tol dem me no talk."

I said, "Look, I only want to ask you one question."

"Fuck you. Me no talk. You no scare me. Fuck you." This guy was starting to piss me off. I didn't come all this way to listen to this shit. I looked at Coop and asked him to take the Lieutenant out and get him a coffee and could he also bring me back one. I looked over at the interpreter and asked if he wanted one. Then I looked at the prisoner and asked him, "You want coffee?"

"No fuck you and fuck coffee." Coop stood and waved North toward the door. North a little reluctantly went with Coop. I pulled out my 45. I unloaded the clip and put it back in the gun. Our guy kept saying, "You no scare me. You no shoot me. Me no afraid."

When I had the clip back in the gun and the bullets on the table, I held the gun by the barrel. Then I asked him, "where is the woman prisoner with the little girl you captured at Loc Dau?"

"I no talk. I not afraid you." I got down on one knee, took his shower shoes off, and with all my might, I brought the butt of my pistol down on his baby toe. He let out a scream that was as much animal as human. I stood and back handed him across the mouth. I said, "Shut up, tough guy – you still not afraid?" Then I turned to the interpreter who now was staring at me, his eyes bulging out of his head and hands shaking.

"I want you to tell him so he understands. What I want is information about this woman and her child. I don't want any military secrets so he won't be betraying his country. Tell him I have one question and he has ten toes. It would be in his best interest to tell me what I want to know."

The interpreter told the prisoner what I said and I could see the prisoner shaking his head. Then I asked him again, "Where is this woman and little girl?"

He started speaking Vietnamese. When he finished, I was told that he didn't take the girls but that he joined up with his company in Cambodia and saw the two of them then.

"Where are the girls now?" The interpreter asked the question. Again he answered in Vietnamese. I was then told that the woman tried to run away with the little girl and was shot.

My stomach dropped. I felt hollow inside. Looking at that little prick, I started getting angry all over again. Next I asked, "Was she killed? Is the little girl alright? If she is okay, where did they take her?!"

He spoke in English, "Woman dead. Little girl go to Thailand. In Bangkok sell little girl. She be made to work in house. She first be taught how to speak Thai and how to be made. The more she learn, the more they pay."

"Where will she go in Bangkok?"

"Don't know. Just know she go Bangkok be sold." I was looking at this heartless little prick talking about selling my little Ling Ling into a life of slavery and my blood started to boil over. I had to do something. I took my gun and started smashing his toes one at a time as hard as I could. He was screaming his head off when I felt people grabbing me – it was Coop and North.

"Rain, stop." It was Coop trying to bring me back to my senses.

North yelled, "what the Hell do you think you're doing?!"

"Interrogating our prisoner. You might want to ask him a few questions now that he's in a mood to talk."

I sat back in my chair and stared into his eyes thinking all the time how much I wanted to twist his head off and piss down his throat.

North started asking him questions. I just sat there staring at him. I never moved, just stared and stared. The prisoner talked and talked. He answered every question without hesitation. And every time he looked over, I was staring at him. The interpreter couldn't' meet my eyes; he kept looking away, wringing his hands.

After an hour of interrogation, North got everything he knew. He told the interrogator to take him up to sick bay and get his feet fixed.

When they had left the room, he looked over at me, "I don't know what you said to him, but you scared him half to death. And that dead-eye stare, where did that come from? At one point, it even had me nervous. You locked eyes on him and didn't blink for ten minutes. Whatever, it worked and I for one want to say thanks. The information we got out of him will save a lot of lives. You guys go and get some chow. After you eat, I'll have my driver take you back to the lab."

With that he left the room. I think I made him a little nervous. While he was talking I was reloading my 45. And I wasn't smiling. Run Run was dead and ling Ling was being sold into slavery. They would probably be better off if I left them with Charry.

On the ride back to the crypto station, I told Coop what I had learned. He agreed we had to go to Bangkok. We had to save Ling Ling. I know when we told Cap, he would do whatever it took to help us.

On the boat ride back to the Danforth, Coop and I were in the pilot house talking to Cap. We told him what we had learned and that we needed to get to Bangkok. I told him I had some leave coming to me and Coop also had some left on the books.

Cap said he couldn't let both of us go; he needed Coop to run my machine gun. "When we get back to the ship, I'll get hold of personnel and see what I can do. I think the crew from the Monkey boat deserves a little consideration," said Cap.

At Loc Dau the rebuilding of the base was going real good. it helped that the Army corps of engineers were part of it. Most of the destruction was to the tents and chow hall. The rest had mostly fire damage and was salvageable.

The crew of the Monkey boat was happy to stay on board the ship anyway. Until we found Ling Ling, the base had lost its appeal.

True to his word, Cap was fighting for me to get leave. I put in a request for fifteen days and Cap was trying to push it through. While waiting for the next mission and to find out about my leave, we worked on the Monkey boat replenishing supplies, cleaning the weapon systems, and general maintenance. After two days of hanging around, word came down we had a mission to go on. It could take a couple days and they chose the Monkey boat because of our experience up the Tiger. There were some LRRPs (long range reconnaissance personnel) that were late getting back to their rally point. The helicopters couldn't' hang around, so we were selected to go up river and hang around until they were contacted and put in contact with us for an extraction.

We were crossing the river for two days in the area where the tam was lost. Big Mouth was constantly on the radios changing frequencies and trying to stay awake. I had gotten few hours' sleep on the pilot house and offered to relieve Big Mouth so he could get a little shut eye. As I was climbing down to the main deck, word came in the LLRPs were headed for the LZ. Big Mouth immediately woke up. He went from half asleep to full alert in one second. I hustled my ass back up to my machine guns.

Big Mouth got on the horn and told them to forget about the LZ, we were going to have a water extraction. He then read them the coordinates to where we wanted them to go. They gave us a ten-four and told us that they could be there in less than an hour. We moved the Monkey boat over to the extraction site and prepared to pick them up. I was on full alert waiting to hear gun fire and was moving my machine guns from side to side.

Next I saw the LLRPs coming to the river. I was thinking, *where's Charlie if the VC ain't chasing them, why are they late?*

When we finally got the LLRPs on board, they told us they were surrounded by a company of North Vietnamese regulars and had to wait for them to pass before they could move out. At times, they were within a dozen feet of the enemy and didn't dare use the radio in fear of being heard.

They gave Big Mouth the coordinates of the enemy and had him call it in. His radio was more powerful than theirs and they wanted an air strike.

As we were going down river, we saw the F14s fly over then we heard the bombs. A minute later, more F14s and more bombs. Big Mouth had the radio on the speakers and you could hear the pilots talking to one another, telling where they saw the Gooks and the position of some of their artillery. We eavesdropped in on their conversation all the way down the river. The three extra days that the long-range reconnaissance team spent in the jungle really paid off. now we had to get them back to base. We got instructions to bring them to the piers at Loc Dau.

When we got to Loc Dau, there were three Marine MPs standing on the pier. I wondered what they wanted. As we were tying up and offloading the LLRPs, the MPs came over.

"We're looking for Richard Elliott and William Cooper." I thought to myself that this had something to do with me breaking that prisoner's toes.

Cap stepped up, 'What do you want them for?"

"They're charged with murdering a civilian. We've been instructed to put them under arrest and take them to Saigon to stand trial."

Cap said, "That's bullshit. We've been up the Tiger River for the last three days."

"We know that. We've been waiting for you to get back. The incident happened six days ago on the outskirts of Saigon. Now if you'll turn them over, we can be on our way."

Coop and I stepped of the boat and headed for the jeep with our three Marine MPs. When we got to the jeep, the MP in charge said, "We know this is bullshit, so we're not going to handcuff you. Just promise you won't try and escape."

Coop and I both said no problem and climbed into the jeep. On the way to Saigon, they filled us in on what was going on. It seemed that the kid we killed with the hand grenade was the son of some influential people close to the South Vietnamese government.

"The parent's contention was that he was no VC and you killed him by mistake. This could turn into a political nightmare."

I am sure glad they didn't handcuff us; the ride back up to Saigon was bumpy as hell, and in some places we had to hang on with both hands.

When we got to the brig, it turned out to be part of the Army base where I interrogated the NVA prisoner. The Marines had to put handcuffs on us before bringing us into the brig. I was thinking of the brig I was in when in boot camp and figured this was really going to suck.

This place was more laid back; the Marines weren't that hard on the prisoners, especially with people like me and Cooper. They knew the charges were bullshit. Our reputation on the Monkey boat was well known, even up here. So we got treated pretty good in jail. Instead of a cell, we got a two-man room, some place normally reserved for officers. They hardly ever locked the door unless one of their officers was around. We had the run of the recreation area, chow hall, and exercise room. We even had a radio.

After we had been checked in that first day, we were introduced to our legal officer. He seemed a little young but was real personable. Lieutenant Michael Lovely, USN. The first thing he told us was that we were charged with manslaughter in the death of Lee Neisung. After telling us basically what we already knew, with the exception of the boy's name, he told us about the government's case against us.

"This is a political problem in which you two are unfortunately stuck in the middle. The government has no evidence except his parents' statement that he is not Vietcong. They are very well connected to the South Vietnam government and pull a lot of weight. What we need is an eye witness. Otherwise it's your word against theirs and politically they have more pull than you. I don't have to tell you that when it comes to international politics, you two are expendable."

I spoke first, "I considered myself expendable from the first time I came over here and my best friend got killed. I won't go down without a fight. I have a few friends in the military, and I'm sure they can get a news agency involved."

"Rain, that is one thing the government wants to avoid. So first things first. Is there an eyewitness. You didn't list one on your report."

Coop answered that one with, "They actually read those reports? Whoppdy do."

"Look guys, I'm here to help you. I'm on your side. I know this is bullshit, but in order to squash this thing and for our government to save face, we need a witness. If you're found guilty, you could face three to five years in Leavenworth."

"Lieutenant, the cab driver is a witness, and I'm sure he'll testify. He couldn't thank us enough for saving his life," I said.

"Where can I find him?"

"He is normally parked outside the crypto lab just south of here. He drives a yellow VW Bug with gray primed doors. He is Vietnamese with some French thrown in. He also speaks four languages fairly fluently – English, French, Chinese, and of course Vietnamese. He is approximately five feet, six inches tall, one hundred fifty pounds, has black hair, brown eyes, and a black goatee."

"Rain, I'll go back down there this afternoon and look for him. This is just what we need to defuse this thing. Anything else before I go?"

"Yes," I asked, "How do you know to call me Rain?"

"Whether you know it or not, Rain, you have a certain reputation. I think Rain is better than 'Toe Man." With that, he winked and walked out of the room.

I was thinking that word does get out and it travels through the grapevine. I'd rather be called Rain than Toe Man. Coop looked at me and said, "Hey, Toe Man, want a coffee? I'm buying. " It was the first time we laughed in a long time.

To pass the time, Coop and I played cards, listened to the radio, or worked out in the exercise room. The food in the place wasn't half bad, and both of us ate a lot.

After three days, legal officer Lovely came back to see us. He had a smile on his face from ear to ear. "I found the cab driver. A very interesting man. He has agreed to testify on your behalf at a motion hearing. The powers that be want this over with ASAP and have scheduled not only a motion hearing but also a pre-trial hearing. The parents' testimony, your testimony, and the testimony of the cab driver will be given at that time. The other option being considered is to present that statement of the cab driver to the South Vietnamese government officials involved in the case and to the parents. They may be predisposed to drop the charges when they see the evidence. So for now, sit tight. I'm trying to set something up for next week."

He didn't ask if we had any questions and obviously we had no other options but to sit tight. We were optimistic about our hearing and his optimism was catchy. We both felt a lot better knowing he found the cab driver.

It was late Wednesday afternoon and we had already been in jail for five days. We figured it would be at least another week before he could set anything up. Knowing how slow the judicial system is, it would probably take a lot longer. Two days later, the guards came into the recreation area and told us to get our things together. We were to go to administration and see Lieutenant Lovely.

When we got there, not only was Lovely there, but also the adjutant General was there. Coop and I looked at each other as if to say *what now?* Lovely's expression was bland and I couldn't read whether he had good news or bad news. Being that the adjutant General was there, I figured it was bad.

They asked us to sit down. Coop sat at the end of the table, and I sat in the middle. The back door of the conference room was slightly ajar, and I figured other people were in the other office waiting to come in and testify.

Lieutenant Lovely spoke first. "This is Adjutant General Paulson. He is the senior officer on the case." He turned, looked at the General and said, "This is second class petty officer Richard Elliott, and third class petty officer William Cooper."

RAIN: A Sailor's Story

To my surprise, the General leaned over and shook our hands. He took a seat at the table so he was diagonally across from both Coop and me. Lovely sat beside him, to his left. I was sitting there, totally baffled. I was thinking *what the fuck is this all about?* I turned and looked at Coop. Coop looked back and shrugged his shoulders.

We both turned and looked at the General. Finally he cleared his throat and started to talk. "First I want to commend you on your exemplary service. Elliott, you have fourteen letters of commendation in your service record. You served over here early last year, came back eight months later on the U.S.S. Cole where you were wounded and put up for a purple heart. After being released from the hospital, you requested duty back here in Vietnam where your reputation for getting the job done and protecting those around you is outstanding.

And you, Cooper – you have seventeen years on active duty with a perfect record. You have six letters of commendation in your personnel file and are qualified as is Elliott for a battle ribbon in the Tet offensive. I am here to tell you personally that the charges against you have been dismissed. After the testimony of the cabbie, the South Vietnamese government had no option but to drop the charges. You may not know that the political climate over here is very volatile. The parents of the boy you killed are highly involved in government policy. They have agreed to drop the charges on one condition – that the two men responsible for the death of their child be removed from South Vietnam and never be allowed to come back. Immediately following this meeting, you, Mr. Elliott, will receive an honorable discharge, not recommended for reenlistment. You will be shipped home, paid in full for your full enlistment, battle pay, and other incentives.

And you, Mr. Cooper, will get an early retirement with full benefits and be advanced to the rate of E5, second class cook as we believe you would reach that rate if you were allowed to stay in the Navy until qualified for normal retirement.

Lieutenant Lovely will stay with you and get all the paperwork processed. If you have any questions, I'm sure he can handle them. Oh, and good luck, gentlemen." With that, he got up and walked out the door.

I looked over at Lovely. "What's that all about – honorable discharge? I have two and a half years left in my enlistment. I also have some unfinished business over here. I'm not leaving – not yet anyway."

"Oh yes you are," replied Lovely. "When a General tells you you're leaving, you are leaving." I will escort you back to the Danforth where you will get your things together. We have forty-eight hours to get you out of the country. We arranged a civilian flight out of Saigon to Hawaii late tomorrow, so let's get to it."

"I'm sorry, Lieutenant Lovely, I just can't go right now."

"What don't you understand, Rain? You have no say in the matter. You're going home and that's that."

I looked at Coop for support. Coop just sat there shaking his head back and forth. Coop finally spoke up, "Rain, he's right. We have no say in this matter, but Cap and the boys are still here. They want what you want. With the help of Lenny and Ronny, I'm sure they'll get the job done. And no one says we can't keep in contact with them." I didn't like the idea of leaving, but what choice did I have?

Back at the Danforth, Coop went to his locker to start packing. I went topside to find the Monkey boat. When I looked over the side, the Monkey was gone. I hustled my ass up to the radio room, asked if there was any word on the Monkey boat.

"Yah, she's on her way back. Should be here soon." I went below decks and told Coop. Then I started packing my stuff. I left most of my uniforms; I figured I wouldn't be needing them.

At the bottom of my locker I found Ling Ling's antlers and red nose. I felt a strong tug on my heart. I had to talk to Cap and Ling Ling's two favorite Seals Lenny and Ronny. They would help; I knew it.

We were all topside when the boat pulled in. Rob was the first one off and grabbed Coop in a bear hug. Then he grabbed me. Soon we were surrounded by everyone – all asking questions at the same time.

Finally Cap yelled, "Hold on! Let's all go down to the mess hall, grab a couple tables and some coffee, and find out what's going on. Lieutenant, you can stay here."

"No, I'm going where they go." I looked hard at Lovely and said, "You heard Cap, you stay here."

"Rain, I have to keep an eye on you two, and besides, I kinda know what you are going to talk about. The legal stuff I can answer and as far as Ling Ling goes, I know nothing."

I knew he was privy to my interrogation of the prisoner, but I didn't think he would put two and two together. I thought for a second and said, "Fine. Come on down. You can probably use a cup of coffee."

After we all got a cup of coffee and sat down, Cap asked, "So tell us what happened."

I turned to Lieutenant Lovely, "So tell him."

When Lovely was finished telling him all about what went on, Cap looked over at Coop and I. "So, what do we do now?"

I looked around, "Where's Lenny and Ronny?"

"Probably over Seal side. Fish, run over and see where they are and ask them to come over."

While waiting for them to come, we talked about trying to find a way to get some information from Bangkok about Ling Ling. When Lenny and Ron got there, we explained what happened and asked if they would help. They both said, "Absolutely, no problem. We loved her too." We talked about maybe the Australians could get some info from the Cambodians. Maybe someone might have a contact in Thailand.

After talking for some time, Lovely spoke up and said, "Come on guys, we've got to go." We got up and said goodbye to everyone, each one promising to keep in touch.

We must have been on somebody's VIP list because we got konan1@comcast.neta helicopter ride to the airport in Saigon. When we got to the airport, we had about an hour to kill before we caught our plane. We watched our flight pull up. Both Coop and I thanked our legal officer for keeping us out of jail and apologized for getting him in the middle of this political nightmare.

He said, "No problem." He had made some good contacts and it might just help his career.

Once on the plane, Coop and I just looked out the windows. Then Coop said something that got me thinking.

"When you get home, Rain, get your passport. Maybe we can't come here in the military, but no one said we couldn't go on vacation to Bangkok."

The tunnel was awfully long and awfully dark, but I think I had just seen a glimmer of light.

* * *

CPSIA information can be obtained
at www.ICGtesting.com
Printed in the USA
BVHW070101171020
591032BV00004B/350